Days Like These

Brian Bilston has been described as Twitter's unofficial Poet Laureate. With over 400,000 followers on social media, Brian has become truly beloved by the online community. He has published four collections of poetry, *You Took the Last Bus Home*; *Alexa, what is there to know about love?*; *Days Like These*; and *And So This is Christmas*. His novel *Diary of a Somebody* was shortlisted for the Costa First Novel Award. He has also published a collection of football poetry, *50 Ways to Score a Goal*, and his acclaimed poem *Refugees* has been made into an illustrated book for children.

Brian Bilston

Days Like These

PICADOR

First published 2022 by Picador

This edition first published 2023 by Picador
an imprint of Pan Macmillan
The Smithson, 6 Briset Street, London EC1M 5NR

EU representative: Macmillan Publishers Ireland Ltd, 1st Floor,
The Liffey Trust Centre, 117–126 Sheriff Street Upper, Dublin 1, D01 YC43
Associated companies throughout the world
www.panmacmillan.com

ISBN 978-1-0350-0166-8

1 3 5 7 9 8 6 4 2

A CIP catalogue record for this book is available from the British Library.

Printed and bound by CPI Group (UK) Ltd, Croydon, CR0 4YY

Contents

January

1st January

For those whose lives are shackled by the temporal constraints of the Gregorian calendar – and I know mine is – today is New Year's Day. Notable traditions of the day include the declaration of New Year's resolutions, as well as the breaking of New Year's resolutions, which takes place several hours later. While it can be tempting to reach for a bold gesture with which to start the new year, decades of experience have taught me that such a resolution becomes increasingly difficult to keep as the minutes roll by. Far better to stick to a goal both realistic and achievable, such as boycotting Turkish croquet matches or not eating bicycle clips.

Resolution

Having failed to keep
A New Year's resolution for
Pretty much ever, this year I resolve to
Play it safe. The trick is to know
Your limits. Keep it simple.

Now what I resolve to do is to
Eschew a poetic form. Abstain from
Writing an acrostic for a whole

Year. A resolution, I think,
Easily done. Eminently achievable.
A piece of cake. Oh,
Rats.

3

2nd January

....

*On this day in 1860, the French Academy of Sciences announced the
discovery of Vulcan, a planet which was believed to exist in an orbit
between Mercury and the Sun. The mathematician Urbain Le Verrier
claimed that peculiar movements in Mercury's own orbit could only be
explained by the existence of another planet. His hypothesis was never
verified, however, and it became known as the 'hypothetical planet'.
In 1915, the publication of Einstein's* Theory of Relativity *offered a
different approach to understanding gravity, and finally disproved the
case for Vulcan's existence with maths far too advanced to relate in a
book of this nature.*

It's Not the End of the World

A hypothetical planet
between Mercury and the Sun
was no sooner discovered
than found itself gone.

Once Einstein's equations
were upheld and fostered,
Vulcan neither lived long
nor prospered.

On hearing the news,
a theoretical crowd gathered
on the non-existent planet
to express its disappointment

while a suppositional spokesperson
vowed to fight the decision
in an imaginary court
of interstellar law.

3rd January

....

The final daily Peanuts *comic strip appeared on this day in 2000,
although the Sunday strips continued to run until 13th February,
the day after the death of its creator, Charles M. Schulz. It had been
a standard feature of American newspapers for nearly fifty years,
serving up a daily treat of heartbreak and laughter, philosophy and
psychology, in four simple tragi-comic panels. Charlie Brown was a
character I could relate to – shy, under-confident, generally incapable
– but, as a child, it was Snoopy I adored the most. Even now I harbour
hopes that all those books he'd write while sitting on top of his kennel,
tapping away furiously on his typewriter, will eventually find the light
of day.*

The Greatest President America Never Had

That Snoopy never became President
is now generally agreed upon
to be one of the great lost opportunities
of twentieth-century politics.

He would have got my vote,
had I been an American citizen
and had an anthropomorphised cartoon beagle
been allowed to run for office.

Yes, I know there were times
when he could be selfish or difficult –
and it's hard not to feel sorry
for Charlie Brown, poor kid –

but look beyond that,
and you'll find loyalty, empathy,
kindness, dogged common sense.
And lots and lots of dancing.

He'd have pulled out of Vietnam earlier.
Carried the flag for civil rights.
Repealed the second amendment.
Sat down with Khrushchev.

Grand claims to make, perhaps,
of an anthropomorphised cartoon beagle;
but nothing is impossible and Snoopy was a guy
who achieved nothing every day.

4th January

Louis Braille, born on this day in 1809, was only fifteen years old
when he developed his reading system – a raised type consisting
of varying combinations of six dots – which was to become
widely adopted across the world. World Braille Day celebrates his
achievements and champions the importance of Braille in the full
realisation of human rights for blind and visually impaired people.
The day highlights the necessity of improving access to Braille
resources, particularly in developing countries and poorer communities.

Once More with Feeling

Look upon these raised dots
which dapple the page
like papery goose bumps.

They are what happens
when spines tingle, pulses race,
and hearts skip beats.

They are what happens
when doors open to your touch,
when dark relents to light.

They are what it feels like
to have the world at your fingertips,
to have it in your sights.

5th January

....

The first public performance of Samuel Becket's play Waiting for
Godot *was staged on this day in 1953, at the Théâtre de Babylone
in Paris. Heralded as one of the greatest dramatic achievements of the
twentieth century, the play consists of the conversations and encounters
of Vladimir and Estragon as they wait for a man named Godot. He
never arrives. I always imagine him waiting elsewhere – standing
under a clock or sitting in a cafe – wondering where on earth Vladimir
and Estragon have got to. Nowadays, a simple 'where r u m8?' tapped
into a mobile phone and any misunderstanding concerning time and
place would be swiftly resolved.*

Waiting on Godot

He was sat on his own at a table for three.
I fetched him the menu. He ordered afternoon tea.

Nothing happened. Nobody came, nobody left.
He bit into his doughnut. He looked quite depressed.

To help pass the time, he stuffed a bun in his face.
The time would have passed in any case.

'Waiter!' he said. 'Give me the impression I exist.'
I brought him a bowl of crinkle-cut chips.

After a vague supplication for a small walnut whip,
he settled the bill and then gave me a tip:

'Don't spend your life waiting. Think later. First, dance!
Act now while you can – while you still have the chance!'

After that, he thanked me and said he must go.
He did not move.

6th January

....

*Sherlock Holmes was born on this day in 1854. Although it may have
been 1853. And not 6th January but 17th October. Unless it was
12th February. Or 21st August – or any other date for that matter.
The stories don't actually tell us but that didn't stop him from being
given a birthday by the Baker Street Irregulars, one of the world's
oldest Sherlock Holmes societies. Various theories were shoehorned
in to justify the date: from references in the stories to* Twelfth Night
to a possible hangover in The Valley of Fear *on what may have been
7th January. At least we can be more certain of Holmes' death – at
Reichenbach Falls in 1893. Oh, hang on a mo . . .*

The Adventure of the Imperfectly Wrapped Parcel

pity poor Sherlock
on his special day
to spend his tenth birthday
deducting away

no mysteries for him
no need to unwrap
his first violin
a deerstalker hat

impossibles ruled out
only improbables left –
some new boxing gloves
a chemistry set

and the plant in the pot
that was wrapped up outside
deduced to be citrus
a lemon tree, he cried

all things known except
the joy of surprise –
how dull it must be
to have a brilliant mind

7th January

On this day in 1927 the first official transatlantic telephone call was made, between Walter S. Gifford, the president of America's Bell Labs (now AT&T), and Sir Evelyn Murray, the secretary of the General Post Office in London. Ever since that date, transatlantic phone calls and teleconference meetings have become commonplace, driving international business forward with varying degrees of productivity, professionalism and competence.

The First Transatlantic Telephone Call

'New York has joined the meeting.'
The violins of Vivaldi's *Four Seasons* announce
the arrival of Spring with zesty triumph.
'London has joined the meeting.'
'Good afternoon, London!'
'Good morning, New York!'

'Thank you for joining me on this historic call
for today is the result of many years of research and—'
'London has left the meeting.'
The violins of Vivaldi's *Four Seasons* announce
the return of Spring with jaunty persistence.
'London, are you there?'

'London has joined the meeting.'
'Sorry, New York. A few gremlins at this end.'
'No problem, London . . . Today we open a telephonic path
of speech between our two great cit—'

'London has left the meeting.'
With irrepressible gusto, the violins of Vivaldi's *Four Seasons*
proclaim the entrance of Spring once more.

'London has joined the meeting.'
'Glad to have you back, London. Where was I? Ah, yes.
Who can foresee where this latest achievement of science and –
I hear barking. London, do you have a *dog* with you?'
'Sorry, I'm working from home tod—'
'London has left the meeting.'

The goddam violins of Vivaldi's *Four Seasons*
announce the re-entrance of Spring with tedious predictability,
followed by the tiresome arrival of Summer,
the insidious encroachment of Autumn,
and the bleak onslaught of Winter,
until they cease suddenly with the news that
'New York has left the meeting.'

8th January

....

Food rationing was introduced in Britain on this day in 1940, as a
measure to cope with wartime shortages and ensure that provisions
were distributed fairly. Initially, only bacon, butter and sugar were
restricted but the list was soon extended to cover many staples, such
as meat, cheese, eggs and milk. Although such restrictions were
undoubtedly hard, poorer sections of society were able to increase their
intake of protein and vitamins, and public health experts now reckon

the wartime diet was far healthier than the one we have today. This has led to calls from some quarters for rationing to be reintroduced, particularly in regard to beefburgers, pizza, and re-runs of Shaun of the Dead *on ITV2.*

Poem

These are tough times for poets.
With the re-introduction of rationing,
many poets are having to live on as little as five similes
and four ounces of metaphor per week.

Haikus have been reduced to twelve syllables.
Brexit has led to a shortage of French villanelles
and Sicilian octaves, while elegy prices
are set to increase by 50 per cent this winter.

Some poets have been forced to burn
their sonnets simply to stay warm;
many can no longer afford to give their poems
more imaginative titles.

And so, think of the poor poets, shivering
in their cedar-clad writing cabins,
wondering where their next rhyme will come from –
and should you have any spare iambs,

odd odes or spent pentameters,
rusting tin cantos or throwaway lines,
please donate them to a Word Bank near you.
Credit card payments will also be accepted at this time.

9th January

....

On this day in 1902, a bill was introduced in New York State to outlaw flirting in public. While that may sound ridiculous, the law was aimed at protecting young girls and women from unwanted attention from men: so not so silly after all. That's not to say that there aren't a lot of rather bizarre laws which remain on the New York statute book: the hosting of a puppet show in a window is rightly banned, as is the throwing of a ball at someone's face for fun. And please remember that it remains illegal there to transport an ice cream cone in one's pocket on a Sunday, following a long-forgotten incident in which 'untold mischief' was caused.

Be Alert, Not a Flirt

Please be aware that flirts
are known to operate in this area.

You are advised to keep
your longings with you at all times.

Kisses have been stolen
and bottoms pinched,

while there have been reports
of batted eyelids, grazed arms,

and gentle teasing.
Should anyone laugh too loudly

at one of your lame jokes,
or take an immoderate interest

in the colour of your eyes,
please report them immediately.

On no account should you
attempt to flirt back

as this may result in giggling,
unseemly canoodling,

irritable looks from bystanders,
and the imposition of a hefty fine.

10th January

....

The Metropolitan Railway – the world's oldest underground railway
– opened between Paddington and Farringdon on this day in 1863,
forming the first line of what would become the London Underground.
Things back then were very different to the Underground we know
today: trains were steam-powered; carriages were lit by gas lamps;
passengers could choose between first- and second-class travel; and
there were fewer adverts showing how to get a better deal on your
home insurance. Gaps were not introduced until 1883, although it
was to be another twenty years before a warning to mind them came
into force.

Love Notes from the Underground

A Monument I will build for you,
my Angel, where nightly I will stroll.
Or Morden that, a shining Temple –
from Brixton mortar, Burnt Oak and gold,
a Plaistow go in worship of you,
to provide a Balham for my soul.

Hainault, I wasn't Holborn yesterday
and I know you like Stanmore than me
but don't let our futures be Edgware,
or leave me Barking up the wrong tree.
It's true, I may not be a Richmond
but you can Bank on me.

It appears, Euston, we have a problem.
You're the bee's Neasden, yes, it's true,
but you Maida Vale I can't see behind
and I'm right at the back of your Kew.
Yet it's never Oval until it's Oval
and I'm Pinner all my hopes on you.

Just say the word and it Wimbledon.
It's time to Acton what our hearts say.
With you, I've found my station in life –
let's walk through the Archway.
Know this – always and without fail –
my love for you shall Perivale.

11th January

The first state lottery took place in England on this day in 1569. It was introduced by Elizabeth I to raise money to strengthen coastal defences, vulnerable to Spanish invasion. First prize was a huge £5,000, paid in 'ready money', plate, tapestries and cloth. It wasn't a success, however. Tickets were ten shillings each, too expensive for most people, and the whole enterprise was regarded with suspicion. Subsequent lotteries proved more popular, and helped to fund the building of Westminster Bridge in the 1730s and the British Museum in the 1750s. But, as gambling increased across the country, the lottery eventually came to be seen as a great moral evil and was stopped in 1826, never to be introduced again, until it was.

Odds

The chances of winning the lottery
are 1 in 45,057,474,
or, to express this probability
in a non-mathematical way,
quite slim.

Statistically, being crushed to death
by a vending machine
is a far more likely occurrence –
particularly for me,
as I use vending machines a lot
and I've never bought
a lottery ticket.

12th January

On this day in 1976, pioneering surfer Dame Agatha Christie died, aged eighty-five. Not only is she regarded as being one of Britain's first ever stand-up wave-riders, she is also the best-selling novelist of all time, having sold between two billion and four billion books (and possibly a few million more by the time this book goes to press). My little grey cells can rarely work out who, amongst her cast of questionable characters, has perpetrated the crime; this, despite the fact they always have one thing in common – they're the person I had least suspected.

In the Drawing Room

And for these reasons, Colonel,
I contend it could not possibly have been you.
Nor, as we have seen, could your housekeeper,
the redoubtable Mrs Payne,
have access to the Remington Home Portable
upon that fateful day.

And while the behaviour of Mr Cedric Guscott
may have been ill-advised,
the issue of his gambling debts
must be regarded as a mere red herring;
a conclusion which may come as some relief
to the impulsive but well-meaning Miss Robson,
who, as I have already proven,
did not set out deliberately to deceive.

May I be the first to congratulate the two of you
on your engagement.

No, there is only one person here
who possessed the means, motive and opportunity.
One person, whose devilish designs
and fiendish plotting sought to mislead us
at every turn; whose little grey cells
fooled us all, and for so long.

Dame Agatha,
perhaps you would like to tell us
how you did it?

13th January

*Michael Bond, the children's writer, was born on this day in 1926.
The inspiration behind his most famous creation came from his
encounter with a small bear as he took shelter in Selfridge's toy
department, on a snowy Christmas Eve. He took him home and named
him Paddington, after the railway station. Later, while sitting in front
of a blank sheet of paper, he felt the bear's hard stare upon him, and
Bond began to imagine what would happen if a real bear had found
himself at Paddington Station, friendless, alone, with a label around
his neck, like a refugee in the war. And if that was to happen now,
what would come next? How the story unfolds tells us a lot about who
we are, and the place where we now live.*

Please Bear in Mind

that the Department of Visas and Immigration
claim he has ideas above his station,
having arrived into this Great Nation
without the proper documentation.

But what they fail to understand
is that this isn't the life that he had planned.
He could no longer stay in his homeland.
He's just looking for a helping hand.

His wellies are red, his duffle coat blue.
He wears a wide-brimmed hat from Darkest Peru.
If you should see him then here's what to do:
Please look after him. That's all. Thank you.

14th January

....

*On this day in 1966, a teenager changed his name. David Robert
Jones was looking to make a name for himself but annoyingly, another
Davy Jones was already out there doing just that: a young actor who,
having hit the big-time in* Coronation Street, *was now becoming
famous by making a Monkee of himself. In response, the young man
did what any out-monikered teenager would do in such a situation:
take the name of a nineteenth-century American pioneer and the
knife he had popularised. This wasn't the only time David Bowie was*

*to reinvent himself: later personae included Ziggy Stardust, Aladdin
Sane, The Thin White Duke, and the Goblin King.*

Ch-Ch-Ch-Changes

It's time to ring the changes.
I shall be braver, be bolder,
grow my hair down to my shoulders,
sport a handlebar moustache,
with a tattoo of my favourite snooker player
inked across my back.

I shall moisturise and wear eyeliner,
shave off a sideburn in protest
against human rights abuses in China.
I shall accessorise with piercings
and a cockapoo. My spirit animal
will be the brindled gnu

and every day, I shall totter off
for a macchiato and chocolate croissant
on silver-glittered platform shoes
and not use the tongs which the cafe provides,
being careful not to get crumbs
on my skin-tight leopard-print strides.

I shall wear star-shaped sunglasses,
even when it's murky out
and regardless of whether I bump into things.

I shall enrol on a course of dolphin therapy.
My in-tray and LinkedIn profile
shall be neglected terribly.

I shall change my name to Marlon DuBois,
Spike Vuvuzela or Dr Atticus Flyte,
and this will all take effect from seven tonight.
Although – come to think of it –
next Tuesday might be better,
or maybe a few weeks after that.

15th January

....

*On this day in 2001, Wikipedia, the free public-generated
encyclopedia, went online. According to Wikipedia, that is. I mean, it
might not be true and I should probably double-check this entry with
some peer-reviewed academic research but I don't have time. Although,
while I'm at it, I might just have a quick read of their featured article
from today on Marwan I (c. 625–685), the fourth Umayyad caliph
– then read up about the goosefish, deconstructivist architecture, the
1945 Prague Uprising, and the complete discography of Leo Sayer.*

A Quick Dip into Wikipedia

the First Republic of Armenia →
Anthimus of Nicomedia →
the playing career of Jimmy Melia →
a quick dip into Wikipedia

the diagnosis of synaesthesia →
the cultural forms of psychedelia →
the definition of oenophilia →
just ten more mins on Wikipedia

the legacy of George Bush, Snr. →
the track listing of *Quadrophenia* →
Vratislaus II of Bohemia →
can't stop reading Wikipedia

the distribution of crocodilia →
the reception of Millais's *Ophelia* →
hypogammaglobulinemia →
whole day spent on Wikipedia

16th January

....

*The original Cavern Club opened at 10 Mathew Street in Liverpool
on this day in 1957. Top of the bill was the Merseysippi Jazz Band,
supported by the Wall City Jazz Men. Through the early 1960s, the
Cavern was to host a number of popular beat combos of the time,
including Gerry & the Pacemakers, Billy J. Kramer, the Merseybeats,
and The Beatles (note: must check spelling). None, though, were able
to repeat the glories of that first evening with the Merseysippi Jazz
Band, featuring the frenzied ivory-tickling of Frank Robinson and
some inspired noodling by banjoist Ken 'Nob' Baldwin.*

Outside the Cavern

He's fiddling with his quiff and tie
when she joins him in the queue.
It stretches the length of Mathew Street

but it's moving, going steady,
getting better all the time. He lights
her cigarette, chatters nervously

about The Coney Island Skiffle Group
while they shuffle forwards,
already halfway across the universe.

Some places have their moments –
in this street which reeks of rotting fruit
and tobacco and cheap perfume,

time stands in line with them,
forms an orderly queue, fifty years deep,
stretches back to this January night,

a night cold enough to see your breath
in the murky light of a Mersey moon.
He reaches out and holds her hand.

She doesn't know it yet, but she loves him;
they stand there on the threshold,
at the start of it all, then head through the door.

17th January

....

It was on this day in 1920 that Prohibition began in the United States,
a nationwide ban on the production, importation, and sale of alcohol.
It lasted until 1933. But if necessity is the mother of invention, then
forced sobriety is the controlling stepfather of deception, and no time
was lost in finding ways around the ban. Illicit establishments, known
as 'speakeasies' (a phrase of British origin, meaning to lower one's
voice), sprang up across the country to sell alcohol. Speakeasies often
contained secret rooms, trap doors, fake walls, or rotating shelves, in
order to thwart the police; assuming, that is, they weren't in on the
secret themselves and being paid to keep quiet.

write-easy

dear reader,   lovelydearreader,
swear to you i' ve not touched a drip
poets, youknow, are a soberbunch
yes, that's write –   i do right like this
%
hey! do not castsuch aspirations
iam   nOt blurringwords allthe time
i haveNOt beento a   write-easy
somethingsomething something moonshine

i'm tellingyou, i am tootally tooteetal
itsprobablyjust   *   autocorrecT
i'll prove it – watch me write these words in one long very straight line
there justlike I sed   it's Prefect

18th January

....

Today is Thesaurus Day. It honours Peter Mark Roget, author of
Roget's Thesaurus, who was born on this day in 1779. Although there
were earlier collections of synonyms, it was Roget more than any other
compiler who became synonymous, interchangeable, analogous with
such works, and his thesaurus remains the standard today. Before the
first thesaurus came along, writers just had to use whatever words were
in their heads – or, to put it another way, whatever terms were in their
noggins.

Roger's Thesaurus

In order to grow, expand, widen
his lexicological corpus,
Roger bought, acquired, purchased
a synonymopedia, a thesaurus.

Soon, presently, without delay,
he no longer ran out of things to say,
speak, utter, express, articulate,
give voice to, pronounce, communicate.

This was all very well, fine, great,
wonderful, super, terrific
but his friends, mates, pals thought him
boring, tedious, dull, soporific.

So let this be a warning,
an omen, a sign, a premonition,
it's all very well to show learning,
education, knowledge, erudition,

but here's a top tip,
a suggestion, some advice,
don't ever let it stop you
from being concise,

brief, short, clear, pithy,
succinct, compendious, to the point.
Breviloquent.

19th January

....

*On this day in 2000 the Austrian-born American actress Hedy
Lamarr died, at the age of eighty-five. Promoted by the Hollywood
studio MGM as 'the world's most beautiful woman', she became a
star with her performances in films such as* Algiers *and* Samson
and Delilah. *What they failed to mention in their publicity was
that she was also a complete brainbox. In her spare time, she liked
to invent things. At the beginning of World War II, she developed
a radio guidance system for Allied torpedoes, along with composer
George Antheil. Although the technology was not adopted by the US
Navy until the 1960s, its techniques and principles have since become
incorporated into Bluetooth technology. So yes, there was that, too.*

Just Stand Still and Look Stupid

So, here's the pitch.
There's this broad, looks a million dollars,
the most beautiful woman in the world we'll call her,
the kind of dame to put the fizz in your soda,
if you catch my drift, and she's got all these men
falling over her, knocking themselves out for her,
yeah, yeah, I know, you've heard it all before,
but here comes the twist, now get this . . .
she's an inventor, yeah, like she's got all these crazy ideas,
some of them even better than a man can come up with,
and she figures out this system, some kooky system,
where ships can communicate in secret,
let's call it frequency hopping or some batshit like that,
and somehow or other, it helps our boys win the war.
Yeah, that's right, we win the war
and all because of some lush in a lab coat.

What's that? Too far-fetched?
OK, then, how about we ditch the inventor bit,
or better still, we get a man to be the inventor,
Clark Gable – or Spencer Tracy, maybe –
and she's the beautiful German spy he falls in love with
but who has to keep her identity under wraps.
Yeah, that should do it – far more believable.
It'll be box office gold.

20th January

In terms of celebration days, penguins do pretty well for themselves: they get today – Penguin Awareness Day – as well as World Penguin Day on 25th April, which roughly coincides with their annual migration. In terms of a few other things, such as their vulnerability to global warming, their vanishing habitats, and their declining populations, they've been doing less well of late. Given that, two days a year dedicated to penguins – and figuring out what we can do to stop them from being wiped off the planet – doesn't seem nearly enough.

Penguin Awareness

I've been aware of penguins since I was three:
I think one may have moved in with me.

The signs are everywhere.
The smell of saltwater in the air.
There are moulted feathers on my chair
Yesterday I found a fish upon the stair.
But when I turn around there's no one there,
for he moves in the shadows, like Tony Soprano;
I am forever stepping in guano.

I don't know why he's come to live with me.
There are better places for him to be.
But when I've gone to bed, I can hear the tread
of his soft heels across the kitchen floor,
and the opening of the freezer door.

And I picture him there,
his head resting on a frozen shelf,
dreaming sadly of somewhere else,
thinking about the hand that life has dealt him,
and I wonder if his heart is melting.

21st January

....

National Hug Day, which occurs on this day every year, celebrates the
act of hugging, an activity which can help to lower blood pressure and
the risk of heart disease, trigger the release of healthy hormones, and
make some of us feel awkward on doorsteps and street corners.

Before You Hug Me, Don't

I've never quite mastered the art of the hug.
I know the benefits. I've read the research
but I'm struck by a fear of being left in the lurch,
of taking the plunge and making a lunge
only to find that it's mistimed or misjudged,
and dismissed with a frown, a slap, or a shrug.

I'd like to hug but I'm not sure I know how.
I come at it from all the wrong angles –
an arm finds itself squashed or else it dangles
useless, forlorn like a broken bough.
And then there's the question
of how much time to allow

and where to put my stupid head.
Off to one side? Or something bolder?
Cheek to cheek? Nuzzled into a shoulder?
What is the optimal pressure of squeeze?
And what would happen if I should sneeze?
Or if one of us had some awful disease?

A hug's no good when born of unease.
The hugged always know. So, please,
let's agree that neither of us will lean forward –
instead, we can just stand there, feeling awkward,
grasp an elbow at most, pull a strange face,
forgo the gauche ballet of close embrace,
and not encroach upon personal space.

22nd January

....

*On this day in 1927, Teddy Wakeham and C. A. Lewis provided the
first football commentary on British radio as Arsenal and Sheffield
United played out a 1–1 draw. The Radio Times issued a Listener's
Plan dividing the pitch into sections, which were then called out as the
ball entered each section during the commentary. It was thought that
the ball being kicked back to a goalkeeper provided the origin of the
phrase 'back to square one', although in the Notes & Queries column
of* The Guardian, *a letter from Mr Norman Brindley, Caddington,
Beds, disputes this etymology, claiming the phrase dates back to earlier
board games. But I'm afraid it's too late now, Mr Norman Brindley,
Caddington, Beds, I have already written this poem.*

Sideways to Square Four

If you are tuning in late, you've not missed much.
The community singing at 2.50 was a rousing affair
and my half-time cup of Bovril – thank you, Sandra! –
has certainly helped to warm the cockles.

As for the game, the Gunners lead through a Buchan header
on a Highbury pitch that resembles an ice rink.
Both teams have exhibited extraordinary pluck
and determination to contend with these conditions.

Remember you can follow along with all the action
on your *Radio Times* Sectioned Pitch Plan.
And don't forget, for those of you listening in black and white,
Sheffield United are the team playing in stripes.

And it's United now, who have a corner (*square 7*).
Tunstall crosses it and there's Gillespie (*square 8*) to nod it in!
United are level! And the game is right back now
to where it started. If only there were a phrase for that.

23rd January

....

Walter Frederick Morrison and his future wife Lucile liked to throw
things at each other. On Thanksgiving Day 1937, they tossed around
a popcorn can lid. At their local beach, they would fling cake pans
back and forth with joyful abandon. When people began to buy the

*cake pans from them, Morrison decided to design and sell his own
aerodynamically-enhanced flying discs: the Whirlo-Way, the Flyin-
Saucer, the Pluto Platter. The rights to the last of these he sold to
the Wham-O toy company on this day in 1957. They renamed it
the 'Frisbee'. Since then, nearly 300 million Frisbees have been sold
around the world, becoming the best-selling toy of its kind – although
in recent times the boomerang has been making a comeback.*

Frisbee

Frisbee whizzing
through the air,
above our heads,
over the sand,
into the water,
onto the waves,
out to sea.

You cried a lot that day.
Frisbee was a lovely dog.

24th January

....

*Scouting for Boys was published on this day in 1908. Written and
illustrated by Robert Baden-Powell, it became used as a manual in
Boy Scout training and is thought to be the fourth-best selling book of
the twentieth century. It must be said that aside from general survival
skills ('Using your eyes', 'Spooring', 'Signs round a dead body') some*

of the original content was rather moralistic in tone ('Good temper and cheeriness', 'Courtesy to women') and has not aged particularly well ('Lion hunting', 'How the empire must be held'). The art of knot-tying was introduced in the 1915 edition, in a chapter entitled 'Saving Lives with Knots'.

Saving Lives with Knots

Similar to the Snuggle Hitch
and Solicitous Bowline,
the Double-Looped Friendship Knot
can save lives
when dealing with a survival situation.

First, tie a simple Tendershank,
left over right then under,
ensuring the loose end is threaded
through the standing end,
like an Outstretched Comfort Bend

but with diagonally-opposed crossings.
This, in turn, should create
two interweaving Sympathy Loops,
which form a rounded elbow
for an Underhand Love Twist.

Pull tight to prevent snaggling,
remove any remaining slack,
and never let go. For extra fastness,
secure with a Compassionate Grip Hitch.
No rope is necessary for this exercise.

25th January

Burns Night, a celebration of the life of Robert Burns, takes place on this day every year in honour of the poet's birth in 1759. It is customary to commemorate the occasion with a Burns supper, a meal traditionally comprising haggis, neeps, and tatties, alongside whisky, speeches, toasts, poems, singing, dancing, bagpiping, and generally, much Scottishness. I've never been invited to attend such a gathering: being an English vegetarian unable to drink a tot of whisky since being hospitalised on half a litre of it at the age of fourteen, I suspect that is just as well.

Address to a Vegetarian Haggis

How warm you make me feel inside,
great chieftain of the veggie tribe!
True bearer of this nation's pride –
beans, nuts, and oats –
in Forfar, Wigtown, East Kilbride,
and John o' Groats.

Abhor the boorish carnivore
who fills his plate with meaty gore.
You give me spice and seeds galore,
not bloodstained guilt.
Upon you, mushroom gravy pour,
mindful of my kilt.

No liver, heart or lung of sheep
to haunt me when I go to sleep.
And should I fancy with my neeps
something foreign,
there's some hoisin sauce that I keep
in my sporran.

O braw and tidy recipe!
Vegan-friendly and gluten-free,
unslaughtered is the poor beastie –
thus removing what the snag is.
Join me – please raise your cutlery
to veggie Haggis!

26th January

On this day in 1926, in a crowded upper-storey room in Frith Street,
Soho, members of the Royal Institution and a few other visitors
gathered to receive a demonstration of a large transmitting machine,
containing a revolving shutter, lens disc, and light-sensitive cell.
They watched as the image of the head of a ventriloquist's doll was
transmitted, first onto a receiver in the same room as the transmitter
or 'televisor' (as its inventor, Mr John Logie Baird, referred to it),
and then in another room. The image was faint, often blurred, but
unmistakably there. Exactly ninety years later, modified versions of
that original televisor were able to receive images of a pair of brothers
taking on two sisters in Builth Wells, Powys, in a brand-new episode of
Bargain Hunt.

Tiny People

Back when I was knee-high to a space hopper,
I used to believe there were tiny people living inside
that magic box in the corner of our front room.

Whenever the box was dark and silent,
it meant there were rehearsals taking place inside –
new jokes tried out, dance routines polished,

so that when, at long last, my mum let me
make the box light up, the tiny people were ready,
word perfect, for their new performance.

Back when I was ankle-high to a pogo stick,
I used to believe that the tiny people in the magic box
were watching me as I watched them –

looking out at somebody else inside a box
and practising, too; a tiny person learning his lines,
preparing himself for the performance to come.

27th January

International Holocaust Remembrance Day is a memorial day which takes place every 27th January. It pays tribute to the memory of the six million Jewish victims of the Holocaust during the Second World War. The date marks the anniversary of the liberation of the Nazi concentration and extermination camp of Auschwitz-Birkenau which occurred on this day in 1945. The day brings people together to think about the tragic events of the past with the intention of preventing further genocides.

On the Importance of Not Forgetting

How soon we try to leave the past,
to think what's done is done
and all that happened years ago
was sad but now it's gone.

Look forward and not back, we say,
the future's coming fast.
We cannot change what came before,
the time to mourn has passed,

while unseen, the shadows gather
until the now resembles then,
and remembrance comes too late to help –
and it happens once again.

28th January

Data Protection Day (or Privacy Day as it's known outside Europe) is celebrated on this day each year. While more rigid data protection has undoubtedly been a pain for all companies and organisations that have to deal with humans, there are serious ethical and safety issues attached to the collection and use of others' personal data. When new regulations came into force in the UK a couple of years ago, I took the opportunity to unsubscribe from all the email lists I had signed up to, or had unknowingly been signed up to. It was after the third week of not having a single new email appear in my inbox, not even from my close family and friends, that I decided to resubscribe to many of those lists.

She's Opted Out of Me

She's unsubscribed from all my lists
She tells me I will not be missed
She only signed up when she was pissed
She's opted out of me

She's updated all her preferences
She's removed me from her references
She can't see what my relevance is
She's opted out of me

She's informed me that she's sick of me
She claims she wants some privacy
I've opted into misery
Now she's opted out of me

29th January

The long-running radio programme Desert Island Discs *was broadcast for the first time on this day in 1942. On the programme, guests (or 'castaways') are invited to select eight recordings they'd like to take with them to a desert island, along with a book and a luxury. The producers have made it quite clear to me that they have no intention of inviting me back after what happened last time (see 25th April), so you will never get to hear what my eclectic, thought-provoking selections would be. Instead, you can have this list of pudding-based songs which I'd listen to should I ever find myself stranded on a dessert island.*

Dessert Island Discs

Sundae Bloody Sundae
Fool If You Think It's Over
Key Lime Every Mountain
Champagne Supavlova

It's a Family Éclair
Don't It Make Your Brownies Blue
In the Gateaux
Brûlée-vous

30th January

On this day in 1649, Charles I was executed outside the Banqueting House in Whitehall. The identity of his executioner, who carried out the royal decapitation in a face mask and wig, has long been the subject of debate. In a seventeenth-century version of conspiracy theory culture, there was much debate at the time as to who it might have been – with suspects ranging from Richard Brandon, London's Common Hangman, through to, somewhat preposterously, Oliver Cromwell himself. Whoever it was, they knew what they were doing: a single blow and bish, bash, bosh, bonce in a basket.

Last Orders in the King's Head, January 1649

'Ere, you'll never guess who I had on my scaffold
the other day. Go on, have a guess! Nah, mate, not him.
John Bigg lopped his loaf off ages ago.

I'll tell you. It was only the King of England, weren't it!
Old Charlie boy – the flippin' Tyrant himself! Ever such
a big crowd there was. They were well up for it.

His maj took it pretty well, all in all. Can't be easy that,
knowing yer royal noodle's gonna be rollin' around
in front of you any moment. Reckon I was more on edge

than him, to tell you the truth. Anyhow, best thing
is to just get on with it, commit yourself
to the job at hand. The last thing anyone needs is me

hacking away at his noble bonce for ten minutes.
A mighty swing and that was it – got him in one.
Usually, I pick up their noggin and shake it at the crowd,

shout, 'Behold the head of a traitor!' or what have you,
but this time I played it cool. Wore a disguise, too, just in case.
You never know what'll happen in the future –

it mightn't look too clever on my CV should this country
ever reject the notion of parliamentary governance
and return to a monarchical system of absolutist authority.

So, if you can keep this conversation under your hood,
that would be much appreciated. And thanks for the beer.
Cheers! To the King's health! Sorry, force of habit.

31st January

April may be the cruellest month but January is by far the longest.
By the time it gets to about the 25th, it seems like it will never end
but I am given to understand that eventually it does.

Mnemonic

Thirty days hath September,
April, June and November.
Unless a leap year is its fate,
February hath twenty-eight.
All the rest hath three days more,
excepting January,
which hath six thousand,
one hundred and eighty-four.

February

1st February

....

In 1857 work began on the Oxford English Dictionary, *the foundational reference work of the English language. Twenty-seven years later the first 'fascicle' was published: in the UK on 29th January 1884 and then in the US, three days later. The fascicle – which means an unbound instalment of a larger work – was 352 pages long, covered words from 'a' through to 'ant' and, as the review below illustrates, was an absolute corker.*

A – Ant: An Analysis

An almost alchemical allegiance
amongst alphabetic allies,
agonisingly accumulated, ably amassed
and affectionately aggregated.
An admirable achievement.

Again and again, alliteration abounds.
Adjectives abut, adverbs adjoin
and ambition advances,
affording ample advantages
and accompanying adventures ahead.

Adored amongst alphabet addicts,
all accord *A–ANT* absolute acclaim.
Accessible, accurate, aidful,
and always accommodating:
an amazing accomplishment. Amen.

Anon

2nd February

....

*Groundhog Day is celebrated on this day in the United States and
Canada. It derives from the superstition that if a groundhog emerges
from its burrow on this day and sees its shadow due to clear weather
and retreats to its den, winter will continue for six more weeks.
However, if the groundhog does not see its shadow, then spring will
arrive early. This tradition was captured in a popular film starring Bill
Murray, which coincidentally is also called* Groundhog Day.

Groundhog Day

Alarm clock flips itself to six
'I Got You Babe' is in my head
I see my shadow on the wall
Think I'll stay in bed

2nd February

....

*Groundhog Day is celebrated on this day in the United States and
Canada. It derives from the superstition that if a groundhog emerges
from its burrow on this day and sees its shadow due to clear weather
and retreats to its den, winter will continue for six more weeks.
However, if the groundhog does not see its shadow, then spring will
arrive early. This tradition was captured in a popular film starring Bill
Murray, which coincidentally is also called* Groundhog Day.

Groundhog Day

Alarm clock flips itself to six
'I Got You Babe' is in my head
I see my shadow on the wall
Think I'll stay in bed

2nd February

....

Groundhog Day is celebrated on this day in the United States and Canada. It derives from the superstition that if a groundhog emerges from its burrow on this day and sees its shadow due to clear weather and retreats to its den, winter will continue for six more weeks. However, if the groundhog does not see its shadow, then spring will arrive early. This tradition was captured in a popular film starring Bill Murray, which coincidentally is also called Groundhog Day.

Groundhog Day

Alarm clock flips itself to six
'I Got You Babe' is in my head
I see no shadow on the wall
Best get out of bed

3rd February

On 3rd February 1959, a plane carrying the rock 'n' roll musicians
Buddy Holly, Ritchie Valens, and 'The Big Bopper' J. P. Richardson
crashed, killing all three along with the pilot Roger Peterson. The event
later became known as 'The Day the Music Died'. Twenty years later,
an envelope was found in a courthouse basement storage vault in Cerro
Gordo, Iowa, which contained various items recovered from the crash
site in the days that followed. Included amongst them was the Big
Bopper's wristwatch and Buddy Holly's iconic glasses.

Personal Effects

contents of manila envelope,
rec'd April 7, 1959:

one cigarette lighter
two sets of dice
two wristwatches,
one with inscription
'KTRM Champion Disc-a-thon 122hrs 8 min,
J P Richardson, 5-4-57'

and one pair of thick,
black horn-rimmed spectacles:
lenses smashed
but frames intact,
unscratched, good as new

4th February

World Cancer Day takes place on this day each year in order to raise awareness of the disease and encourage its prevention, detection, and treatment. You might be forgiven for thinking that cancer scarcely needs any more awareness raised for it, given that none of us are left untouched by it, either directly or through its impact upon those around us. But there is much that can be done – from improving education to enabling access to life-saving cancer treatment and care for all. And if medical science should fail us, we can always unleash a plague of terrifying British curses upon it until it disappears for good.

OK Cancer, That's Enough Now

I hate you, cancer.
I wish on you a plague of curses.
May you be forced to memorise the *Mahabharata* –
all two hundred thousand verses.
Or twelve of mine.
May there be engineering works on your line
on a Sunday evening
and you have to use the bus replacement service
and sit next to a sweaty, gassy Morris dancer.
That's how much I hate you, cancer.

I hate you, cancer.
May your tea get ruined
when you dunk a biscuit and it falls into your mug.

May you step on an upturned plug
having had to get up in the night with chronic indigestion.
May you finally get invited
onto *Who Wants to be a Millionaire*
only to use up all your lifelines on the £1,000 question,
and still not know the answer.
That's how much I hate you, cancer.

I hate you, cancer.
May your passport go astray
when you most need it.
May your boiler break down on Christmas Day
and you sit and shiver in your front room
watching the film adaptation of *Cats*,
including all the deleted scenes, interviews with the cast,
and a two-hour documentary on how it got made,
followed by *Grown Ups 2*, starring Adam Sandler.
That's how much I hate you, cancer.

I hate you, cancer.
I shall summon all the friends you've taken,
and bring them back here from the dead.
And when you wake up,
may you find your milk has curdled
and there is mould upon your bread
and knotweed is spreading silently
from your toes up to your head.
Yes, that's right – I'm training to be a necromancer.
That's how much I hate you, cancer.

5th February

....

The Greenwich Time Signal – commonly known as the pips – was
introduced on this day in 1924. It has remained one of Britain's most
popular time signals ever since. From 1990, BBC Radio stations have
used them to mark the precise start of each hour, except for when
there's an afternoon play on or Celine Dion is in full flow. In recent
times, the advent of digital broadcasting – and delays in the digital
signal – have affected the accuracy of the pips, causing their use and
usefulness to diminish. This may lead to the eventual retirement of the
pips or to their retraining as bleep censors should public broadcasting
become swearier.

Tempus Fugitive

one of the pips went missing
and a world of chaos beckoned
everything started too early
by one-tenth of a second

nobody knew which pip it was
but the time flew by that week
no beep beep beep beep beep beeeeeeep
only beep beep beep beep beeeeeeep

out of the blue, the pip came back –
from where, it did not disclose
where time goes, we haven't a clue
all we know is that it goes

6th February

On the afternoon of 6th February 1958, British European Airways
Flight 609 crashed on its third attempt to take off from the slush-
and ice-covered runway at Munich-Riem Airport. Twenty-three
people on board died in this tragedy, including eight Manchester
United footballers, dubbed the Busby Babes for their youth and
success. Amongst them was Duncan Edwards, who at the time was
the youngest footballer to play for England and was regarded as the
greatest player the country had ever produced. He was twenty-one
years old when he boarded that plane, with a European Cup semi-final
to look forward to, and the whole world at his feet.

Black Country Boy Goes Home

1966. In a parallel universe,
he pops back home to see his mum.
The whole of Dudley's painted red
to cheer on their famous son.

Boys wave books at him like rattles;
smiling, he stoops to sign his name.
Fathers offer up their ciggies,
opinions on tomorrow's game,

while he wonders how he got here,
this unparalleled afternoon.
Three FA Cups. Five league titles.
One World Cup – another soon?

Perhaps. Only the past is known:
what is done cannot be undone,
no more than the memory of snow
can be melted by the sun.

7th February

....

*Periodic Table Day is not a periodic celebration of tables (and related
furniture), but of the Periodic Table more specifically, on 7th February
every year. It commemorates the first appearance of the table (designed
by the English chemist John Newlands) in 1863, when it contained
only 56 elements. These days, the table totals 118 elements, and has
been redesigned several times. Its significance cannot be overstated,
both as a critical information reference tool for scientists, and as a
source of low-scoring answers for competitors on the popular teatime
quiz show* Pointless.

Periodic Updates

Radox – Crouton – Jargon – Bourbon –
Brassic – Jolene – Oxymoron

Decaf – Sliver – Shebanganese –
Aquarium – Pleather – Anti-freeze

Horlix – Triptych – Pandemonium –
Antipathy – Einsteinagogium

Zilt – Pantyline – Podium – Tedium –
Kimkardashium – Lint – Delirium

Feline – Bosphorus – Condominium
Nectarine – Vermouth – Thanksamillium

8th February

The architect and designer Sir Giles Gilbert Scott died on this day in 1960. As well as designing Liverpool Cathedral and overseeing rebuilding work at the Houses of Parliament after the Second World War, Scott designed the iconic red British telephone box. With the advent of the mobile phone, the need to fiddle around for the right coins while inhaling the stench of stale urine has receded but I still miss the phone box with its connections to the past. Thankfully, there remain plenty of them about. Some now host miniature libraries, art galleries, or memorials, without a working phone in sight: not that many had working phones in the first place, as I recall.

The Phone Box on the Corner

It stood there in all weathers,
a sentry guarding entry to an old world,
glass framed in poppy red
and a proclamation of love
sprayed on the door.

It brought me the news –
plans for the spare room, Dad's
sciatica, benedictions from the dog –
as I fumbled with change
two hundred miles from home.

The pips would go then so
would I, returning each Sunday,
and finally no longer, until
time-travelling back to the town
I left thirty years ago,

it stops me in my tracks,
standing on the corner
of a new century – the phone
now a defibrillator
in a box still saving lives.

9th February

It was on this day in 1986 that Halley's Comet was last visible in the
inner Solar System. Like the appearance of Birmingham City in an FA
Cup Final, the comet only comes around every seventy-five to seventy-
six years. This means it won't pop up in our night skies again until
2061 – by which time I shall probably have to be unfrozen from my
cryogenic state in order to see it. In fact, I have informed the cryonic
company Frozen Slumbers Inc.® to do just that, alongside instructions
also to wake me should Birmingham City ever reach the FA Cup Final.

A Brief History of Halley's Comet

It is thought that Pliny the Elder may have seen it,
and Tigranes the Great, that most brilliant
of Armenian kings, may have had a comet
with a distinctive curved tail carved into his crown.

Chinese astronomers recorded its apparition
in the Book of Han in 12 BCE, the same year
it was believed to have hovered over Rome
to portend the end of Marcus Vipsanius Agrippa.

It heralded the defeat of Attila the Hun in 451
while in the Bayeux Tapestry we see it depicted
for the first time, auguring badly for ill-starred Harold.
Genghis Khan was said to have turned to Europe

because of it, and by 1705 Edmund Halley could tell us
when next it would return. In 1835, observatories
around the world were watching out for it; in April 1910,
the first photos were taken; while its last appearance

(which I missed) took place in 1986 as I was making
an unsuccessful attempt to chat up Sarah Crosbie
at Lisa Todd's party. I doubt I'll live to get another chance
but frankly she's the one who's missing out.

10th February

....

Today is World Pulses Day, a designated United Nations event which
recognises the importance of pulses as a global food. You can't beat
a good pulse: they're packed with nutrients, full of protein, and have
tons of economic and environmental benefits. A few years ago, I'd have
probably produced a poem with 'finger on the pulse' as its punchline,
but I like to think my writing has evolved a good deal since then.
Instead, here's a poem, which starts with the punchline and goes
nowhere fast after that.

At the Speed of Zero Beats per Minute

To set pulses racing
is not quite as exciting as it sounds.
For one thing, they don't move very quickly –
not even the top seeds,
like the runner bean,
their lack of mobility doing them no favas.

Undeterred, we placed our bets.
Your heart was with the kidney,
I put a fiver on the black beluga
while opinion concerning the pea was   split.
One sharp blow on your flageolet
and they were off.

Two hours we sat there, watching them,
during which the old adage
of a lentil being as inanimate as a chickpea
never seemed more apt
until, outpaced by boredom and hunger,

you went upstairs to read your book
on the danger of misinterpreting idioms,
while I swept up the field,
dropped them into a large pot
and made dinner.

11th February

Although there has been much progress over the last twenty years in dismantling gender stereotypes within science, it is estimated that less than 30 per cent of scientific researchers worldwide are women. What's more, those women who have found their way into STEM fields are paid less, and do not progress as far as men in their careers. The International Day of Women and Girls in Science, which occurs on this day each year, aims to address this by creating full and equal access to, and participation in, science for women and girls: it's a kind of women's lab movement, if you will.

Equipment

For today's practical you will need:

a **set of scales** on which to weigh gender imbalances

a **tripod** for mounting a sustained attack on inequality

a **pipette** to squeeze out every last drop of bias

a **mortar and pestle** to grind centuries of stereotyping into a fine, powdery dust

a **magnet** to attract more women into science

a **petri dish** to cultivate interest from girls at an early age

a **microscope** to examine impediments to progress

a **pen** to rewrite the history books

and, finally, a **Bunsen burner** to put some heat under it all.

12th February

....

Today is Darwin Day, a commemoration of the naturalist, biologist
and geologist Charles Darwin, who was born on this day in 1809.
It highlights the contribution he made to the science of evolution,
and his theory that we all descend from common ancestors. In spite of
the rather trivial matter of Darwin having scientific truth on his side,
there are still those who continue to think that God created the Earth
in six days, between 6,000 and 10,000 years ago – thus giving some
credence themselves to the theory that not all life forms evolve.

Who Do You Think You Are?

I guess it must have been several months
since I'd popped my saliva in the post
so the lab results when they arrived,
came as something as a surprise,

not least the news that I was related
to a chimpanzee called Alan,
about 300,000 generations back,
on my father's side.

I googled him. I discovered that Alan
had once been a big wheel
in the personal grooming industry.
Beyond that, I couldn't find much.

But I couldn't stop thinking about him,
wondering what we might have in common.
These ears? A haplessness at DIY?
Had he dreaded dinner parties as much as me?

At the same time, I couldn't help thinking
the ancestry company had got it slightly wrong.
If my calculations were correct,
Alan would have been swinging around,

cracking open nuts and shotgunning beer,
more like 320,000 generations ago,
but then maybe that's just me:
I always have been a bit of a nit-picker.

13th February

....

*I listen to the radio a lot. Actually, that's not quite true. I have the
radio on a lot, and only sometimes do I listen to it. It's a gentle
murmuring in my kitchen, a defence against silence and solitude as
I eat cereal or empty the dishwasher. And then a song will catch my
attention, or there'll be a wicket, or a sudden clanging will occur and
I will realise that for the last twenty minutes people have been talking
about their shared passion for campanology. Once a year, on 13th
February, I might hear the phrase 'Radio Day' and wonder what that's
all about, having not tuned in to the rest of the feature, distracted as
I am by the construction of an elaborate lunchtime sandwich.*

Tuning the Dial

We're lost in music, caught . . . . at second slip,
low down, by the outstretched hand of . . . .
Deputy Prime Minister, Dominic Raab, who was
. . . . working as a waitress in a cocktail bar
when . . . . Shostakovich's Symphony No. 7
was premiered in the . . . . Forties. South
or southwest 5 to 7, occasionally gale . . . .
from Croydon is on the line, who wants to talk to
us about . . . . why Aviva life insurance
is right for you and . . . . offers me
protection, a lot of love and affection whether I'm
right or . . . . left wing but there's nobody
in the centre and the ball gets cleared to . . . .
. . . . Oscar Wilde, who famously announced
'I have nothing to declare except . . . .
. . . . . . I can boogie, boogie woogie all night long.'

14th February

St Valentine's Day is celebrated on this day by lovers young and old, tall and short, bewhiskered and smooth-skinned. Non-lovers are advised to stay indoors on this day, steer clear of social media feeds, and avoid listening to 'You Belong with Me' by Taylor Swift on repeat for twelve hours. As for the patron saint of love himself, little is known about Valentine beyond his martyrdom on this day in AD 269 and his ownership of a successful franchise of florists, chocolatiers, and greeting-card shops.

The Annual Valentine's Day Massacre

All the other boys seemed to get one,
pressed between the pages of their French textbook
or falling out of a locker after swimming.
But not for me, that kind of luck.

Every year, the postie's sack would bulge
with expectation. *Pour moi, une lettre d'amour?*
Mais, non. The latest Kay's catalogue
and the water bill. *Oh, zut alors!*

Until, at the age of fifteen, I got my first.
In my schoolbag, amongst leaky pens,
snapped shatterproof rulers, biscuit crumbs.
'From a secret admirer,' I read.

The next year, same message, same hand;
each Valentine's Day, from that point on.
I rang her, in the end, my biggest fan.
'Thanks, Mum,' I said. 'But I'm forty-one.'

15th February

....

The UK and Ireland decimalised their currencies on this day in
1971. Public information campaigns had run for two years prior to
the switch-over on Decimal Day, or D-Day as it was referred to at
the time. Some worried that unscrupulous shopkeepers might take
advantage of the confusion as people adjusted themselves to this weird
new system which seemed complicated and unintuitive, particularly
after the simplicity of the £sd currency of pounds, shillings, and pence.

£sd

Look, it's perfectly simple.
A pound's a pound – whatever you call it –
and there's twenty shillings in a pound.
You've got twelve pennies to every bob
(a bob is what we sometimes call a shilling)
so that makes two hundred and forty pennies in a pound –
or nine hundred and sixty farthings
on account of there being four farthings to each penny.
Of course, if you're still working in groats,
they're as good as fourpence,
so that's a third of a bob, or a sixth of a florin.

Now, your half-crown, that's two and six –
why are you looking at me like that? –
two and six is thirty pence, so that means a crown
is worth five shillings or quarter of a pound.
A half-guinea's ten bob and six,
and it almost goes without saying
there are two half-guineas to a guinea,
so that's twenty-one shillings, although it used to be twenty.
And thirty. Anyway, we don't use those now.

I've not gone through the ha'penny,
the threepenny bit, or the sixpence,
but I'm sure you've got the hang of it by now –
it's a perfectly sensible system.
Why would you want to mess with it? There'd be havoc.
Some people aren't very good with change.

16th February

On this day in 1923, Howard Carter unsealed the burial chamber
of Tutankhamun, revealing the Egyptian king's 3,200-years-old
mummified remains. Inside they found jewellery, gold, a chariot,
weapons, and a stone sarcophagus containing three coffins nested
within each other. Inside the final coffin, made of solid gold, was King
Tut himself. Stories later spread about a curse on anyone who dared
to break into a pharaoh's tomb. This, of course, was ridiculous and
the subsequent deaths of eight members of Carter's team in violent or
peculiar circumstances were entirely coincidental.

Tutankhamun

was what we said to Ian Watkins that day
to express our disbelief about what he had just told us,
an utterance accompanied by a mimed elongation
of our chins in imitation of the late Pharaoh's beard.

Jimmy Hill would sometimes get used in a similar context,
as would *chinny reckon*. None of us knew back then
about the mandibular prognathism suffered
by the Habsburgs after centuries of interbreeding

or we might have been tempted to utter *Charles V*
in recognition of his abnormally protrusive jaw.
It was only later, too – and much too late for Ian Watkins –
that we were to learn of King Tut's curse

and how our disbelief at the story he told us
did not mean it to be untrue, and how some things
are in need of air, require an opportunity to breathe
and should not be sealed back into their tomb.

17th February

....

*Random Acts of Kindness Day, which occurs on this day each year, was
set up to encourage kindness which, one imagines, can only be a good
thing. Recent acts of kindness have included the offering of a seat on*

*the number 367 bus from Stranraer to Portpatrick; a compliment paid
concerning a dusk blue lambswool cardigan; the lending of a pair of
pinking shears; and the sending of a tweet to congratulate someone on
their impeccable grammar.*

Random Acts of Kindness

help old ladies cross the road
write your friend a thoughtful ode
hand out jerkins dyed with woad
random acts of kindness

reduce a colleague's large workload
nurse to health an injured toad
make someone with joy explode
acts of random kindness

hand out with joy an injured road
write someone a large workload
cross a jerkin with an ode
kindness acts of random

help old ladies dyed with woad
reduce a colleague's thoughtful toad
make a friend or nurse explode
random kinds of actness

18th February

In the same way that 25th December is now inextricably linked with Christmas Day, 18th February has become synonymous with National Battery Day. Well, it has in the US anyway. And why not – because, when you think about it, batteries are everywhere! They're in our phones and our watches; they're in our cars, smoke detectors, and hearing aids. They're even in that box on the shelf in the utility room you use to store spare batteries. The date commemorates the birth of Alessandro Volta in 1745, the Italian physicist who was to later go on to invent the volt.

(2%) Battery Will Get You Nowhere

Oh dear, what can the matter be?
My phone has run out of batt

19th February

EastEnders *made its first appearance on this day in 1985. Set in the fictional borough of Walford, E20, the long-running TV soap opera began in dramatic fashion with the discovery of local resident Reg Cox (played brilliantly by the actor Johnnie Clayton), unconscious in his armchair. He will later die in hospital and we discover that he's been murdered by Nick Cotton for his war medals. Fortunately, the show has taken a lighter turn since, with the possible exceptions of when Tanya buried her husband alive, and when Albert Square was rocked by the news that the bin collections would be changing from weekly to fortnightly.*

A Weep and Wail of Unrequited Push and Shove

you're the real Ian Beale, babes,
make no Cadbury Flake,
but to find a way to your cherry tart
ain't no piece of cake

when I see you down the Fatboy Slim
or in the field of wheat,
I'm a great big bag of West Ham Reserves
to think that we might meet

a fog comes over my watch and chain,
stops it working as it oughta,
dicky-birds stick to my Brigham Young,
and come out Allan Border

oh, to hold you in my Chalk Farms
as the currant bun starts to rise
let me press my filter tips to yours
& gaze into your mince pies

one day I'll get you off my George Best
& at last I will be free
'til then I walk in the pleasure and pain,
the poor fridge freezer that is me

20th February

It was on this day in 1877 that the world premiere of Tchaikovsky's ballet Swan Lake *took place at the Bolshoi Theatre in Moscow. Although you could also say it was on 4th March. It depends which calendar you use – and whether you go with the date convention used at the time, or convert the date to what it is now. Russia, you see, didn't move to the Gregorian calendar until 1918 so 20th February was the date that the ballet premiered under the old Julian calendar-based system and now I've wasted all of this introduction in discussing the problems inherent in Old Style vs New Style calendar conventions, and have run out of space to discuss the exquisite enchantment of* Swan Lake *or, indeed, the beauty of swans themselves.*

The Truth about Swans

It is a myth, of course,
that a swan can break your arm,
but they are capable
of flipping you onto your back
through a smartly-executed *seoi-nage*.

Don't be fooled into thinking that all swans
exhibit proficiency in judo;
many never make it past the rank of first kyu,
while in recent times,
there has been a resurgence

in capoeira, particularly
amongst the more enlightened cobs and pens
keen to instil in their cygnets
a love of music and dance,
alongside all the honking and fighting.

Another long-perpetuated myth
is that all swans belong to the Queen –
that would be ridiculous.
The Queen only owns the unmarked mute ones,
which is in itself ridiculous.

21st February

The first telephone directory was published on this day in 1878. It took the form of a piece of card that listed the fifty individuals and businesses with telephones in New Haven, Connecticut. The first phone book covering the whole of Britain was published in 1896; it contained 81,000 numbers and 1,350 pages. The 1970s are now regarded as the Golden Age of the Telephone Directory. Estimates for that era indicate there were an awful lot of them knocking about. With the advent of the internet, however, the phone book's days were numbered, and now they are only produced in order to be ripped up at the annual competition for the World's Strongest Man.

The Telephone Directory: A Book Review

To the uninitiated, this is a book
which, at first glance, may appear to be
a somewhat daunting read
with an overly long cast of characters.

However, the author is to be commended
for the single-mindedness of his vision
and unwillingness to sacrifice his Art
or let the reader off the hook.

This is no publishing-by-numbers exercise.
Each line connects the reader
to the lives of this small-town community,
sometimes with engaging results.

Who is the mysterious Pemberton, C.?
What is the significance of 01236 443 788?
Will the Smiths be able to keep up with the Joneses?
What is the area code for Stoke-on-Trent?

With echoes of *Calls of the Wild*
and *Lord of the Rings*, it is a worthy successor
to the author's previous book,
1001 ISBNs I Have Known and Loved.

22nd February

....

The cloning of Dolly the Sheep was first announced on this day
in 1997. Dolly (surname unknown) had been born seven months
earlier, and became the first mammal ever to be cloned from another
individual's body cell. The announcement propelled Dolly into the
spotlight: a whirl of newspaper articles, television adverts, chat shows,
and theatrical roles resulted, including an ill-advised foray into the
world of celebrity fragrances. The cloning of Dolly was to lead to
concerns that human cloning would be next, until such research was
banned by United Nations protocol following the Jedward Scandal
of 2009.

Send in the Clones

Isn't it strange?
Isn't it weird?
To find myself jumping around
And sometimes sheared.
Where are the clones?

Oh, how it hurts
My ovine skull,
To be just cells on some glass
Then to have wool.
Where are the clones?
There ought to be clones.

Don't you love grass?
Isn't it fab?
Far better than hanging around
In some old lab.
But where are the clones?
Send in the clones.
Don't bother, I'm here.

23rd February

....

On this day in 1947, the International Standards Organization (ISO)
was founded, with the goal of promoting worldwide standards across
industry and commerce. You may be familiar with them through their
ground-breaking standard ISO 27001:2013 and the controversial
but robust 31000:2009. Out of all of the competing and conflicting
international standards organisations out there, the ISO is my
favourite; far better than the Organization for International Standards
(OIS), the International Organization for Standards (IOS) or those
absolute clowns at the Global Council for Organizing Standards
Internationally (GCOSI).

Standards in Modern Poetry

Please note that this poem conforms
to ISO standard 478182-1:2021
which states that no poem be confined
by fixed regulations concerning meter or rhyme scheme

nor require strict adherence to form and structure,
unless the poet deems it necessary
in the writing of the poem.
ISO standard 478182-1:2021 supports the move

to a new stanza whenever the poet wishes,
    the indentation of lines,
                not   to mention
            allthis   kindof thing.
the employment of capital letters
or a full stop at the end of sentence
is not compulsory

ISO standard 478182-1:2020 also recognises
that the poet may elect to write about any subject
of their choosing. This includes – but is not limited to –
the moon, the human condition, the passing of time,
love, death, work, the joy or horror of having children,
guilt, loneliness, bicycles, darts, penguins, doing the bins,
or imagined international standards in poetry.

Please note that this poem also conforms
with ISO standard 526-9001:2015
making it fully compliant
with most English-language poetry anthologies
and can also be used in the construction
of ISO-approved paper aeroplanes
or as a sleeping aid for the chronic insomniac.

24th February

On 24th February 1786, the folklorist Wilhelm Grimm was born, brother of Jacob, his co-compiler of Grimm's Fairy Tales. The two brothers' retelling of German folk tales was criticised in early editions for including unsuitable material: the wicked queen in 'Snow White' was the princess's biological mother; Rapunzel has a 'merry time' in the tower with the Prince and falls pregnant; and some stories, such as 'How Some Children Played At Slaughtering', were cut and so lost the opportunity to become Disney feature films. And so the volumes were revised to make them less scary for adults – much to the disappointment of children, who tend to love that kind of stuff.

A Few Take Home Points from Grimm's Fairy Tales

Avoid, where possible, all houses situated in dark forests,
particularly ones owned by bears or witches,
or those constructed predominantly from gingerbread.

As tempting as it may be to scythe off the end of your feet
in order to squeeze them into a pair of glass slippers,
do be aware this is unlikely to provide a long-term solution.

An inability to distinguish your gran from a cross-dressing wolf
may indicate more regular eye tests are needed.
Unless, that is, you are also a wolf – in which case,
wait together companionably for a passing woodcutter.

Steer clear of talking animals, with the possible exception of parrots. Be similarly wary of talking severed fingers, quarrelsome brooms, hitchhiking millstones, overly familiar blood sausages, and so forth.

While there may be the odd occasion when a frog will transform into a handsome prince upon receipt of a kiss, mostly he will just blink back at you, leaving you both to feel a little embarrassed.

25th February

If this book hasn't long since been pulped and you happen to be reading this entry on 25th February 2031, then Happy Shrove Tuesday to you. But if you're reading it on 25th February 2024 then Shrove Tuesday will have happened twelve days previously. That's one of the problems of writing about moveable feasts: they can land anywhere, like a flip of a coin – or a toss of a pancake for that matter. But anyway, if it isn't Shrove Tuesday when you're reading this, why not treat yourself to one anyway – pancakes aren't just for Pancake Day, you know.

Flippin' Eck

I wrote a pancake poem.
Instead of eggs I used some nouns,
poured in verbs in place of milk,
added adjectives for flour.

I whisked the words together,
cooked them until golden brown
then tossed my poem in the air.
It landed upside down.

26th February

The American doctor, nutritionist and cornflake inventor John Harvey Kellogg was born on this day in 1852. He developed the cornflake as one of the chief weapons in his war on masturbation, believing such bland breakfast fare would almost certainly lead to a reduction in hands wandering off to places in which they really shouldn't wander. Ironic then that, like many inventors, he did not foresee the consequences his creation would have; neither that its recipe would be improved immeasurably by Anthony Tiger's addition of a frosted sugar coating, nor that the 'Frostie', as it came to be known, would end up becoming one of the world's most powerful aphrodisiacs.

Kellogg's Cornflakes are Really Terrific

I am writing this poem about cornflakes
in the hope that it might be spotted
by a senior manager in the Kellogg's marketing department,
who – moved by its tender, lyrical beauty
and the sincerity of its sentiment –
shares it on social media and then bestows upon me
a lifetime's supply of cornflakes.

As a rule, poets don't tend to receive much
by way of freebies, with the exception of Larkin
and his deal with a leading bicycle clip manufacturer.
They're too busy scribbling sad thoughts
about love and death and whatnot
to realise the commercial opportunities
afforded by the medium.

In this poem I shall make good use of alliteration
as I describe how the toasted flakes of corn
tantalise my tastebuds
to create a mouthful of happiness.
The word 'golden' will probably feature a number of times.
If I feel in the mood, I may make a joke
involving the phrase 'poet aureate'.

But before I crack on with all that,
I first need to finish this bowl of Cheerios,
the wholegrain Os which make my mornings ooze with oomph,
and which I also really like.

27th February

....

On this day in 1964, the Italian government asked for help to stop the Leaning Tower of Pisa from falling over. It was in serious danger of toppling, being seventeen feet out of alignment with the base, the tilt increasing every year. Proposals came in from around the world and a multi-national taskforce of engineers, mathematicians, and historians gathered to discuss solutions. It wasn't until 1999 that an answer was found, involving the removal of soil from underneath the raised north side. It seems to have arrested the movement of the Tower, aided by the millions of tourists who take photographs of it each year and prop it up with their giant hands.

A Lean Spell

You prop me up
 and I'll prop you,
  it's the least
   that I can do,
    when you find
     it hard to cope,
      and each day's
       a long, steep slope,
        the world has
         gone aslant
          and your bed
           you can't recant.
            A day will come
             to see things straight
              but until this
               spell abates,
                then, lean on me,
                 I do not mind,
                  should you feel
                   that way inclined.

28th February

An editor at the Merriam-Webster publishing house noticed the word 'dord' in the second edition of their New International Dictionary (now Webster's Dictionary) on this day in 1939. It was defined as a synonym for density. The word was an error, one which had gone unnoticed for eight years. It was caused by the dictionary's chemistry editor sending in a slip reading 'D or d, cont./density' meaning to add 'density' to the existing list of words that the letter D can abbreviate. The phrase 'D or d' was misinterpreted as a single run-together word. D'oh! The word 'dord' itself has come to represent a non-existent word which appears erroneously in a dictionary or other work of reference.

Selected Entries from *Bilston's Dictionary of Non-Existent Words*

Garblehop v.
To run down a street in dressing gown and slippers, with bin bags in hand, in the futile pursuit of a waste-disposal truck.

Misversification n.
The act of giving
a piece
of prose
the appearance of poetry

through the strategic
                deployment
of line-breaks.

Pringleton n.
A train commuter who provides unwanted assistance
with a fellow passenger's cryptic crossword.

Snagwort n.
A strand of loose wool attached to a cardigan which, when tugged,
leads to the unravelling of the whole material universe.

Umbidextrous adj.
Able to fall in effortlessly with another person's height and stride
upon being invited to share their golf umbrella.

29th February

....

*If you've woken up to find that it's 1st March already, please do not
linger here. I've only included this entry for completeness' sake and
have low expectations of it ever being read. The mathematics are
against it:*

frequency of Leap Days		readers of this book		probability of this ever being read
1/1,460	x	1/1,000,000	=	unlikely

Given these numbers, I could use this entry to write about
anything at all. Something outrageous. Scandalous, even. But I
probably shan't.

An Extra Day

If every year had an extra day, the things that I might do –
I'd paddle down the Amazon in a fibre-glass canoe
I'd write a five-part symphony with the cello and kazoo
I'd topple this bad government in an unexpected coup

If every year had an extra day, there'd be no stopping me –
I'd fix the dripping tap upstairs, I'd save the honey bee
I'd brush up on my Mandarin and earn my black belt in feng shui
I'd stop the Earth from warming and learn to water ski

If every year had an extra day, the things I might achieve –
I'd launch my own cosmetics range and make sculptures out of
    cheese
I'd bring lasting peace to the Middle East and help the refugees
I'd drive around the country collecting honorary degrees

But when an extra day does come by, it always seems the same
Just another square on which to land when playing at life's game
I should care about each one of them as I'm travelling around
Life shuffles by in smaller steps, not in leaps and bounds

March

1st March

Today is St David's Day, a day of celebration in Wales. Unlike the other nations comprising the British Isles, Wales had no need to import their patron saint from distant shores. Born in sixth century Dyfed, St David was a Welsh lad through and through, with a flair for teaching, preaching, miracles, and (probably) rugby union. One of his most famous miracles was the summoning of a hill in Ceredigion, an impressive feat and one which represents a far greater achievement than the summoning of a cardigan in Hull.

Welsh Customs

I can't deny that ever since Wales
declared itself an independent republic,
it's been something of a pain
having to go through Welsh customs.

For one thing, I dislike dressing up
in a shawl, red gown and Welsh hat.
The Customs Officers can sometimes be
overly critical of my baritone

when we sing 'Land of My Fathers',
and I can see them struggling to keep
their faces straight at my efforts
to pronounce Llanfairpwllgwyn-

gyllgogerychwyrndrobwllllanty-
siliogogogoch. My leek soup
is in need of more cream, they tell me.
With all this added rigmarole,

the queues to get across the border
are horrendous. Thank heavens
for Gwyneth, with her coal-black hair
and a smile to gladden any valley,

who'll send you through fast-track
for a bunch of golden daffs
and the timely bestowal
of a hand-carved lovespoon or two.

2nd March

....

On this day in 1995, the discovery of the top quark was announced.
I'm sure you know this already but the top quark is considered to
be the most massive of all observed fundamental particles. Whilst
researching this topic, I have learnt that there are another five types –
or flavours – of quark: up, down, charm, strange, and bottom. I have
no real idea what any of this means despite having read the Wikipedia
article about it five times, but given that a quark is a fundamental
constituent of matter, I'm sure it must all be very important.

QUARKS!

they're in my desk
they're in my chair
they're even in my underwear
they're in my boots
they're in my bed
they're burrowed deep inside my head
QUARKS!

i hear them
when i try to sleep
can't block out their blare and bleat
not quite a quack
not quite a bark
quarking at me in the dark
QUARKS!

they're in the shed
they're in the trees
they're swimming in my cup of tea
they're in Stranraer
they're in Rangoon
they're in the stars, the sun and moon
QUARKS!

not quite a bark
not quite a quack
i'm living in a quark soundtrack

i can't escape
their chirp and chatter
that's the fundamental matter
QUARKS!

they're in you, too
they're in this book
don't believe me? take a look
or bring your ear
close to this page
can you hear them quark with rage?
QUARK! QUARK! QUARK! QUARK! QUARK!

3rd March

....

*World Wildlife Day, which is held on this day every year, was
established to celebrate the world's wild animals and plants and
raise awareness of the issues affecting them. In particular, it tackles
themes of conservation, sustainable development, and the importance
of biodiversity. Barely a day goes by without there being some kind of
awareness-raising celebration in honour of a particular creature or
habitat under threat. It's almost as if a theme is developing.*

International Human Awareness Day

'The poor creatures are running out of ivory,'
said a Galapagos penguin to his fellow committee members,
at the Annual General Meeting.

'There are fears this will result in a major decline
of the luxury chess set business.'
At this, there was a general shaking of heads.

'I've heard reports of softness in the tiger skin market,'
said a whooping crane, giving his neck a good stretch,
for the session had been a lengthy one.
'Rug sales – in particular – have been affected.'
'But what will their rock stars lie on?' came a tiny voice.
It belonged to a tiny, concerned harlequin frog.

'It's not only essentials like chess sets and rugs,
handbags and jewellery,' added a Mexican wolf,
pounding a paw on the table. 'It's food, too!
The price of orangutan meat nowadays!
And they can't chop the rainforest down fast enough
to keep up with the demand for beefburgers!'

'How about we hold an awareness day for them?'
suggested an armadillo. There was no answer
from the committee chairperson: a Pinta tortoise.
Her seat was empty. And so was that
of the black rhino. And the Caribbean monk seal.
And the Yangtze River dolphin.

In fact, when they looked around the room,
they saw hundreds of seats, all now unoccupied.
Even since the meeting had begun, their numbers
had reduced. 'Let's not,' said an Amur leopard,
taking charge and bringing the item to a close.
'I think we're aware of them enough as it is.'

4th March

The Royal National Lifeboat Institution (RNLI) was founded on this day in 1824. It's estimated that RNLI lifeboat crews and lifeguards have saved more than 140,000 lives since then. In 2021 alone, it aided nearly 13,000 people and saved 408 lives. Amazing then, that the RNLI is staffed largely by volunteers – or, as the charity itself says, 'ordinary people doing extraordinary things'.

Deep Water

Lifeboat, please come rescue me!
I'm in deep water – all at sea.
I'm lacking in some buoyancy.
Lifeboat, please come rescue me!

Lifeboat, are you ocean bound?
I'm on the rocks – I've run aground.
The chances are that I'll be drowned.
Lifeboat, are you ocean bound?

Lifeboat, look I'm over here!
I fear the end will soon be near.
These waves will make me disappear.
Lifeboat, look I'm over here!

Lifeboat, bring me to your shore.
Hold me tight until I thaw
And life begins to flow once more.
Lifeboat, bring me to your shore.

5th March

The Dutch painter Jan van der Heyden was born on this day in 1637. Although famed for his acutely observed and finely detailed cityscapes, his talents didn't stop there. He was also a draughtsman, a printmaker, an engineer, and an inventor. Amongst his inventions was the firehose, created through the sewing together of fifty-foot lengths of leather. Not only that, he wrote the first firefighting manual and reorganised the Dutch fire brigade, making him the most celebrated fire-obsessed polymath of his era, with the possible exception of the French mathematician, physicist, philosopher, and theologian 'Blaze' Pascal.

Uncharted Waters

chucking buckets
of water
is OK, I s'pose

but how about
we squirt it
out of a hose?

just putting that out there

         and there

    and here

      and another one over there

6th March

It was on this day in 1899 . . . I think . . . that aspirin was patented by . . . oh, who was it . . . no, it's no good, I can't face doing this today . . . Look, I'll write this entry tomorrow. Maybe come back to this page in a day or two . . .

The Morning After the Night Before

I'd appreciate it if you could read this poem
a little more quietly than some of my others.

Thing is, it was a bit of heavy night
at the Great Orpington Poetry Festival,
and I think I may have heard one Pindaric ode too many –
sorry, please excuse me one moment –

That's better. Where was I?
Ah yes, the Pindaric odes . . . although, come to think of it,
I do remember one particular Petrarchan sonnet
sounding a little off, and it makes me wonder now
if it may have been spiked –

Look, you're reading this poem far too loudly,
practically shouting it.

Right, let's try one more time. This morning,
I thought I'd try necking a quick villanelle,
hair of the dog and all that,
but I could only keep down a couple of lines or so –

No, you're doing it again . . . this isn't going to work.
Either you need to stop reading, or I should stop writing.
Tell you what, how about I do the latter
and then let's see what happens.

But quickly – before we part – don't suppose
you've a couple of aspirins to hand, do you?

7th March

....

*On this day in 1933, unemployed electrical engineer Charles Darrow
finished creating a board game. He called it Monopoly. It was based on
a design of The Landlord Game by Elizabeth Magie but Darrow took
the credit and the money. The original Monopoly board used the streets
of Atlantic City, and a London version of the game was produced two
years later. Since those early days, more than 250 million sets are
estimated to have been sold, including the limited edition spin-off
version 'Bonopoly': like Monopoly, but where the streets have no name.*

Monopoly

They met at a beauty contest. She came first, he second.
They monopolised each other. Prosperity beckoned.
Chancers of the exchequer, they advanced straight to go.
These were the good times. How the money did flow!

Stock sales and dividends. A building loan matured.
Bank errors in their favour. An inheritance secured.

97

And every birthday – to celebrate the pleasure –
each of their friends would pay them a tenner.

They owned the streets. But it began to unwind.
Found drunk in a sports car. A small speeding fine.
Doctor and hospital fees. The cost of street repairs.
The perilous state of their financial affairs.

The Super Tax hit them. They took out a loan.
They were dispossessed of their grand Mayfair home.
They're in jail now. But no sign of contrition.
Last week, they won a crossword competition.

8th March

Today is International Women's Day, a day to celebrate the achievements of women around the world, raise awareness of bias against them, and take action for equality: an activity which bizarrely still needs to happen at – checks watch – half-past two in the twenty-first century. And yes, before you happen to ask, there is an International Men's Day and it's on 19th November.

Suggested Further Reading

The last thing anyone needs
on International Women's Day
is a poem about how brilliant women are
and the need to create a world free
of gender inequalities,
all expertly mansplained by a man
whose first name is Brian.

A poem by Maya Angelou, though,
is a different matter entirely.
Or one by Leona Gom. Or Audre Lorde.
Or Carol Ann Duffy, Salena Godden,
Selima Hill, Margaret Atwood, Adrienne Rich,
Sylvia Plath, Wendy Cope, Caroline Bird,
Hollie McNish, Stevie Smith, U. A. Fanthorpe,
Nikita Gill, Jackie Kay, Imtiaz Dharker,
Emily Dickinson, Amanda Gorman, Dorothy Parker . . .

I could go on,
but there are only so many hours
and I've got a lot of reading
to be getting on with.

9th March

The Barbie doll made its first appearance on this day in 1959, at the American International Toy Fair. The idea of a doll which was an adult, not a baby, took off quickly and more than 300,000 Barbies were sold in the first year. Other dolls were soon in production, most notably Ken, who was introduced in 1961 as Barbie's boyfriend. While Barbie has never been far away from controversy, she has also been a strong role model for girls over the decades: teacher, pilot, doctor, astronaut, scientist. Rather more bizarrely there has also been a Hitchcock Barbie, based on Tippi Hedron, complete with removable, menacing birds.

Plaything

Ken sits around in his pants all day,
not knowing what to do with himself,
while he waits for her to come home.

She shouts goodbye every morning
before she heads out through the door,
space suit on, helmet in hand.

Ken's enlightened as the next man doll,
but ever since she got that job with NASA,
his frozen smile is wearing thin,

and not even an afternoon flipping
plastic burgers on his summer grill playset
can restore the sheen to his moulded hair.

He thought she'd gotten this career stuff
out of her system when he'd hidden
her last outfit – brown boots, khaki shorts

and red safety hat with headlamp detail –
but he regrets now he didn't disappear
her tools, too, because he feels like a fossil,

and that it's only a matter of time
before she comes for him with
her palaeontologist's hammer and chisel.

10th March

....

*The first census of Great Britain took place on this day in 1801. At
the time, the Government only had the vaguest idea of how many
people were living in Britain, and fuelled by worries of an imminent
Malthusian catastrophe in the wake of a population explosion brought
about by the industrial revolution, they thought they had better find*

out. It revealed that the population was around nine million – and
remarkably, the returns showed that, at that time, there was not one
Jedi knight living in Great Britain, a figure which was to rise to a peak
of 330,000 by the time of the 2001 census.

It's Time to Complete Your Census Questionnaire

Section 1

Who usually lives here? Starting with yourself,
please list the names of everyone included in the last question,
including children, babies, lodgers, goldfish, and chinchilla.

Apart from everyone counted in the last question,
who else is staying overnight here on the date of this census?
Please remember to check under beds and in wardrobes.

How many members of this household are related to each other?
If you are a family, how close would you say you are?
How often do you argue? Do you ever wish you lived alone?

What type of accommodation is this? Have you ever been tempted
to go for a bigger, brighter look by knocking that wall through
between your sitting room and kitchen? Are you happy?

Section 2

What is your name? What is your date of birth? What is your sex?
If you are female, how safe do you feel when
walking home in the evening, on a scale of *uneasy* to *terrified*.

What is your country of birth? If you were not born in the UK, when did you arrive here? Over the last seven days, approximately how many times have you been a victim of racist abuse or prejudice?

Do you have a job? What is the main activity of your employment? Is there *anything* about your current position you find fulfilling? Have you ever thought about retraining as a dog walker, or namer of clouds?

Over the last seven days, how many times have you done any of the following:
a) despaired at the government b) watched *Pointless*
c) eaten chutney d) filled in a census form e) worried about bees

Consider your answers above alongside everything else that is going on in the world at the moment.
Again, *to the best of your knowledge and belief,* are you happy?

11th March

....

Douglas Adams was born on this day in 1952. A brilliant comic writer and humourist, he is best known as the author of the Hitchhiker's Guide to the Galaxy *series. In the first volume, he introduces us to Vogon poetry, at the time the third-worst poetry in the universe – behind that of the Azgoths of Kria, and the work of Paula Nancy Millstone Jennings of Essex – but now fourth, following the publication*

of this book. Vogon love poetry, like the example below, is best read
slowly, with the insertion of a gap of several weeks between each line.

To My Crinkly Slobberfrock

What swang humburgle drips from thee,
More frujious than the vimhorn tree,
Thy dropsy dewflaps splotter me,
And fruggle me with globjuice.

My turgle-scented jibberblotch,
You giberate my bindledrops.
Explunge my clanker in your spotch
And jimmy like a squirmtoad.

If I speck Jangrood in your bed,
I will hammersplice his spurgled head,
And gruncheon on his dundledrebs,
So tell him to do one.

Prithee, my furtled foontling-pot,
Let's grawp like bunglebirds do frot.
Conciliate my gruntle-spot
While I jurgle on your plumbles.

12th March

On this day in history, some people were born – Jack Kerouac in 1922, for instance. Some others, like Terry Pratchett in 2015, died. Coca-Cola got sold in glass bottles for the first time on this day in 1894. Exactly eighteen years later, the frozen remains of Robert Scott and his exploration team were found on the Ross Ice Shelf in Antarctica. But a lot of other things have happened on this day, too, as they have on other days. Somewhere, a girl was kissed. A precious hat was lost. A really terrific sandwich got made. Such things may not be historically significant but that does not make them unimportant. It's not possible to write about everything but here, at least, amongst all these extraordinary days is some recognition of the ordinary which, in its own quiet way, is full of the extraordinary.

Just an Ordinary Day

It was just an ordinary day.
Why on earth would anyone say
it was a day worth repeating?

Long hours were spent reading.
I heard the sound of your laughter.
We drank some wine. We ate some pasta.
The two of us had slept in late.

Nothing much to celebrate.
It would be a mistake to think there was.

We watched a paper bag blow by.
There were vapour trails in the sky.
The leaves danced gently in the breeze.
The blossom gathered in the trees.
A dog barked. A seagull cried.
The moon reached down to pull the tide
quietly, with age-old practice.
The world turned slowly on its axis.

It was nothing much to shout about.
Who would ever say
today was an extraordinary day?

– – –

Today was an extraordinary day.
Who would ever say
it was nothing much to shout about?

The world turned slowly on its axis.
Quietly, with age-old practice,
the moon reached down to pull the tide.
A dog barked. A seagull cried.
The blossom gathered in the trees.
The leaves danced gently in the breeze.
There were vapour trails in the sky.
We watched a paper bag blow by.

It would be a mistake to think there was
nothing much to celebrate.

The two of us had slept in late.
We drank some wine. We ate some pasta.
I heard the sound of your laughter.
Long hours were spent reading.

It was a day worth repeating.
Why on earth would anyone say
it was just an ordinary day?

13th March

....

*Open an Umbrella Indoors Day, which is celebrated on this day
by about thirteen people around the world, encourages defiance of
superstition. It challenges people to take on age-old superstitions, and
then use scientific, empiric evidence of the consequences of their action
to demonstrate whether there is any truth to be found in them. About
150,000 people tend to die on this day every year.*

Consequences

I opened an umbrella indoors
and waited for misfortune to rain down upon me.
Nothing happened.

I walked beneath a ladder
and waited for the sky to fall.
Nothing happened.

I placed a pair of shoes on a table
and waited for fate to trample me down.
Nothing happened.

I hung a horseshoe upside down
and waited for the luck to drop out.
Nothing happened.

I smashed up a mirror with a hammer
and waited to be pierced by the shards of seven years' suffering.
Nothing happened.

I shouted 'Macbeth!' at the top of my voice, in the Globe Theatre,
and waited for the woods to march on Dunsinane.
And still nothing happened.

With the third light of a match, I set fire to a chain letter
which had been sent to me by a raven,
with a forwarding on date of Friday the 13th,
and waited, somewhat nonchalantly.
Not a sausage.

Three years later, I lost my house keys down a storm drain.
The following week, Brexit happened.
Five months after that, Donald Trump was elected president of
the United States.
Later, there came a deadly pandemic and war in Europe.

How easy to think the things we do
carry no importance.

How easy to imagine our actions
are without consequence.

How foolish we are
to ignore the old stories.

14th March

....

*Pi Day is an annual celebration of the constant Pi (π), which appears
in many formulae in mathematics and physics. It's observed on this
date since 3 (March), 1 and 4 are Pi's first three significant digits.
Given that the day is based around a US calendar convention, maths
bods in the UK get rather sniffy about this date, and moan about it to
at least fifty decimal digits.*

π in the Sky

He'd think about her
Constantly – well, 22/7 –
never completing.
He even stopped eating.

Then, one day – at 3.14 –
a chance meeting.
But, sadly,
not repeating.

15th March

Today – the seventy-fourth day in the Roman calendar – is known as
The Ides of March. Traditionally a date for the observance of religious
ceremonies, such as slaughtering a sheep in honour of Jupiter, it also
became regarded as a deadline for settling debts. One such settling
occurred in 44 BCE, *with the assassination of Julius Caesar at the*
hands of senatorial conspirators, including Brutus and Cassius. The
tragedy of Caesar's fate was later movingly reconstructed in Kenneth
Williams' dignified and noble portrayal of him in the 1964 biopic,
Carry On Cleo.

Et tu, Chute

today i clambered
up some steps

to the apex
of the arch

then hurtling down
i hurt my back

              be-
                  ware
                       the
                            slides
                                 of
                                      March

16th March

On this day in 1926, Robert Goddard successfully launched the first liquid-fuelled rocket, in Auburn, Massachusetts. It reached the lofty altitude of forty-one feet, lasting two seconds and averaging sixty miles an hour. Goddard's work on rocket propulsion made a huge contribution to the later exploration of space and he is now regarded as the father of modern rocketry. His research and experiments were frequently ridiculed at the time, however, both in the press and by other physicists. It's hardly rocket science, they may well have said. How wrong they were.

The Escape Rocket

The animals are building a rocket
to go in search of the stars.

It's made from coffee cups and plastic straws,
rusty Coke cans and old jam jars,
disposable cutlery, stirrers, lids,
takeaway boxes, fishing nets and rigs,
ice-lolly wrappers, cotton buds and fags,
washing-up bottles, carrier bags.

They need a large rocket to fit them all in,
as they look for somewhere to start over again.
It won't be easy but they have to give it a try.
Materials, at least, are in ready supply.

It's not the first time they've had to reset.
Project Ark had gone well, with one big regret,
a mistake they've corrected in their new plan:
this time, they will not invite Man.

17th March

....

St Patrick's Day is celebrated on this day every year, in honour of the
patron saint of Ireland. A lot of green gets worn by its celebrants, and
shamrocks find themselves shaken with wild abandon. It is believed
that the large amount of drink traditionally consumed on this day
has its roots in the lifting of Lent restrictions on eating and drinking
alcohol; it is not known from when the tradition of singing 'Pride
(in the Name of Love)' outside my house in the middle of the night
comes from but it has been happening for several years now. St Patrick
himself is famous for driving the snakes out from Ireland; this was
seen by many as a miraculous achievement, not least because there
weren't any.

How the Snakes were Driven Out of Ireland

across the lowlands
and highlands of the island of Ireland,
a gang of snakes slithered hither and thither,
bringing terror to   locals unable to resist
their green   lidless eyes, the
                             lilting brogue
                             of their hiss.
                             But then came
                             St Pat – or so says
                             his hagiography –
                             who cried, *'Snakes!*
                             Hey, ger offa me!'
                             and drove them
                             along the clifftop
                             and then over
                             in his multi-terrain
                             5-seater land-rover –
                                          though some still claim they were driven from Eire
                                          in a nineteen eighty-seven Ford Sierra

18th March

....

Ethelred the Unready became king on this day in 978.
Disappointingly, the state of unreadiness which attached itself to his
name did not signify the word as we know it today but rather, that he
was badly advised. Ethelred had it easy: other nicknames knocking

113

around in medieval times included Charles the Silly (French king, went mad, thought he was made of glass), Alfonso the Slobberer (King of León and Galicia, foamed at the mouth when angry), and the gloriously monikered Constantine the Name of Shit (Byzantine emperor, supposed to have defecated into the baptismal font when an infant).

Anglo-Saxon Form Register

Ethelred the Unready?	*Looking for his pencil case, miss.*
Dunstan the Unsteady?	*Fell over on his way to school, miss.*
Godric the Furious?	*Too angry to come in today, miss.*
Eadwulf the Curious?	*Followed a cat down Dead End Lane, miss.*
Frideswide the Flaxen-Haired?	*At the hairdressers, miss.*
Eadmund the Ill-Prepared?	*Helping Ethelred, miss.*
Wigmund the Lazy Article?	*Couldn't be bothered to come in today, miss.*
Oswald the Unremarkable?	
Leofstan the Sorcerer?	*Not done his spelling, miss.*
Hilda the Slaughterer?	*Off murdering Picts today, miss.*
Wemba the Vague?	*Said he had to do a thing, miss.*
Mildgyd the Plagued?	*Not feeling well, miss.*
Sigeberht the Squanderer?	*Wasting time at home, miss.*
Wilburg the Wanderer?	*Got lost on his way here, miss.*
Eadburg the Effervescent?	*Says his enthusiasm for school has fizzled out, miss.*
Winfred the Ever-Present?	*Here, miss.*

19th March

....

The Academy Awards were televised for the first time on this day in
1953. Winner of Best Picture that year was Cecil B. DeMille's The
Greatest Show on Earth, *which remains one of the best films ever*
made about competing trapeze artists. I've never sat through an Oscar
ceremony myself although I was once invited to the prestigious APM
Project Management Awards (West Midlands section), held in the
Bonser Suite at the Bescot Stadium, Walsall. I imagine the Oscars to
be very much like that, albeit with cheaper lager and less histrionic
acceptance speeches.

And the Academy Award Goes To . . .

I feel honoured and humbled to find myself here,
clutching the Oscar I was robbed of last year.
I'd just like to say (through teeth white and flossable)
thank you to those who made all this possible:

to my director, of course, and the producer;
my leading lady, who let me seduce her;
all the rest of the cast and the hard-working crew
(I'm not sure of their names but I hope that will do);

my many fans who flocked to the cinema screens;
the critics who loved me (but not those who were mean);
my family, especially my mother and father,
who sold their spare yacht to put me through RADA;

the friends who were there for me each step of the way;
my life coach Leona, who taught me feng shui;
America, for letting me into your heart,
(reassuring to know you're aware of Great Art);

the poor and the needy who would all struggle to cope
without me in their lives like a beacon of hope;
and God's vast panoply of beautiful creatures
(it's such a shame they lack my classical features);

but there is one without whom this just couldn't be:
hardworking, handsome, humble, I'd like to thank . . .
me.

20th March

....

Today is the first day of spring, as well as International Day
of Happiness. To thrill two birds with one ode, here is a suitably
uplifting poem.

A Suitably Uplifting Poem

The mornings
are getting lighter,
a little more so
every day.

I shall tie them
to my bedpost
so that they don't
float away.

21st March

Today is World Poetry Day so if you happen to be reading this entry on the day itself, then thank you for participating in it. Much poetry can often seem forbidding to the uninitiated, both for the reader and the budding poet. World Poetry Day helps to break down barriers to poetry – and while it's completely understandable to feel in awe of the great poets as you're struggling to knock out a simple limerick for a co-worker's birthday card, do not forget that even they had to start somewhere.

Selected Early Writings of the Poets

I

the roses are red
and all the violets are blue
oh look, a haiku

Basho

II

Roses are red,
unlike those daffs,
I wander lonely
as a ~~giraffe~~ cloud.

William Wordsworth

III

Look – the roses are red!
They make my heart sing!
They fill me with hope –
Like a feathery thing!

Emily Dickinson

IV

ROSES ARE . . . NO!
WHAT HAVE I DONE?
I MUST HAVE LEFT
MY CAPS LOCK ON

ee cummings

V

Roses are dead,
see how they droop.
All of us die:
life's only truth.

Philip Larkin

VI

Got there too late.
The roses had gone.
Bought this instead –
Have an onion.

Carol Ann Duffy

22nd March

It's easy to take water for granted. After all, more than seventy per cent of the Earth's surface is covered in the stuff and sixty per cent of the human body is made up of it. But there are more than two billion people who live without access to safe water. World Water Day, celebrated annually on this day, raises awareness of this issue as well as promoting the role of water in the fight against climate change by spotlighting sustainable, affordable water and sanitation issues.

For Sale: One Glass of Water

Description: this large glass of water is suitable for drinking; bathing; showering; swimming; diving into after a hot summer's day; filling water pistols and paddling pools; the making of ice-cubes; the washing of clothes and dishes; the flushing of toilets; the brushing of teeth; the boiling of rice and the steaming of vegetables; the irrigation of plants and agricultural crops; the production of paper and textiles; the manufacture of semiconductors; the generation of hydroelectricity; industrial cooling systems; baptisms and other non-oil-based anointments; the extinguishing of fires; magic tricks; dousing; spilling; flinging (in the faces of enemies); the avoidance of thirst; the regulation of body temperature; healthy digestion; the removal of body waste; the functioning of brains; and life, more generally.

The auction is now open.
Who would like to start the bidding?

23rd March

....

On this day in 2020, the UK went into full lockdown in response to the Covid-19 pandemic. People were allowed to leave the house once a day for purposes of exercise. While it was better than nothing, the health advantages gained from such daily outings were almost entirely neutralised by the sheer terror of encountering someone else.

On Leaving My House and Encountering Another Human Being

I'm sorry I dived into the bushes.
It's not personal, please understand.
You happened to walk in my direction
and my nerves got the upper hand.

Didn't mean to scream when you came near me.
Don't take my angry shrieks to heart.
Idiomatically, let's stay in touch –
and physically, six feet apart.

Apols if it seems like you repulse me,
that I recoil when you come near –
in other times, we might have spoken,
shared a joke or had a beer,

or waltzed together along the footpath,
perhaps we may yet still one day.
But, just for now, please embrace the margins
and wave to me from far away.

24th March

Today is World Meteorological Day, an annual celebration of meteorology and the contribution it makes to our understanding of the weather. I could do with paying more attention to what the weather forecasters are saying: my 'just look out of the window' approach isn't really working. It explains why I've spent most of my life being inappropriately dressed for the outside – and I don't just mean my mustard-coloured cardigan and check flared trousers.

And Now for the Weather

Today is set to be agreeably alliterative
across an assortment of areas
although the occasional metaphor
may cause some faces to cloud.

Idioms will be coming down like stair rods
in northern regions, while the south
may experience the odd outbreak of similes,
like an unexpected shower of arrows.

In coastal, littoral, and seaside areas,
synonyms remain likely.
Further inland, sudden gusts of hyperbole
look set to take your breath away

and a series of scattered euphemisms
will have you reaching for your wellies.

If you're driving, please be aware that tautologies
of frozen ice are still affecting some roads,

after a heavy and prolonged flurry of oxymorons.
And finally – from tomorrow evening –
expect to see the return of some light litotes,
making next week's outlook hardly the best.

25th March

....

John Lennon and Yoko Ono began their bed-in for peace on this day
in 1969. They were on their honeymoon and invited the press to hang
out with them in their suite at the Amsterdam Hilton Hotel while they
lounged around in bed. With signs over their bed proclaiming 'Hair
Peace' and 'Bed Peace', the bed-ins were intended to be a non-violent
protest against war. By a curious coincidence, it was exactly fifteen
years later that I attempted a similar protest, until my mum told me to
stop being silly and get up, or I was going to be late for school.

The Haiku of John and Yoko

Peace talks from a bed
as the world's press gather round.
Blanket coverage.

26th March

On this day in 2015, Richard III was reburied in Leicester Cathedral,
his remains having been found three years earlier beneath the city
council's car park. Rumours of his presence there had originally been
dismissed – hardly surprising given that Richard III had died in 1485
and the motor car wasn't invented until the late nineteenth century.
It has led historians to revise their thinking about the much-maligned,
twisted-spined monarch, not least his famous cry of despair at the Battle
of Bosworth Field: 'A Porsche, a Porsche! My kingdom for a Porsche!'

Richard the Reinterred

can you imagine it?
in a car park in Leicester,
the last Plantagenet
left there to feicester

with no valid ticket,
he determined to quit it
before the council had time
to issue a fine

he picked up his bones
in a grand upheaval
and found a new home
in Leicester Cathedral

27th March

....

Today is World Theatre Day, an annual celebration of theatre and drama. For anyone unfamiliar with the concept of theatre, it's like going to watch a film but with real people acting instead of glamorous Hollywood superstars. Also, there are no trailers and you get a chance to go to the loo about halfway through without clambering over people in the dark and upturning their popcorn. Plus, there will almost certainly be at least one person in the cast you will vaguely recognise from the telly, most likely from their fleeting appearance on Casualty *or* Holby City.

A Tale of Two Exits

Exiting the theatre, pursued by a bear,
I ducked into M&S, hoping to lose him in the crowds.
I was just catching my breath
by the knitted casuals,

when a shadow loomed over me
and I was confronted by a towering mass
of hair and claw, holding out my programme.
I'd left it on my seat, he said.

Over cake and coffee, the bear told me
of his love for the theatre, and how
he was trying to scratch out a living as an actor
but that the parts were hard to come by.

There was *The Winter's bloody Tale*, of course,
but the rest were mainly musicals –
like *The Lion King* or *The Jungle Book* –
and he had an awful singing voice.

He'd expected more from the Russian dramatists,
he opined bitterly, biting into a yum yum,
but even the plays of Chekhov
contained a mysterious absence of bears.

It was then that he climbed up onto the table,
cleared his throat, and launched himself
into a powerful and stirring rendition
of 'All the world's a stage'.

'Not in here, it isn't,' said the manager sharply,
and the two of us felt compelled
to make a sudden and hasty exit from the store,
pursued by a security guard.

28th March

....

It was on this day in 1964 that Radio Caroline – the first pirate radio station – started operating. Broadcasting from a ship off the Suffolk coast in order to circumvent licensing requirements, it challenged the orthodoxy of the BBC and catered for younger audiences, whose tastes and attitudes were changing. Fearful of the collapse of civilisation, 'pop music' on the BBC had been rationed to six hours a week, just long enough to fit in three Bob Dylan songs. Radio Caroline was to change all that, carrying the songs of The Rolling Stones, Sandie Shaw, and Herman's Hermits across the airwaves and ocean waves, corrupting young ears everywhere.

Pirate Radio Playlist

Blackbeard (singing in the dead of night).
I Left Me Hearties in San Francisco.
I'm Ahoy. You Got the Hook.
Wake Me Up Before You Heave Ho.

Come As You Arrrghhh. Take a Chance on Smee.
You're Bootyful. Pegleggy Sue.
Avast! In the Name of Love.
I Only Have Eye For You.

The First Cutlass the Deepest.
You'll Never Walk the Plank Alone.
Band on the Rum. 99 Gold Doubloons.
Me and Davy Jones.

29th March

....

Now more commonly known as the London Snickers, the very first London Marathon took place on this day in 1981. Over the last forty years, it has developed into one of the major sporting showcases for cosplay enthusiasts. In 2016, Eliud Kipchoge broke the course record by running the 26.2 miles in two hours, two minutes and thirty-seven seconds, which is approximately two minutes and thirty-seven seconds longer than it typically takes me to get out of bed on a Sunday morning in springtime and switch on the television to watch the London Marathon.

The Foolishness of the Long-Distance Runner

Upon further reflection,
it may not have been my best idea
to run twenty-six point two miles,
on the hottest day of the year so far,
in an inflatable sumo suit,

having undergone minimal training,
beyond my weekday workout
involving the negotiation of three flights of stairs
and the retrieval of a Twix
from the sixth-floor snack machine,

but that's just how life is sometimes,
and who knows – if I can evade capture –
the experience might be good for me,
and next year, I may even decide
to enter a marathon.

30th March

....

Vincent Van Gogh, the brilliant post-impressionist artist who was born
on this day in 1853, was famously unfamous in his lifetime. He is
thought to have only sold one painting before his death, for a paltry
400 francs, and his mother is said to have later disposed of crates full
of his work. A hundred years later, Van Gogh's Portrait of Dr Gachet
was to sell for $82.5 million: a fact of which I frequently remind my
own mother, whenever she tells me it's about time I had a proper clear
out of my old love sonnets and limericks.

Vincent Van Cough

Is it Van *Goff* or Van *Go*?
Most people don't knogh.
They could more easily scogh
an unripe mangogh
than toss ogh his name
with cheery gustogh.

Yet neither's right much.
Well, at least for the Dutch,
who pronounce it as *Gogh*,
as a Scot might say *loch*.
But that's a sound I find tough
without wanting to cough.

These mispronunciations
could be cured in an instant,
if we could all just agree
to call the man Vincent.

31st March

....

On this day in 1596, the philosopher René Descartes was born. His most famous statement was 'cogito, ergo sum' ('I think, therefore I am'); in other words, that philosophical proof of existence is based upon our ability to form thought. This can be a reassuring notion, not least for those times when someone makes a thoughtless remark about your shoes or a poem you've posted up on Twitter, and you can console yourself with the fact that they do not exist.

Cogitations at Two in the Morning

I think, therefore I am.
I am, therefore I breathe.
I breathe, therefore I inhale and exhale air.
I inhale and exhale air, therefore my throat tissues relax.
My throat tissues relax, therefore my throat tissues vibrate.
My throat tissues vibrate, therefore I snore.
I snore, therefore I am prodded in the ribs.
I am prodded in the ribs, therefore I groan.
I groan, therefore I am told to stop creating a disturbance.
I am told to stop creating a disturbance, therefore I turn over in
      a huff.

I turn over in a huff, therefore I am now wide awake.

I am now wide awake, therefore I hear the water dripping from the drainpipe outside.

I hear the water dripping from the drainpipe outside, therefore I put my head under my pillow.

I put my head under my pillow, therefore I cannot breathe.

I cannot breathe, therefore I take my head out from under my pillow and turn back again the other way.

I take my head out from under my pillow and turn back again the other way, therefore I am told to stop fidgeting about and go back to sleep.

I am told to stop fidgeting about and go back to sleep, therefore I lie on my back, perfectly still, and listen to the rain as it drips from the drainpipe outside.

I lie on my back, perfectly still, and listen to the rain as it drips from the drainpipe outside, therefore I cannot sleep.

I cannot sleep, therefore I think.

I think, therefore I am.

April

1st April

....

Today is April Fool's Day, the only day of the year when you have a legal obligation to smile when somebody tries to play a practical joke on you. This only applies to pranks played before midday, of course. After that time, even if you do happen to be covered in a thick gloopy substance and your favourite blue cardigan is completely ruined, the joke is on the prankster, apparently.

An Awful Lot of Foolishness

On the first April the First
someone thought it might be funny
to balance a bucket of water on top of a door,
and see what happens.

As it turns out, it *was* funny –
so much so that the following year,
the incident was not forgotten
and there developed a fashion

for the stretching of cellophane
across toilet seats, and the tying together
of shoelaces. A few years after that,
the fake dog turd was invented.

It wasn't long before everyone was at it.
Clever hoaxes were constructed
involving Martian landings
and left-handed toilet paper,

and each year the pranks
became ever more elaborate,
and might take months or years
or centuries in the planning –

genetically-modified spaghetti trees,
the creation of large-scale shifts
in weather patterns, the extinction
of the black rhinoceros –

until it seemed as if such tomfoolery
was what we lived with every day,
and that all the high jinks and the tricks
and the hoaxes were no longer

distinguishable from truth.
Well, *that* escalated quickly, the people said,
slapping each other on the back
and laughing.

2nd April

....

International Children's Book Day, an annual celebration of children's
literature, takes place on or around 2nd April, the birthday of Hans
Christian Andersen. Books can have a transformative effect on young
minds. As a child, they would transport me to faraway worlds and
magical places: Toytown; Narnia; Dictionopolis and Digitopolis;
Fundindelve; Smethwick Public Library. In fact, it's quite possible I

may never have become a writer at all if it hadn't been for the wonder of those early picture books – Where the Wild Things Are; The Cat in the Hat; Not Now, Bernard; The Very Hungry Caterpillar – *books which are still enjoyed by millions of children today.*

The Very Angry Caterpillar

In the light of the moon a little egg lay on a leaf, minding its own business.

Far too early one Sunday morning, the stupid sun came up and – POP – out of the egg came a tiny and very angry caterpillar.

He started to look for things to feel cross about.

On Monday he ate an apple and found a worm in it, but he was still angry.

On Tuesday he had a row with a frog who was trying to jump a queue, but he was still angry.

On Wednesday he wrote to *The Daily Telegraph* concerning the disappearance of the word 'Easter' from the packaging of chocolate eggs, but he was still angry.

On Thursday, he took part in a demonstration against the Highways Agency's proposal to increase capacity on the busy section of the A14 between Ellington and Fen Ditton, but he was still angry.

On Friday, he joined Twitter and corrected five people on grammatical mistakes in their tweets, but he was still angry.

On Saturday, he enrolled on an anger management course and was shown how to bring gentleness to the physical sensations of anger he was experiencing while using a variety of breathing techniques 'to cool the flames of negative emotionality within himself'.

That night he felt physically sick.

The next day was Sunday again. The caterpillar shouted at one unsuspecting crane fly, and after that he felt much better.

Now although he was still angry, he wasn't a little caterpillar any more.

He was a big, fat, angry caterpillar.

He built a small house, called a cocoon, and the flat-pack assembly instructions made him very angry indeed.

He seethed inside for more than two weeks.

Then he punched a hole in the cocoon, pushed his way out . . . and . . .

he was a beautiful, angry butterfly.

3rd April

....

Doris Day was born on this day in 1922. One of the leading film stars of the 1950s and 60s, she came to be seen as Hollywood's archetypal 'girl next door' through a series of romcom and musical box-office hits. It was an image she might later have escaped from had she not turned down the role of Mrs Robinson in The Graduate, *but – as she famously sang in Hitchcock's remake of* The Man Who Knew Too Much – *que sera, sera.*

International Doris Day

is that special day of the year
on which we celebrate the unique contribution
Dorises have made to our culture and society.

From literature to medical science,
space exploration to the serving up
of shepherd's pie in a school canteen,
there is no field of human endeavour
which has not benefitted
from the presence of a Doris.

Maybe a Doris has helped you.
A teacher, perhaps, or kindly aunt,
marine biologist or part-time nail beautician.
It's hard to imagine what our world might be like
without their welcoming blousy embrace.

However, like the Gladys and Hilda before her,
the Doris is sadly disappearing,
hunted for her horn-rimmed spectacles,
unable to survive in a habitat
populated by Olivias and Shaznays.

But all hope is not lost.
Through a combination of conservation techniques –
such as the establishment of Doris-only sanctuaries
and the reclassifying of Patricias –
there are signs that the Doris is beginning
to thrive once more.

Awareness days play their part, too.
So, if there's a Doris near you,
don't forget to thank her for all that she does
and say hurrah, hurrah,
whatever will be, will be.

4th April

It's not easy now, in the first quarter of the twenty-first century, to
imagine a world without reflective road studs. But that's exactly what
it was, until this day in 1934 when the first cat's eyes were laid by
Percy Shaw. The Halifax-born inventor is said to have come up with
the idea having seen his car's headlights reflected back to him by the
eyes of a cat, enabling him to readjust his driving and remain on the
road. It was suggested by the comedian Ken Dodd that had the cat
been facing the other way, Shaw might have ended up inventing the
pencil sharpener.

Cat's Eyes and Other Modern Atrocities

What kind of a world is it that are we living in
when nobody bats an eyelid
at the sight of cat's eyes marking our roads?
Nor does anyone appear to be
in the least bit beetle-browed
towards the surgical removal of bee's knees
and dog's bollocks to supply
the booming trade in compliments.

The government never does anything.
You can badger them until the cows come home
but they're too busy horsing around
with the electorate and making a pig's ear
of running the country. No, like that
rarely discussed fly-on-the-wall documentary
about the elephant in the room,
the proboscis does not look good.

But back to cats. It seems like only yesterday
that the whole business of them being kept in bags
was accidentally divulged. That their eyes
are now being used as road markings
is something we all need to reflect upon further.

5th April

....

*Birkenhead Park opened on this day in 1847. What's interesting about
that? you ask. Parks open every day and then they close – at about
5pm in winter time, later in the summer. But when I say Birkenhead
Park opened, I mean opened for the first time – and what was
noteworthy about that, is that it was the first publicly funded civic
park in the world, the vision of a local industrialist who saw the need
for open space amidst all the factories springing up. Oh, and Joseph
Paxton's design of Birkenhead Park heavily influenced Central Park in
New York, so I think that's rather remarkable, too, and I'll thank you
next time not to be so dismissive of what it is I have to say.*

The Man in the Park

Central heating wouldn't go amiss,
particularly on days like this

when the frost cracks your knuckles
and the pond is glass so the ducks

spend more time waddling than swimming,
but what with the cost of living

these days, who's he to complain
and there's always the bandstand when it rains.

Home is where you can hide your trolley.
He hides his behind the folly,

late Victorian, tattooed with spray paint:
a hundred declarations of love and hate

to make you despair, or believe and hope.
On the grass beyond, kids throw down coats

for goalposts, pick teams, chase a ball.
He'd like to watch, but he knows the score,

they don't want him here. Got spat at once.
Instead, he begins to look for lunch,

the bin by the duckpond is usually the best –
last night's chips, some scraps of bread –

then after that, he'll head back to his bench
for an unexpected social event

or afternoon nap. He sleeps there most nights,
beneath the gleaming chandelier of the sky.

6th April

....

Today is World Day for Physical Activity, a day on which people
are encouraged to participate in regular physical activities, such as
walking, running, swimming, and Greco-Roman wrestling. Poets
are not particularly well known for their physical prowess, unless it
concerns jostling at a crowded bar. But regular physical exercise can
have a very positive impact on mental dexterity, too, and that's why
the ideas for many of Simon Armitage's best poems have come to him
while working out at his weekly Jazzercise class.

How Poets Keep Fit

I may look unfit.
but that's just an illusion.

Already today,
I've been JUMPING
to conclusions

and RUNNING
the bath taps.

And then, after
a brief power nap

(a few more
calories burned),

I've been WORKING OUT
my tax return,

the numbers SWIMMING
before my eyes,

before THROWING
the towel in

and SKIPPING
further exercise.

7th April

....

*William Wordsworth, the celebrated poet and hill-clamberer, was
born on this day in 1770. He wrote one of his most widely known
poems, 'Daffodils', following a walk with his sister Dorothy around
Glencoyne Bay, Ullswater, and an encounter with a 'long belt' of the
flowers. Never a fan of mass tourism, he would most likely be appalled
by the thousands of visitors clumping around the Lake District these
days, inspired not only by the area's glorious landscapes but his own
poetry: 'I thundered loudly at the crowd / that tramps on high o'er
vales and hills.'*

Status Update: A Lonely Cloud

Status update: a lonely cloud,
As wretched as a songless thrush.
When all at once my back unbowed
To see her playing Candy Crush;
Lemonade Lake and Treacle Trees
Did dance before me in the breeze.

So vividly her sweets did shine,
A bright twinkle displaced my frown.
How gay they stretched in endless lines
To reach as far as Candy Town:
And now at last her face was seen
Reflected in her iPhone screen.

Her eyes to me were liquorice whirls,
And her skin was peppermint cream,
Her thick, thick hair did flow and swirl
Like a golden syrup'd stream.
The sweetest girl I've gazed upon!
But I could not get past level one.

Those times, when on my couch I lie
And even daffs can't lift my mood
I remember that fine lady
Whose rare confections I'd pursued;
For then my heart with pleasure meets,
And candy-dances with her sweets.

8th April

....

The Entente Cordiale was signed between Britain and France on this day in 1904. Contrary to how it sounds, this was not a trade deal concerning the import and export of orange squash. Rather, it signalled the introduction of an era of cooperation and closeness between the two nations, who had been at each other's throats for a thousand years or so. These friendlier diplomatic relations were to remain in place for nearly a century until the two countries fell out in a dispute with the Swiss over fondue-dipping rights.

Entente Cordiale

it's time to act, let's make a pact,
an entente cordiale,
i'll obey each clause that we draw up
i promise you i shall

promise not to grind your teeth
and i promise not to snore
or pick my nose if you will pick
your clothes up off the floor

promise you won't bite your nails
or leave the milk out of the fridge,
and i promise to put the loo seat down,
and do bath time with the kids

i promise i'll suppress my jeers
when a royal is on TV
if you promise when the football's on
not to talk to me

and promise me you'll never leave
your hair to clog the drain
and i'll always get the washing in
when it starts to rain

on second thoughts, what need have we
for promises and vows?
we're trusted allies, we'll make it work –
vive l'entente cordiale!

9th April

....

Today is Unicorn Day, which commemorates the tragic plight of those
white, pink, purple, or rainbow-coloured horse creatures with the
horns on their heads. No one quite knows how the unicorns died out,
although one explanation is that they were hunted into extinction:
their fur highly prized in the manufacturing of fluffy earmuffs for
children; their glitter used in the adornment of sparkly pencil cases.
Other theories include their annihilation following an apocalyptic
world event, and that they didn't really exist anyway.

Departure Day

The animals went in two by two, Hoorah! Hoorah!
The animals went in two by two, Hoorah! Hoorah!
The animals went in two by two, while Doug
looked out of the window of their third-floor apartment
and wondered if the rain would ever stop.

Perhaps that crazy old guy had a point, after all.
Those two baboons on the ground floor had got back
from work last week to find their flat flooded,
their winter store of seeds and bark floating past them
in the driveway. They'd been living on the roof ever since.

Doug had been sceptical, though. It'll pass, he told Brenda,
after that first week of rain. By the end of the second week,
with still no respite, he was less sure, and he was glad
when he'd swum back from the hospital, after a busy day
healing wounds, and she showed him the tickets.

We sail on Sunday morning, she'd told him. At eleven.
At least that's what he thought Brenda had said, because
by then he'd become a little distracted by the game.
The Centaurs were trailing. As usual. He watched Brenda now,
asleep on the hay. She looked so beautiful lying there,

her long neck, slender and graceful, that strong jawline,
the wayward tufts of hair which sprang up around her horn,
and which he'd tease her about when she woke up.
Talking of which, he supposed they should get moving.
It was after ten – and it would take thirty minutes or so

to get to the ark. It would be fine to be a few minutes late, he was sure of it. Not that they would be. They had plenty of time – assuming it was leaving at eleven, that is. He should probably double-check that, he thought, reaching for Brenda's bag. Yes, he would check the tickets first, then wake her.

10th April

....

The first recorded appearance of bananas in London occurred on this day in 1633, when the apothecarist, herbalist and merchant Thomas Johnson displayed a bunch of them in his shop in Holborn. It's believed the bananas were from Bermuda although we don't know much about them beyond that, except for them being yellow and bendy. Their introduction was to revolutionise British life over the coming centuries and a new era of creative and artistic endeavour was ushered in, which saw the development of the banana skin routine in slapstick comedy (1741–5), the invention of the banana split (1904), and the batting around of a giant inflatable banana by football crowds (1987).

Bananas!

they're yellow
they're bendy
they're exotic and trendy
Bananas!

they're long
they're pleasant
they're shaped like a crescent
Bananas!

spotty or stripy
we stock a variety
they're silky and piratey
Bandanas!

they're sweet
and they're ripe
they're better than tripe
Bananas!

buy 'em quick
'cos they're lush
they'll soon turn to mush
Bananas!

11th April

....

National Pet Day is celebrated annually on this day in both the US and the UK, although as every pet owner knows, barely a day goes past without their pet being celebrated in some way. And deservedly so, too, as pets bring with them all sorts of benefits: companionship; exercise; the combating of depression and anxiety; the lowering of blood pressure. These typically far outweigh the deficits: the clearing up of excrement; the distraction from an urgent work deadline; their taking up of half the sofa. Please note that these last two deficits do not apply to goldfish. Or at least not the low-maintenance ones.

Pet Peeve

Keeping
a chameleon
for a pet

is something
that I now
regret.

At first,
as far as
I could tell,

he seemed
to blend in
very well,

but he's
changed a lot
in many ways

I've not
seen him now
for fourteen days.

12th April

Bill Haley recorded 'Rock Around the Clock' on this day in 1954. The song had been written two years previously by Max C. Freedman and James E. Myers, but Haley's version went on to become a number one single in both the US and the UK charts and an anthem for rebellious youth everywhere. Quite what the teenagers of the 1950s found so interesting about the daily routine of a rock is difficult for us to appreciate today.

A Day in the Life of a Rock

One, two, three o'clock, four o'clock – rock
Five, six, seven o'clock, eight o'clock – rock
Nine, ten, eleven o'clock, twelve o'clock – rock
I'm a rock around the clock all right

I spend all day in the rain or sun
It ain't much fun when the clock strikes one
I'm a rock around the clock all right
I'm a rock, rock, rock, it's my daily plight
I'm a rock, I'm a rock, around the clock all right

When the clock strikes two, three and four
I'm telling you now that it's such a bore
To be a rock around the clock all right
I'd like to travel the world and see the sights
But I'm a rock, I'm a rock, around the clock all right

When the chimes ring five, six and seven
I'm a paid-up member of the rock profession
I'm a rock around the clock all right
Just a great big nothing of dolomite
I'm a rock, I'm a rock, around the clock all right

When it's eight, nine, ten, eleven too
I'm a rock, not a tulip or a kangaroo
I'm a rock around the clock all right
I'll never eat sushi or learn to fly a kite
I'm a rock, I'm a rock, around the clock all right

When the clock strikes twelve, I'm still a rock
And when the new day starts – well, hey, guess what?
I'm a rock around the clock all right
I'll never fall in love in the pale moonlight
I'm a rock, I'm a rock, morning, noon and night

13th April

....

Scrabble Day recognises the inventor of that popular word game,
Alfred Mosher Butts, who was born on this day in 1899. Originally
called Lexico, the game was launched in 1931 and has been creating
insurmountable rifts in relationships ever since. Theoretically, the
highest scoring word to put down in Scrabble is 'oxyphenbutazone',
played across three triple word tiles, and which bags a whopping
1,778 points. This puts my best ever word – 'quinx' (on a triple word
score, 120 points) – in the shade somewhat, not least because it was
disqualified over the small technicality of it not being a word.

Sometimes There Are Just No Words

Let's lockdown with the Scrabble board,
have a rummage in the tiles,
and join up words of hope and love
to pass the time awhile.

And if you're short of consonants,
you can have a few of mine.
But, hang on – what does 'PRAXY' mean?
No, that's OK. I'm sure it's fine.

And now you've set down all your tiles,
on a triple word score, too.
Oh great, I've just picked up the Q –
when you've got the final U.

Used to think we were meant to be
but now I'm not so sure.
You've gone where I had planned to go.
Your word says 'IMMATURE'.

14th April

The first Highway Code was published on this day in 1931. It was much needed. The accident rate per vehicle was a staggering twenty times worse in 1930 than it is today; a fact less surprising when you consider there were no driving tests, no restrictions on drink-driving, and no speed limits. As a non-driver, I have never read the Highway Code. This inability to drive is not uncommon amongst poets who, as a rule, prefer to stare distractedly through their passenger windows at assorted cows and the shapes of clouds, before getting shouted out for a missed turning.

L Plates

Here come the kids, inching
round the corners, L plates on, unsure,
steering clear for now of all main roads,
hoping they don't stall

as they try to get familiar
with the gears, the clutch, the knobs,
how hard to press the pedals,
to accelerate and stop.

They learn the Highway Code by heart
and hope to make the grade.
Too fast, too slow, turn left just there,
let's try that once again.

15th April

....

It was in the early hours of this day in 1912 that the luxury steamship Titanic *sank, after striking an iceberg. It led to the loss of more than 1,500 lives. Contrary to the mythology which has grown up around the event, the ship had never been described as 'unsinkable' before the tragedy, at least not without qualification. One myth which is true, though, is that the band did play on as the ship went down, themselves with it. As one passenger said: 'The music they played served alike as their own immortal requiem and their right to be recalled on the scrolls of undying fame.'*

The Iceberg Cometh

Why do I always get portrayed as the bad guy?
The one with the heart of ice, the cold-blooded killer.
There's more to me than that. People don't appreciate
I've got a lot more going on beneath the surface.

I started out as a snowflake, you know,
back in the time of King Tut – not that we ever met,
although I'd often dreamt of living somewhere warmer.
I suppose that's why, after a few thousand years

the Arctic started to get to me. One day, I snapped.
I didn't have any plans as such, thought I'd drift around
for a while, take in some sights, see what happens.
And that's how I ended up in the North Atlantic.

Now let's get one thing clear: the ship crashed into me.
It was midnight. And there I was, minding my own business,
silently floating along, trying not to worry about
why I'd been dripping so much recently, when WHAM!

and there's all this shouting and screaming and crying
and the rasp of tearing metal, a right palaver.
And you know what? Nobody ever stopped to ask about me
or to apologise for the fact that souped-up bath-tub

had taken a big chunk out of my rear end. Unthinkable!
The next six months were tough. I can't deny it hit me hard.
I was shattered. I had survivor's guilt. Post-traumatic stresses
all over me. Then came my much-reported meltdown.

And yet, apparently, I'm the bad guy. If you ask me,
that ship was travelling too fast, should have slowed down,
shown more caution. But no one ever did listen to my advice.
That's just the tip of the iceberg, they say.

16th April

*Rosalind Franklin, the pioneering British biophysicist, died on this
day in 1958. Four years after her death, James Watson and Francis
Crick shared the Nobel Prize for their discovery of the double helix
structure of DNA. But what was less widely known at the time was
that Franklin's data – including her now famous 'Photograph 51',*

which captured the X-ray diffraction pattern of DNA – had played a major part in the breakthrough. Whilst her contribution is now widely recognised, she was far from being the first woman – nor indeed, the last – to find her scientific work overlooked in her lifetime.

Rosalind Franklin

Rosalind Franklin
could do with more thankin'
for her contribution to the knowledge pool
concerning the structure of the deoxyribonucleic acid molecule.

17th April

....

Today is International Haiku Poetry Day. The haiku, a type of short form poetry from Japan, consists of three phrases, typically in a 5-7-5 syllabic pattern. The form can often produce contemplative results, an enigmatic distillation of thoughts and feelings filled with reflection and piquancy. The perfect form, then, for chronicling my hopes and aspirations, actions and emotions, as 2020 unfolded. It was a year which held immense promise for me, both professionally and personally, and how better to capture it than in a haiku for every month.

2020: A Year in Haiku

January
it's twenty twenty
what a time to be alive!
the world at my feet

February
how busy I am
making plans and chasing dreams
days buzz with purpose

March
a curious month
not quite what I'd imagined –
I'm sure it will pass

April
how pleasant it is
to have this time to reflect
a life rebalanced

May
daily exercise
spent diving amongst bushes
screaming at oak trees

June
noticed a chickpea
at the back of the cupboard
we've since become friends

July
still sane, thanks to Greg
(that's the name of the chickpea)
I will get through this

August
engulfed with feelings
of guilt, shame and loneliness
have eaten my friend

September
no longer sure
what a haiku
is

October
the leaves are falling
and the year is getting old
unlike Greg, of course

November
there is a vaccine!
how happy Greg would have been
still can't face houmous

December
the year has taught me
that life is a fragile thing
how precious it is

18th April

On this day in 1930, nothing happened. The BBC's news announcer came on air and declared, 'Good evening. Today is Good Friday. There is no news.' Piano music was played for the rest of the fifteen-minute segment. I write this the day after the US Capitol was besieged by a right-wing mob, more than a thousand British people lost their lives in a single day to Covid-19, reports of the NHS being overwhelmed following a huge rise in new cases, and news of a growing sense of unease from traders trying to cope with the new border rules ushered in by Britain's exit from the European Union. I would quite like a day with no news, please. Just one. The piano music would be nice, too, but not essential.

Serenity Prayer

Send me a slow news day,
a quiet, subdued day,
in which nothing much happens of note,
save for the passing of time,
the consumption of wine,
and a re-run of Murder, She Wrote.

Grant me a no-news day,
a spare-me-your-views day,
in which nothing much happens at all,
except a few hours together
some regional weather,
a day we can barely recall.

19th April

The first ever space station, Salyut 1, was launched on this day in 1971. Sent into space by the Soviet Union, it orbited the Earth almost three thousand times during its 175 days up there before it crashed (intentionally) into the Pacific Ocean. There are times when the idea of life on a space station seems perfect: floating serenely above Earth in all that quietness and tranquillity, far away from noisy neighbours and inept governments. But then I worry about having to head outside to fix a dodgy lunar panel, forgetting to tie my safety cord properly and hurtling off into a starry void, and it makes me think better of it.

Spacecation

Feel the weight of modern life lift
in this spacious and stylish detached modern residence,
that's perfect for a cosy romantic getaway.

Orbiting fashionably in outer space,
this luxurious property affords stunning views
of the inner solar system,
while being just four hundred kilometres
from the bustling planet of Earth.

After a busy day out repairing the air filters,
or enjoying a short lunar walk
on a neighbouring moon,
why not strap yourself into one of the station's comfortable sofas,

or simply float about from room to room
and take in the glorious sunset,
every forty-five minutes,
from one of the property's cosmic viewing areas.

Worried about circadian desynchronisation?
Cast space fatigue into the outer reaches of the galaxy,
with the station's state-of-the-art slumber module –
pressurised and well-ventilated,
with the capacity to hold up to six sleeping bags –
so you'll wake up feeling refreshed
and ready for the morning
and your dehydrated breakfast pouch.

For those wishing to enjoy
the calm and serenity of outer space,
this makes the perfect retreat.
No smoking. Check-out time: 10.30.

20th April

....

BBC Two was launched on this day in 1964. It was the third national TV station and was responsible for bringing a huge range of acclaimed series to a wide audience, including Match of the Day, The Likely Lads, Horizon, Life on Earth, Fawlty Towers, The Young Ones, The Office *and* Yes, Minister. Top Gear *has been another one of its programmes. And when I say BBC Two was launched on this date . . . well, that is and isn't true. A huge power cut on launch night caused*

a blackout and all that ended up being broadcast was the news from
Alexander Palace.

This Poem Will Start Shortly

Well, good evening.
Thank you for tuning in to today's poem,
which will start shortly
start shortly
start

Sorry about that.
Unfortunately, today's   poem
appears to be
experiencing a few technical difficulties
so while we attempt tempt empt
to get it fixed,
here's a block of white space
for you to stare at

Thank you for bearing with us.
I am pleased to inform you
our engineers have now fixed the problem
with to
da
    y's
  p

In a change to our scheduled poem,
here's one with no words:

21st April

....

On this day in 1934, The Daily Mail *caused a sensation by publishing a photograph of the Loch Ness Monster. Taken by a travelling gynaecologist, the 'Surgeon's Photograph', as it was known, appeared to show the head and neck of a creature just breaking the waves of the Scottish lake. It was after this that the myth of Nessie really took off and since then over a thousand sightings have been recorded and approximately zero Loch Ness Monsters have now been found.*

Who's the Real Monster?

[*Daily Mail*, Monday]
LOCH MONSTER PHOTO! NEW AND EXCLUSIVE!
Surgeon takes snap. The proof is conclusive.

[*Daily Mail*, Tuesday]
PHWOAH! WHO'S THAT RISING UP FROM THE WATER?
Saucy pics of Nessie's teenage daughter.

LOONY RED NESSIE IN PALACE SNUB SHOCK
Queen rebuffed by Marxist monster in loch.

[*Daily Mail*, Thursday]
MONSTERS: HOW MANY MORE CAN BRITAIN TAKE?
Country overwhelmed by creatures in lakes.

[*Daily Mail*, Friday]
NASTY NESSIE: THE PEOPLE'S ENEMY
Drag the loch. Lock her up. Throw away the key.

22nd April

....

Earth Day has been taking place on this day every year since 1970.
It remains one of the most popular planetary celebration days in the
entire solar system and loads better than Mercury Monday or the,
frankly, rather showy Lord of the Rings Day celebrated on Saturn.
Environmental issues are at the heart of Earth Day and it serves as
a reminder for us all, should we need it, that we need to take care
of our planet. The consequences of not doing so are too miserable to
contemplate.

Birdsong

There is a bird who sings to me,
each morning from the old lime tree.
I wonder what he's trying to say?
Stop fucking up. It's not too late.

It's such a happy, joyous sound!
Little bird who chirps so loud
And brightens up my day with song.
Stop standing there. You've not got long.

I wish I could translate your words,
my faithful, a cappella bird,
who sits upon the lime tree bough.
And still you wait. You must act now.

All's quiet in the tree today.
I think perhaps he's moved away.
There's silence these days everywhere,
the ghost of birdsong in the air.

23rd April

There's a lot going on today, given that not only is it the feast day of St George, patron saint of England, Bulgaria, Georgia, Portugal, and Spain (how splendid it is to share saints across borders – no wonder the English are so proud to flaunt their flag like that!), but it's also the anniversary of the death of William 'the Bard' Shakespeare in 1616. It may also be the anniversary of his birth, too, but no one is entirely sure. What we can be sure of is that the man was very good at writing, particularly words; the best, in fact.

The Very Condensed Shakespeare

A terrible storm rages, and two gentlemen –
one a Venetian merchant, the other a Trojan prince –
are washed up on the shores of the Forest of Arden.
When Angelo is chased off by a bear wearing
yellow stockings, the prince (who calls himself Falstaff
but whose real name is Beatrice) encounters Puck,
a fairy-like shrew, who enchants the woods to march
on the nearby hamlet of Dunsinane. There, Falstaff meets
a passing traitorous Roman senator, who tells him
of a blind, hunchbacked tyrant named Henry VI,
ruler of three parts of the kingdom, alongside Henry IV
(two parts), Henry V, Henry VIII, a couple of Richards,
and John who have one part each. The king, fearful
of a merger between powerful rival families, has abducted
two star-crossed teenagers and cooked them in a pie.

On his way to avenge these crimes, Falstaff falls in love
with a shepherdess called Goneril (but who is really
Antiphonus, eldest son of Henry VI) and woos her
through the recital of one hundred and fifty-four sonnets.
Upon reaching the court, Falstaff takes advantage
of the disloyalty of Henry's general, Iago, to overthrow
the king, who runs away to a cave and kills himself by asp.
Goneril succeeds to the throne – and Falstaff becomes
his queen – following a joyful double wedding
with Angelo and the yellow-stockinged bear,
who have also fallen in love (just as the three witches
had prophesied), and all's well that ends well.

24th April

*On this day in 1184 BC, an elite squad of Greek soldiers emerged from
the inside of a wooden horse which had been dragged inside the walls
of Troy and went on a rampage to take the city. The Trojans believed
the horse to be a gift from the Greeks to congratulate them on winning
the war; only a few were more circumspect. Laocoön, a Trojan priest,
began to strike the horse with his spear, only for the goddess Athena to
send two giant sea serpents to strangle and kill him and his two sons
which, frankly, seems a bit harsh by today's standards.*

The Fall of Troy

Every now and then, perhaps once a decade or so,
I think about how the city of Troy fell
because of a ruse involving a wooden horse,

and I can never help but wonder
at exactly how clever the Trojans were
to have fallen for a cheap trick like that.

Had I been there at the time, I like to think
I might have spoken up, pointed out
the unlikely retreat of the Greek forces,

the curious coincidence of a votive offering
large enough to house forty crack troops,
and what appeared to be the outline

of a trap door carved into the creature's underside.
But then I consider the fate of Laocoön
and suspect I'd have kept my mouth shut.

And I trace back my knee-jerk suspicion
of any giant wood-carved creature delivered to my door
to my childhood fascination with this story

and so, I hope you understand why it was
that today I had to turn away the deliveryman.
It's not that I don't appreciate the skill and care

with which you carved its oaken contours,
the sweeping curve of its tail, the delightful detail
of the acorn clutched between its paws,

the eight-feet high scale of your ambition,
but you have to admit it is a strange birthday gift,
particularly for somebody who suffers

from a fear of being murdered in his sleep,
somebody who has never previously
revealed a fondness for giant wooden squirrels.

25th April

Robinson Crusoe, *Daniel Defoe's famous novel about a shipwrecked castaway, was published on this day in 1719. It is thought to be based on the adventures of Alexander Selkirk, a Scottish privateer, marooned by his captain on a South Pacific island. The book was a phenomenon. Defoe wrote two sequels and by the end of the nineteenth century no other book had received so many editions, translations, or spin-offs. It also led to the emergence of 'Robinsonade': a whole genre of books, films, and television series based around the castaway narrative and not, as the name suggests, a type of fizzy barley water.*

Robinson in Hounslow

Imagine my surprise when, en route to Broadcasting House
to appear on *Desert Island Discs*, my bus – swerving
to avoid a heavy slice of irony – capsized and sank,
and coming round, I found myself washed up on the central island
of a traffic roundabout, on the outskirts of Hounslow.

Having dragged myself to safety, I rested awhile
to regain my strength before I set about exploring.
The island appeared uninhabited, although a Twix wrapper
suggested the place had been no stranger to castaways.
For some time, I wandered amongst its rich vegetation,

admiring the mauve and yellow crocuses arranged
to form the word WELCOME. But the skies were darkening,
and I got to work on my shelter. I had no idea how long
I might be stranded here but I knew my fortifications
needed to be sturdy and watertight to contend

with the weather extremities that the edge of Hounslow
might entertain. By a stroke of good fortune, my records
had washed up on the island, too, and I was able to construct
a shelter out of 1980s synth-pop album sleeves,
several of which had come with a helpful gatefold design.

How many months I resided there, living on rain-water
and crocuses, I cannot say; by the time I was rescued –
a passing floral designer had spotted my desperate waving
of Howard Jones' *Human Lib* – I was bearded and thin,
and had befriended a black and white directional arrow sign.

You can get the Number 26 from there, she said,
indicating a bus stop, along one of the busy thoroughfares
radiating out from the island. It dropped me off practically outside;
although on my arrival at reception, the producer told me
I was far too late, and they'd ended up getting Sue Barker in.

26th April

....

*Ludwig Wittgenstein was born on this day in 1889. He went on to
become one of the greatest philosophers of the twentieth century as
well as a really good person to quote if you want to appear clever at a
dinner party. Wittgenstein's 'what cannot be imagined cannot even
be talked about' is perfect with garlic mushrooms, while his 'whereof
one cannot speak, thereof one must be silent' complements a Chilean
merlot delightfully. He also said, 'I don't know why we are here, but
I'm pretty sure that it is not in order to enjoy ourselves', which in itself
is a pretty good description of a dinner party.*

Wittgenstein's Cat

It's not easy, living with a philosopher.
When I pad into his bedroom in the morning
at the very reasonable hour of five o'clock,

to remind him it's time for breakfast
he lies there in silence until it becomes necessary
for him to remove my claws from his eyelids.

Philosophy should not be a theory, I miaow,
but an activity, particularly one
which involves the refilling of my bowl.

On several occasions, I have mentioned
that even if it *were* possible for a human to talk,
we cats could not understand him,

yet he persists in making these strange noises
in the hope I might him answer back.
And sometimes, when my eyes are closed

and I am deep in thought upon his lap,
pondering how the tenets of logical positivism
can help me catch more mice,

he will suddenly leap up in the air,
as if a crash of cymbals has sounded behind him,
sending me and my thoughts flying

and so, I ask you, is it any wonder
there are so many questions
I have yet been unable to solve?

27th April

Samuel Morse, the American inventor and painter, was born on this day in 1791. He helped to invent the single-wire telegraph system and co-developed Morse code. The first message to be sent in Morse code occurred in May 1844 when it travelled between Washington DC and Baltimore. The message read said: 'What hath God wrought?'; not the catchiest of opening lines, perhaps, but the communication was a success and thought to be a vast improvement on banging drums, producing smoke signals or climbing hills to wave a flag around a bit.

.-.. --- ...- . / .-. --- . -- --.-- / .-- -.- .. - - -.-. / ... -.- / -- --- -.-. . . . . / -.-. --- -.-. .

-.. --- - / . . . . -.-. .-. .-. . . . . / .. -. / .-- --- -.- .-. / .-. -.-. .-.
-.-. . . . . -.-. . / . . . -.-. .-. .-. --. .... - / .-. --- -.-. / -.-. --- .-.
.-- --- -.-. .-. . . . / --- .-. / .-.. --- ...- . / . .- .-. .-. .-. .-. / --- .- - / .. -. / -.-. --- -.- . .
-.. .. - / -.. .- .- / -.. .. - / -.. .- .... / -.. --- .

-.-. .- -. / .-. --- --- .- / ..... .- .-. / --- . / - ..... .-. .-. .-. ... / - ..... . / .- ..... .-.
. -.-. .-. .-. . . . / .-- --- -.- .-. .-. / .-. -.-. .-. / .- -.-. . .-... -.
--- --- .. -. / - ..... / -.. --- --- - . . . / -.. --- --- / -. ..... .-. . . . . / -- --.-- / .... --- --. ... .
-.. .. - / -.. .- .... / -.. .. - / -.. .- .... / -.. --- .

.-. .-. -.-. . . . . / -.- .-. -.-. .- . . . . / - ..... .- . / . . . .-. .-. .-. .-. -.-. -.. .. . . / -- . . . . -.-.
-. ..... .-. - / .. / .-- -- / -.. .- --- --- .-.-.- / .- -.- .- --- -.. .- - / .-. --- -.- .-.
.. / ..... .- . .- . / . . . . . . -. .-. -.-. -.-. .-. -.-. .-. .-. / -- .-.-.- / .. .-. . . .-. -.-. .- --- -. . . ....
-.. .. - / -.. .- .... / -.. .. - / -.. .- .... / -.. --- .

Love Poem, Written in Morse Code

Dot signals in your area
Dashing straight for you
Words of love tapped out in code
Dit dah dit dah do

Can you hear me through the ether
Transmitting clear and true?
Join the dots . . . don't dash my hopes
Dit dah dit dah do

Please excuse this slapdash message
But I am dotty about you
I have signalled my intentions
Dit dah dit dah do

28th April

....

Today's date has become one of the most significant in the modern calendar as it marks the occasion in 2011 on which the former British politician Ed Balls accidentally tweeted his name. Intending to search for a recent article about himself on Twitter, he typed his name in the wrong box, sending out a tweet just consisting of the immortal phrase 'Ed Balls'. The day has been celebrated in the UK ever since with the hosting of street parties, the exchanging of gifts, ceremonial dancing around an Ed Balls tree, and the writing of encomiastic verse.

Tweet

I don't think I shall ever meet
A sight as joyous as his tweet.

A tweet to set a heart astir
And make it flutter like a bird.

A tweet that strikes a merry chord
And cheers me up when I am bored.

A tweet that towers over all,
To sing each day, to learn at school.

A statement proud, a song of hope,
Through long, dark days, a way to cope.

Leave poetry to other fools
For none compares to this: *Ed Balls*.

29th April

....

Today is International Dance Day, in honour of the birth of Jean-Georges Noverre, the creator of modern ballet, in 1727. The day celebrates all forms of dance, from the bolero to body-popping, and aims to encourage more people to strut their stuff. This may not be advisable in my case. I don't consider myself to be a particularly good dancer, having two left feet when it comes to such matters; a disadvantage only partially offset by my one right foot.

do you remember the first time we danced?

how the dancefloor cleared of all but us
how each song segued into the next
how were we to know the music would not stop,
we'd have no chance to catch our breath?

yes, we've cut some shapes, you and I,
jived to the music of time
we've breakdanced, lindy hopped and twerked
we've grown a conga line

bolero, salsa, boogaloo –
oh, how well we know these steps!
the night sky is a spinning glitterball,
and our feet aren't tired yet

30th April

*International Jazz Day occurs annually on the last day of April.
Within jazz itself there exists a huge variety of sounds and styles,
but at its heart lies improvisation, rhythm and freedom. And that
freedom of expression applies not only to the smokin' of saxes, noodlin'
of clarinets, and bangin' of tubs. The art of 'scat' allows an escape
from the straitjacket of meanings that come from words: that's why
it's remained such a powerful form of communication for jazz
vocalists and Conservative cabinet ministers alike. Doo-yah-dah-
dah-dit-dip-bah!*

experimental jazz poem

in honour
of international jazz day,
this poem
is one hundred percent
        freestyle

                and
                                imp-ro-vised

        yeah!

    words written just as they come to me

                                100 %
                freestyle

                                        andimprovised

                okay!

    wild!
                                yeah!

            umm . . .
                    that's it

May

1st May

....

Today is International Workers' Day; also known as Labour Day in some countries. It commemorates the historic struggles and gains made by workers and the labour movement, and gives a platform for discussion concerning workers' rights and conditions, including pay. The day, of course, is also known as May Day, which can be used as a distress signal to shout in times of emergency. In terms of my working career, which has been largely based around sitting at a computer watching the emails in my inbox grow, this may be no coincidence.

Ten New Emails

Ten new emails waiting there for me
Eleven new emails waiting there for me
And if my computer should accidentally beep
There'll be twelve new emails waiting there for me

Twelve new emails waiting there for me
Thirteen new emails waiting there for me
And if one new email I should accidentally read
There'll be twenty new emails waiting there for me

Twenty new emails waiting there for me
Twenty-one new emails waiting there for me
And if one new email I should accidentally respond to
In a brisk and business-like fashion,

Only for me to have to re-send it because I'd forgotten my
    attachment,
There'll be thirty new emails waiting there for me

Thirty new emails waiting there for me
Thirty-one new emails waiting there for me
And if my computer should accidentally be hurled against the wall
There'll be no new emails waiting there for me

2nd May

....

*Leonardo da Vinci died on this day in 1519. He was the original
Renaissance man. Although still regarded primarily as an artist,
Leonardo was much more than that – engineer, scientist, geologist,
musician, general legend – as the thousands of surviving pages from
his notebooks show. He wasn't without his flaws, though; his rival
Michelangelo often taunted him for his inability to complete his
work. He hadn't even finished dabbling with the* Mona Lisa *by all
accounts but, as Leonardo himself once said, 'art is never finished,
only abandoned'.*

A Comparison of Genius

sure, that elusive sfumato smile
of his most famous portrait may reveal
an impressive mastery of technique,

an intimate understanding
of not only the muscles which move our lips
but the retina's processing of perception,

a profound insight into happiness
and what it is to be human,
and yes, I guess there is a strong argument

for saying that *The Last Supper* possesses
a dramatic narrative without parallel
in the history of Western art,

and I will grudgingly admit
that his pioneering studies of geology,
engineering, optics, and anatomy

represent a fair accomplishment
when you consider they involve
the first ever drawing of the thyroid gland,

an investigation into the cirrhosis of the liver,
the invention of the armoured car,
helicopter, flying machine, parachute,

self-powered vehicle, diving suit,
as well as several new types of bridge,
but then again, I have just balanced

twelve Pringles on the bridge of my nose
and made you laugh at a time
when you had forgotten how to,

and while I am not saying
that makes me a genius, it's hard to deny
the scale of my achievement

3rd May

....

World Press Freedom Day takes place annually on this day to
remind all governments around the world of the need to respect
their commitment to freedom of the media. It also serves as a day of
remembrance for those journalists who lost their lives in the pursuit of
a story. We seem in need of this day more than ever, in a world where
even the most long-established democracies are under threat from
states' control of key media and a pandemic of misinformation, 'fake
news', and 'alternative facts'.

Broken News

We interrupt this poem to bring you reports of   an explosion
of wild untruths and other signs that the news   is broken.

Eye-witness statements from those first to arrive   on the scene
describe how they watched as the truth was blown   to
      smithereens

following a frontal assault on the facts   and a
prolonged barrage of   propaganda.

A government spokesperson has blamed the attack on the influx
      of   immigrants
amid widespread fears that further fabrications   are
      imminent.

This latest outbreak of misinformation is believed to form part
      of   a familiar pattern.
But back to the poem. We'll bring you more news   as it
      doesn't happen.

4th May

....

Today is Star Wars Day, an annual celebration of the popular Star
Wars *media franchise. The date was chosen for its pun on the films'
catchphrase 'May the Force be with you' (May the Fourth be with
you). Given the continued popularity of* Star Wars, *it seems hugely
surprising, then, that my space opera,* Under the Moons of Love
*– concerning a doomed love affair between a Wookie in the rebel
alliance and a droid in the service of the Imperial Guard – remains
available for production. Should any theatre producers be reading this,
please do feel free to contact my agent if you would like to discuss
further.*

Love Duet for Wookie and Droid

[Wookie]   Yyyurrruggnhh aarr wgh grrbokgh
                 Rrraughh muurggh karaaa
                 Rowrigghh murgbushk rwww hrungh
                 Nyyrrrnyrrr aarrgghhrmph
                 Grrrwwwwrrrrrrrrwr

[Droid]   Beep. Beeeep. Boop. Boop.
                 Whirr. Booooop. Beep.

[Wookie]   Grrrrrgeeer rwww mrowgh nwurr
                 Muurrrgh brrr-annnn goowwrrrgh
                 Aarrr wgh ggwaaah ahh
                 Grrbokgh wyaaaa mwoygh hhummmghhra
                 Grrrwwwwrrrrrrrrwr

[Droid]   Beep. Beeeep. Boop-boop-boop.
                 Whirr. Booooop. Beeeep.

[Together]   Ggwaaahhh mwowgggh weedle-beep-boop
                 Wghh aarrrr mwworyghh kaarr beeep
                 Whirr hurnngh brr-annnghgh weedle-boop
                 Grrrwwwwrrrrrrrrwr beedle-ee-beep

5th May

Today is International Midwife Day, a day to celebrate the role played by midwives in ensuring healthy outcomes for women and their babies. I'm in awe of these individuals, not least from having undergone the experience of delivering my own daughter, simultaneously the most exciting and terrifying episode of my life. Well, I say I delivered her, but my partner did it all really; I just held my hands out, closed my eyes, and hoped for the best.

Home Delivery

I'm sure you could have waited,
if you had put your mind to it.

I appreciate it can't have been a bundle
of laughs, cooped up like that,

but what made you think this day
carried with it anything more exciting

than the resumption of county cricket,
a guest appearance from the sun,

and a midwife cursing the traffic,
while two rookies on a landing

are handed surprise debuts: one,
mid-delivery, doing all the hard work,

the other, at first slip, bending low,
preparing to catch.

6th May

The Channel Tunnel opened on this day in 1994, connecting Great Britain and France by a fifty-kilometre railway tunnel. The first proposal for a tunnel was put forward in 1802 by Albert Mathieu; it included an artificial island halfway across for changing horses. When the project did eventually get underway, it took six years to complete and involved more than thirteen thousand workers. Eleven boring machines were used to dig the tunnel – apologies if that sounds harsh but I'm just not very interested in excavation technology.

Chunnel Vision
Poem Written on the Opening of the Channel Tunnel

With the opening of this tunnel,
it's time to put old scores aside;
for our future lies together,
not determined by the tide.

No more splendid isolation.
No more separate plans.
For no man is an island
(except the Isle of Man).

Europe, we are at one with you –
let our shores be joined to yours!*

* Postscript: June 2016
Oh, flipping 'eck! Oh, zut alors!

7th May

One of the most significant developments in recent British political history occurred at the general election held on this day in 2015, when people began to share photographs of their dogs waiting outside polling stations on social media. This development was seen as an important breakthrough in making the whole election process slightly less awful, and the redeeming feature in a day typically filled with bad news and misery.

Dogs at Polling Stations

There are dogs
at polling stations,
sitting outside

waiting
for their democratic right
to exercise.

8th May

Sir David Attenborough, the natural historian and broadcaster, was born on this day in 1926. More than any other television presenter, he's been responsible for foregrounding the impact humans have had on our planet and the challenges that confront us. Prior to his involvement in documentary-making, he was controller of BBC Two, *commissioning programmes such as* Match of the Day *and* Monty Python's Flying Circus. *But it is as a naturalist and all-round national – no, global – treasure that he is best known, and it's hard to think of what this world would be like without him.*

Unimaginable Death of a Naturalist

I don't want to think about it
but when that day comes
the sloths will get up early for once
the crocodiles will cry real tears
the flamingos will line up in pink, long-legged salute
the birds of paradise will parade in their finest
the seals will participate in a minute's clapping
the elephants will entwine their trunks in solidarity
the penguins will huddle together for comfort
the gorillas will act out stories of his visits
the lyre birds will mimic his voice
the ostriches will bury their heads in the sand
the blue whales will use their blowholes as trumpets
the electric eels will be in shock
the lions will stop chasing the wildebeest for one day
and they will stand together side by side on the Serengeti plain
the glow worms will light up the dark
and the humans will sit and watch documentaries
but not for long, he will be hoping,
because Earth is a ticking bomb
and there's much to be done

9th May

Roger Hargreaves, author of the Mr Men and Little Miss books, was born on this day in 1935. The two series became instant classics, as young children (and their parents) fell in love with the bright and variously shaped inhabitants of Mister Land. The books have become popular all around the world, with some of the titles working even better in other languages than they do in English: Herr Dumpidump *(the Norwegian* Mr Bump*);* Monsieur Bing *(the French* Mr Bounce*); and* Don Confuso *(the Spanish* Mr Muddle*).*

The Lesser-Known Mr Men and Little Miss Books

I

Cantankerous man
makes amazing things with yarn –
Mr Crotchety

II

Friendly man gets drunk,
having lost concentration –
Mr Cordial

III

Lethargic young girl
loses plan of what to do –
Little Miss Listless

IV

Tedious bore with
his contrabass saxophone –
Mr Long-Winded

V

Smug-faced irritant
points out missing syllable –
Mr Pedant

VI

Girl finds life absurd,
embraces surrealism –
Little Miss Fridge Hat

10th May

....

'You're making me angry. You wouldn't like me when I'm angry.'
The first issue of The Incredible Hulk *by Marvel Comics went on*
sale in the USA on this day in 1962. Dr Bruce Banner is the brilliant
scientist who, following a laboratory experiment that goes awry,
transforms into a giant green monster called the Hulk whenever he
finds himself under extreme stress. It's a difficult condition to live with,
and one which I feel much empathy for – as anyone who has seen me
attempt to assemble flat-pack furniture will firmly attest.

Anger-Management Techniques for Superheroes

1. Identify triggers. Take stock of those situations
   which light your fuse, such as traffic jams, HMRC forms,
   or confrontations with mutant supervillains
   intent on taking over the world, and plan accordingly.

2. Find a word or phrase to help you calm down
   and refocus. Repeat it again and again.
   'Relax' or 'Be cool' are good examples of this.
   'SMASH' or 'DIE, YOU FREAK', less so.

3. Go to your happy place! Close your eyes
   and take yourself there. Focus on the details—
   What colour is the water? How tall are the mountains?
   How stringent are the health and safety regulations
   concerning the handling of gamma radiation?

4. Try counting up to ten.
   Or, if you're feeling really mad, up to a hundred –
   unless, that is, you are being hit over the head repeatedly
   with a heavy metal object by a gang of hoods
   beneath the Santa Monica Pier,
   or your throat is being gripped
   by the tentacle-like appendages of a mad, evil scientist –
   in which case, forget all this advice
   and channel your anger
   into dealing with the task in hand.

11th May

....

Salvador Dalí, the Spanish surrealist artist, was born on this day in 1904. He pioneered the 'paranoiac-critical' method, designed to help him access his subconscious by staring at a fixed object until something different was found within it, or by keeping himself in a state between sleep and wakefulness. A similar effect can be achieved through demolishing three packets of custard creams in one sitting. As part of a paternity suit, Dalí's body was dug up in 2017, when it was discovered that his famous moustache was still intact, in its customary ten past ten position: a finding that can only be regarded as somewhat surreal.

Portrait of Man with Head of Purple Delphiniums Gazing Out of a First-Floor Window

Life has become far more interesting
since I discovered surrealism.
I don't think the peanut butter trees
have ever seemed more vibrant,
nor cloud song more beautiful.
My fitted wardrobes are in full bloom.

Each morning, I draw back the painted curtains
with my giant carrot fingers,
and look out on a world of improbability –
dogs on stilts, giraffes with umbrellas,
chimneys swaying in the breeze. A violin
stoops to pick up his hat, a tree chuckles,
and the postman scuttles by. I wave at him
and he lifts a happy claw in response
then posts himself through next door's letterbox.

How I wish I could stay here all day
watching the sundrops run down my window
until green liquid night pours in,
but even here, in this land of the not normal,
there are responsibilities, deadlines –
my drooping clock says it's half past thirteen,
and this fridge won't knit itself, you know.

12th May

Established in honour of its most popular exponent, Edward Lear, born on this day in 1812, today is National Limerick Day. To those who don't know much about poetry, a limerick takes the form of a five-line poem consisting of anapaestic trimeter with a strict AABBA rhyme scheme, if that helps. Lear himself wrote 212 limericks but sadly most of these were of the nonsense variety which, as everyone knows, is not as good as the smutty ones.

Nantucket Man Has Had Enough

There once was a man from Nantucket
who, tired of being a puppet
in crude, smutty rhymes,
said goodbye to those times

by moving
to a new stanza
in a vacant piece of free verse,
just five miles away
from the thriving market town
of Ludlow.

13th May

....

It is thought that on this day in 1637, Cardinal Richelieu of France created the table knife. The story goes that the eminent French statesman was so repulsed by his fellow diners stabbing their daggers into chunks of meat and then using them to pick their teeth at the end of the meal, he ordered his kitchen staff to file off the sharp points of all the house knives. Debrett's Guide to Etiquette and Modern Manners *would have been appalled by such behaviour and dictates that a knife should never be licked nor held like a pen. The latter instruction is all very well but I happen to hold my pen like a knife, and now I don't know what to do.*

Cutlery Etiquette When Under Attack from a Grizzly Bear

Should you ever happen to find yourself
to be the recipient of a frenzied attack
from a grizzly bear whilst dining,
remember, the usual principles apply.

Always work from the outside in.
Begin with your soup spoon, which should make
a pleasing *thwock* when brought down
upon the advancing bear's cranium.

Your butter knife should remain on your bread plate,
unless you are using it to warn the bear off
through a series of violent, jabbing motions.
The hurling of bread rolls is not considered good form.

Should the bear fail to pick up on the social signals –
such as its exclusion from your conversation
concerning the on-trending of Portuguese wine,
or the screaming of your fellow diners –

you should prong it with your dinner fork,
ensuring the tines are pointing downwards at all times.
Your dinner knife should be held in the right hand
with the handle firmly tucked into the palm,

until the moment presents itself for a sudden lunge.
If you accidentally drop your cutlery on the floor,
leave it! The waiter will replace it for you,
assuming they remain unmauled. And finally,

use your napkin to indicate when you are finished,
leaving it semi-folded at the left side of your place setting,
signalling that the dishes may now be removed
and the bear's bloody carcass discreetly dragged away.

14th May

Eric Morecambe was born on this day in 1926. Together with his comedy partner Ernie Wise, he formed one of the funniest and most loved double acts Britain has ever produced. Born John Eric Bartholomew, he took his stage name from his home town, the seaside resort of Morecambe, and where a statue now stands in his memory. It was the duo's Christmas Day television specials, in particular, which were to become iconic, with their natural chemistry and masterful comic timing and delivery, always seeming to hit all the right notes, in the right order.

'Just a Statue'

A selection of one-star Trip Advisor reviews of Eric Morecambe's statue.

The intrinsic nature of statuary requires only
for it to be a representation of a person or animal,
fashioned from stone, wood or metal.
And yet, for some, it appears this was not enough.

'You can't do anything with it,' opined one reviewer.
Another declared it 'Boring! Takes three seconds
to look at . . . then done,' not questioning whether
this in itself might constitute an achievement,

given how it's possible to shamble through
the Museum of Modern Art while checking
the football scores on your phone, and barely give
Van Gogh's The Starry Night a second glance.

'Disappointingly small. Perhaps 120% life size,'
was one verdict, suggesting the whole experience
might be improved with a giant Eric, a Brobdingnagian Eric,
towering over the town of Morecambe,

casting it in shadow and blocking out the views
of the Cumbrian hills behind. It was
an inconsistency concerning the statue's presence
which was very much on one visitor's mind,

a woman who had journeyed all the way from Heysham,
a not inconsiderable distance of three miles,
only to find the figurative funny man missing.
'All that remained was a bronze foot,' she reported.

'Don't like it! Where is Ernie?' exclaims another,
unaware that Ernie's a hundred and thirty miles away,
on Queen Street in the centre of Morley,
clutching a brolly and tipping his hat to his friend,

bringing sunshine, laughter and a rainbow big enough
to stretch across the Pennines and join them together
once more, while a man from Withernsea stares
then taps into his phone, *'looks nothing like him.'*

15th May

The International Day of Families is observed on this day annually and celebrates the importance of families as a foundation of society. It raises awareness of the challenges to families such as education, poverty, health, and work–family balance. Given the strain that some families find themselves under, bickering about the state of the bathroom or what to watch on the TV seems rather trivial in comparison. George Burns may have got nearest to the truth, though: 'Happiness,' he said, 'is having a large, loving, caring, close-knit family in another city.'

Kith and Kin

To distinguish between kith and kin,
here's a good place to begin:
the best way to regard one's kith
is those we *choose* to spend time with,
whereas kin conform to no such plan,
and must be endured as best we can.

16th May

Today is the International Day of Light, a celebration of light and the role it plays in science, culture and art, education, and sustainable development. It's held on the anniversary of Theodore Maiman's first successful operation of the laser in 1960. Light is one of the most

important factors in the survival of animals and plants on Earth and,
for that reason, it should never be hidden under a bushel, nor indeed
any pile of grain or fruit.

Look for the Light

look for the light
in the darkness,

the light which
makes its way

among the bombs
and broken lives,

offers blankets
and shoulders to cry on,

puts on kettles
and bandages,

mends what it can
and asks

for not one thing back,
as it wraps

in its arms
the troubled night,

cradles it
in its soft, pale light.

17th May

Bob Dylan performed a show at the Manchester Free Trade Hall on
this day in 1966. At the time, he was seen as a traitor by some of the
folk community for daring to use an electric guitar. He played two sets.
The first, on his own, was acoustic. The second, an electric one, was
with his backing band. Some people walked out, there were slow hand
claps and while waiting to play the final song of his set, 'Like a Rolling
Stone', there came a shout of 'Judas!' from the crowd. It was a word
which was to follow him around for years to come.

Dylan Goes Electric

1. Manchester, 1966
A crowd gathers in the Free Trade Hall.
They've heard there's nowt so queer as folk.
Dylan plugs in, like a Rolling Stone,
a shout, intended to provoke . . .
JUDAS!

2. Bathroom, 1979
Dylan's bedtime. A new toothbrush.
It starts to hum, its bristles whirr.
He chucks his old one in the bin.
The lid snaps open, says that word . . .
Judas.

3. Garden, 1995

He takes the lawn into his own hands.
Its edges have never looked so trim.
Zimmerman's a Strimmer-Man.
A whispered word blows in the wind . . .
Judas.

4. Desolation Row, 2015

No more acoustic cigarettes
for the times they are a-vaping.
But Dylan, in his lime drop fug,
sees a word there's no escaping . . .
Judas.

18th May

*Today is International Museum Day, which celebrates the role
museums play in communities as well as raising public awareness
of the challenges facing them. Growing up in Birmingham, I was
lucky to have a very fine museum – and art gallery – on my doorstep.
Or a half-an-hour bus journey away, at least. There were Egyptian
mummies, hoards of treasure, and the most important collection of
Pre-Raphaelite art in the world. Not that I thought any of that back
then, when the prospect of setting foot inside the place would fill me
with abject fear.*

How the Dinosaur Died Out

Unlike modern day prehistoric monsters,
this one was made out of real dinosaur.
The height of a hundred terrified young boys
(or of one terrifying Tyrannosaurus rex),

he patrolled the entrance hall
of the Birmingham Museum and Art Gallery
where he would roar at regular intervals,
and at one terrified young lad, in particular,

thus preventing the boy from venturing further,
unless hoicked up in a fireman's lift
and carried swiftly through the vestibule
to the room beyond and the safety of its mummies,

where he would eventually calm down
and stop making an exhibition of himself.
What drew a Tyrannosaurus rex to Birmingham
was a mystery to us all, unless he'd come

to battle King Kong, who was busy bemusing Brummies
in the Bull Ring, before moving out to occupy
a car dealership on the Ladypool Road.
But everything must come to an end, some time –

even dinosaurs. Some say it was a comet;
others claim he ended up in a skip after a falling out
with the museum's senior management.
Carnage, by all accounts. Papier-mâché everywhere.

19th May

On this day in 1536, the second of Henry VIII's six wives – Anne Boleyn – was executed. There has long existed an effective aide memoire to help poor students remember the running order of his queens. But while it's helpful in the establishment of some basic facts, it's less useful when faced with the prospect of writing a 2,000-word essay on Anne Boleyn, particularly when you've left it to the last minute and can't remember your password to get into the university's online library. To redress the balance, here's a mnemonic offering a more critical, analytic approach to her involvement with the crown.

Mnemonic to aid understanding of the role of Anne Boleyn in the Succession Crisis of Henry VIII

In the hope of finding a wife who would bear him a male heir, Henry VIII divorced Catherine of Aragon and

Wedded Anne Boleyn, whom he then

Bedded in pursuit of that dynastic goal. However, their marriage failed to provide him with the male heir

he so desired and rumours of high treason, incest, adultery, and witchcraft were

Spreaded in order to allow the king to remarry, or so it is

Saided As for poor Anne Boleyn, she got

Beheaded and, not long after, found herself

Deaded

20th May

Not to be confused with World Bidet, an international solution for washing one's nether regions, World Bee Day is a celebration of the famously buzzy insect which occurs on this day every year. It is not only the knees of a bee which are so wonderful, but the whole package of one: they're Earth's top pollinators and the vast majority of the plants we need for food rely on them going about their pollinating business. In other words, without them, we're done for – and that's why the decline in their population is alarming and we need to stop using pesky pesticides, grow more bee-friendly plants, and stop wrecking the planet in general.

The Last Bee

After the last   ee
had   uzzed its last   uzz,
the   irds and the   utterflies
did what they could.

  ut soon the field lay   are,
few flowers were left,
nature was   roken,
and the planet   ereft.

21st May

....

*Mary Anning, the fossil-hunter extraordinaire, was born on this
day in 1799. She became known around the world for the finds she
made at Lyme Regis, discovering an ichthyosaur at the age of twelve,
the complete skeleton of a plesiosaurus in 1823, and the remains of
a pterodactyl five years after that. Her discoveries were to rock the
scientific world, and made a major contribution to the development of
scientific thinking about prehistoric life and the history of the Earth.
Remember that next time you're lying on a beach, soaking up the
sun, and trying to summon up the energy to get yourself a mint choc
Cornetto.*

Mary Anning

Mary Anning
was forever beach-scanning.
Every day she would hunt for fossils.
Her contribution to palaeontology was colossals.

22nd May

....

*This day in 1885 saw the death of Victor Hugo, the acclaimed French
poet, novelist and author of* The Hunchback of Notre-Dame *and* Les
Misérables. *The latter work is believed to be one of the longest novels
ever written, containing 365 chapters, 1,400 pages and 655,000
words. In spite of this, a few years ago I decided to read it. I've been*

reading it ever since. Given that in 1959, this date also saw the birth of Mancunian miserabilist Morrissey, here's a reworking of one of his songs which describes how I feel about making that kind of investment with my time.

Heaven Knows It's *Les Misérables* Now

I was happy in the days of a hunchback's tower
But heaven knows it's *Les Misérables* now
I was looking for Valjean, and then I found Valjean
And heaven knows it's *Les Misérables* now

In my life
Why do I give valuable time
To novels I will read until I
Lay down and die

Two summers combine, pass me by
And heaven knows it's *Les Misérables* now
I was looking for Valjean, and then I found Valjean
And heaven knows it's still *Les Misérables* now

In my life
Why do I give valuable time
To lengthy tomes I'll never get through
Before I die

'What's next?' she asked, at the end of the day
'*À la recherche du temps perdu.*'
'You keep on choosing books too long,' she said
As I doggedly read

In my life
Why can't I be
Like people who would much rather
Just watch TV

23rd May

....

Today is World Turtle Day. Contrary to what the mainstream media might have us believe, only some turtles are teenage, very few are mutant, and hardly any at all happen to be ninjas. But lots of them are endangered, hence the need for days such as this one, which raises awareness of their plight. Poaching, habitat destruction, climate change and accidental capture in fishing gear are threatening the extinction of several species and unless we tackle these issues soon, not even Leonardo and his gang will be able to do much about it.

Turtle Recall

Oh yes, there've been a few changes
over the last 120 million years, I can tell you –
not that I'm that old myself, of course –
I know I might look prehistoric
but that's life beneath the waves for you,
it plays havoc with your skin.

I'm a whippersnapper really –
ninety-four years young this very day!

But that doesn't mean I don't know
the old stories. They wave to us
from history, like thick sea-grass
swaying in the murky depths of time.

Take the Early Cretaceous – what an epoch!
Crabs, shrimps, whelks, jellies . . .
whatever you could lay your flippers on,
and none of the plastic we get nowadays;
no nets, either, to trap and tangle;
long, quiet beaches to lay your eggs.

Time is brittle. But my shell is strong
and so I shouldn't grumble – not today,
my special day. The party's starting soon
and I'd best get on and tend this reef.
Won't be long until my friends are here –
there's less of them that come each year.

24th May

....

On this day in 1956, the very first Eurovision Song Contest was held.
It was established to promote cooperation between European countries,
and unity across the continent. It's a tradition that continues to this
day, as all nations come together as one to humiliate the United
Kingdom. Here are the lyrics of the Faroe Islands' 2016 entry, which
later went on to become a surprise hit in the thrash disco charts. The
United Kingdom was to finish last that year.

Europe Together

(The Chiff-Chaff, Twit-Twit, Chirp-Chirp, Tweet Song)

Come here, my little turtle dove
And sing with me this song of love
We'll make some sweet music tonight
The whole of Europe shall unite

Chiff-chaff, twit-twit, chirp-chirp, tweet
Let's join together when we meet
On the one thing we agree upon –
United Kingdom gets nul points

Our feathers may not be the same
But yet we share a common aim
Come sit down here, my branch is strong
You know the words so sing along

Chiff-chaff, tweet-tweet, chirp-chirp, twit
Let's all agree their song was shit
It does not matter where you're from
United Kingdom gets nul points

For one night may we be allied
Our differences all shoved aside
So come and gather in this tree
To sing this song of unity

Chiff-chaff, twit-twit, chirp-chirp, tweet
Sing it loud! Vote with your feet!
The one thing we agree upon –
United Kingdom gets *nul points*

25th May

Bank holidays were established in the United Kingdom on this day
in 1871, with the passing of the Bank Holidays Act. It was repealed
in 1971 and superseded by the Banking and Financial Dealings Act
1971, a piece of legislation I am unable to discuss at length in this
book due to dullness. In recent decades, the May bank holidays have
traditionally been reserved for getting on with some DIY and watching
the snooker. My interests lie more with the latter, being hopeless at
the former: a haplessness shared with Arctic Monkeys' frontman, Alex
Turner.

I Bet You Look Good With a Hand Saw

My house is despising me, and I can't face B&Q
What it is that surprises me is that I really need someone like you
Because my shower is broken (and the grouting's a sight)
Oh, and the boiler is smoking (something's not right)
For you, it's a breeze – oh, but I don't understand.
When I change a fuse, it results in a bang, in a bang-oh

I bet that you look good with a hand saw
I don't know if you're looking much to sand floors
Don't know what you're looking for
I said I bet that you look good with a hand saw
Or using a Black & Decker Workmate from 1984
Well, from 1984!

My neighbour's ignoring me because my house is in disrepair
Rain gutters need installing, see, and I'd rather not go up there
And my dishwasher's broken (so the kitchen's a sight)
And I haven't a notion (to make it all right)
I'm quite good with tea, though. Come and lend me a hand,
Come and make the boiler's 'bang and a clang' go

I bet that you look good with a hand saw
I don't know if you're looking much to sand floors
Don't know what you're looking for
I said that I bet that you look good with a hand saw
Or using a Black & Decker Workmate from 1984
Well, from 1984!

No, it ain't no help, no, looking on the internet
Got no power drills, no staple guns, no,
just a Christmas cracker screwdriver set

26th May

....

'Persons of small courage and weak nerves should confine their reading of these gruesome pages strictly to the hours between dawn and sunset' is not an early reader's report of the book you're holding in your hands but a review in The Daily Mail *of Bram Stoker's* Dracula, *published on this day in 1897. Although the book was popular on publication, it was cinema which propelled Dracula (much to his own displeasure) into the limelight. He's now the most filmed fictional character ever, from early classics such as* Nosferatu *and Bela Lugosi's* Dracula *through the Hammer film series of the 1960s and 70s with Christopher Lee, to George Lucas's experimental 'Dracula in space' movie,* The Vampire Strikes Back.

Bride of Dracula

Yes, it *is* rather draining,
having a vampire come and feast on your neck
every single bloody evening,
particularly when you've got work the next day
and a pile to get through
because it's the run-up to year-end.

I know Mr Bradshaw is getting concerned
about my productivity levels
but that's the thing about having the life sucked out of you
by an eight-hundred-year-old fanged demon,
it plays havoc with your vitamin D.
I'm on supplements now.

Sandra thinks I should ward him off
with a bit of garlic or something –
at least until we've got the accruals finished –
but she spends half her day
flirting with Clive Pickering in purchase ledger
so she's a fine one to talk,

and besides, I enjoy his nightly visits,
the hungry way he looks at me
before he leans in towards my neck,
it makes me feel dead special,
and after a long, boring day of chasing invoices
who wouldn't want to feel like that?

27th May

It's World Otter Day, celebrating all things otters. By now, it will
come as little surprise to know that sea otters are endangered, thanks
to a combination of the fur trade, pollution, and global warming.
I have always felt a particular kinship with these furry aquatic beasts.
This may be because I am good at holding my breath underwater.
Or possibly because I also eat 25 per cent of my body weight in food
every day.

What Don Corleone Did Next

upon retiring
from the Mafia

he wove aquatic mammals
out of raffia

let me tell you
how I learnt this news:

he made me an otter
I couldn't refuse

28th May

....

*Ian Fleming was born on this day in 1908. Now mainly known for his
classic children's story about a magical car,* Chitty-Chitty-Bang-Bang,
*Fleming had, prior to that, penned a few other novels about some spy
or other, whose name he took from the author of the field guide* Birds
of the West Indies. *The ornithologist was to have the last laugh,
though, as his popular field guides were to provide the inspiration
behind a whole flock of blockbuster Hollywood films, including* From
Russia with Dove, Goldfincher, *and* On Her Majesty's Egret
Service.

Bond, off duty

It's rare for the movies to show him
wielding a hoover, or unloading a dishwasher;
presumably not making for good box office,
or maybe they just don't have the budget.

It could be that he employs a cleaner,
although that runs the risk of someone snooping
through his drawers. M would never sanction
such a potential security breach.

The cutting-room floor must be littered
with footage of him ringing around
to get a new quote on his home insurance,
filling in his expense forms – the itinerary

of an international secret agent is complex:
he'll be drowning in receipts. And what about
the days he needs to catch up with his laundry,
take his wetsuit to the dry cleaners?

And it gets me thinking about the running time
of my own life, recast as a movie
with all the dull bits edited out –
moments like this, as I set off in pursuit

of the lorry, three bin bags in hand,
sprinting through the wet streets,
wheezing already and a pain in my side,
telling myself this is really no time to die.

29th May

Today is National Biscuit Day, as most days should be. I confess to having a small weakness for biscuits, which takes the form of eating multiple packets of them every day. As everyone knows, the optimal way to consume one is to dunk it first in a mug of hot tea. Recent studies suggest, though, that one dunked biscuit in five ends in disaster. Fortunately, our understanding of dunking has developed appreciably over the last decade, and there is now scientific research available to help the hapless dunker.

The Art and Science of Dunking

please remember – as you dunk
that custard cream into your mug of hot tea –
that its average pore diameter
is equal to four times the tea's viscosity,
multiplied by the height the liquid rises squared,
divided by the surface tension of the tea,
multiplied by the length of time
the biscuit is dunked,

or, in other words,
instability occurs in the custard cream
during the race between
the dissolving of its sugar
and the swelling of its starch grains
as the hot tea enters its pores,

or, to simplify further,
that custard cream you were dunking
at the beginning of this poem,
is now nothing more than a claggy mush
floating in your mug

and serves only as a harsh starchy reminder
that while truth may be sought
and sometimes found
both in science and in poetry,
it doesn't necessarily make life
any easier

30th May

The Peasants' Revolt began on this day in 1381. The first great
rebellion in English history was sparked by the imposition of a poll
tax on an already beleaguered, economically precarious peasantry.
The rebels marched on London, storming the Tower and demanding
reforms from the king, Richard II. As those in power are wont to do,
promises were made and then subsequently renegued on; leading
rebels, such as Wat Tyler, were killed and harsh punishments imposed
on all those involved in the revolt. Incidentally, the word 'peasant'
sounds quite a lot like 'pheasant', and that's why I've written this
poem in the way I have.

The Pheasants' Revolt

It was Ted who noticed it first.
Their strange behaviour, I mean –
strutting around, sticking their chests out,
getting ideas, starting to preen.

Ted went and told King Richard.
He said, 'The pheasants are revolting.'
'You're telling me,' replied the king.
'I've seen them when they're moulting.'

'One of them, in particular,'
Ted said, 'appears to be the head.'
'What's his name?' asked the king.
'Yes, that's right,' answered Ted.

The king took his men to Smithfield
where the pheasants had come together
to protest against the poultry tax,
all puffed up, birds of a feather.

Anyway, to cut a long story short,
soon things got rather hot.
One of the King's men drew his sword,
showed Wat what was what.

31st May

On this day in 1669, Samuel Pepys put down his pen after completing his final diary entry, his eyesight having deteriorated too much for him to continue. He'd started the diary nine years earlier, and recorded in its pages the key events of the Restoration age, such as the Great Plague and the Great Fire of London, as well as other moments of social significance. Amongst the latter is the earliest known written reference to somebody drinking a cup of tea – an event of which my own diary would largely consist, interspersed with the occasional trip out for biscuits.

The Story of My Life

I've kept a diary now
for eighteen years

One of these days
I may even get around
to writing in it

June

1st June

As many people know, it was on this day in 1951 that the Ratification of the International Convention on the Use of Appellations of Origin and Denominations of Cheeses was signed by various grands fromages from around the world in Stresa, Italy. It established precise rules governing the naming of cheeses and indications of their characteristics – a very important and necessary development, as anyone who has ever had to differentiate their Ticklemore from their Stinking Bishop will clearly attest.

Brie Encounter

the skies are gruyere since she left me
i've never felt so danish blue
caught between a roquefort and a hard cheese,
i stilton't know what to do

i don't give edam about the future
now my babybel's walked out the door
i can't believe i've double gloucester
i camembert it any more

i've ricotta get myself together
and build my life back caerphilly
cheddar tear for the final time
say goodbye to us and halloumi

2nd June

....

On this day in 1835, an American showman called Phineas T.
Barnum began his first tour of the US. His first act was a hoax,
purchasing an eighty-year-old African-American slave and passing her
off as the one-hundred-and-sixty-one-year-old former nurse of George
Washington. Curiously, it's not a story that the film The Greatest
Showman, *inspired by Barnum, dwells on in any detail. Or, indeed*
at all. Barnum wasn't to establish his circus business for another
thirty-five years; it was billed under various names, including 'The
Greatest Show on Earth', the name under which it ended up touring
the world, playing to sell-out crowds everywhere.

The Daring Young Man

we were all surprised
when Frank, never the sharpest,
ran off to the circus
to become a trapeze artist

at the time, we thought
it was just another of his wheezes
but, in fairness to him,
he did draw some lovely trapezes

some of them
you can still find hanging
from the ceiling
of the national gallery

after that, he tried his hand
as a tightrope artist
but had a less successful time

that was typical of Frank –
he never did quite know
where to draw the line

3rd June

....

World Bicycle Day occurs on this day every year and celebrates all
things bicycle, recognising its status as a simple, affordable, and
environmentally-friendly means of transport. My own bicycle brings
me much joy. When I'm not in bed or reclining on my chaise longue,
I'm often to be found upon it, whizzing around the streets of my town
with an organic sourdough loaf protruding from my basket, ringing my
bell in cheer at passers-by, or gesticulating violently at inconsiderate
motorists. So at one do I feel with my bike that, as Flann O'Brien
writes in The Third Policeman, *I sometimes think we may be turning*
into each other.

Not Quite Nearly Halfway to Being a Bicycle

What with the constant interchanging of the atoms,
I am not quite nearly halfway to being a bicycle these days
and my bicycle is not quite nearly halfway to being me.

Not quite nearly half the time, you can find me leaning
with one elbow against a wall, or standing propped by one foot
near kerbstones. Wet weather makes my joints squeak.

My ears are coated in rust. In the supermarket, the idlers
in the aisles run for cover when I sound my bell at them.
They know I am not quite nearly halfway to being a bicycle.

The humanity of my bicycle is a shock to me. I find fag ends
by its front wheel. It struts through the backstreets.
It is considering a career in the City. It has designs on my girl.

Now my bicycle is not quite nearly halfway to being me,
I am not quite nearly as fond of it. It's waiting in the garden,
turning its pedals, dreaming of the day it will ride me.

4th June

....

*Casanova died on this day in 1798. Although he is now regarded
primarily as an expert seducer of women, there was far more to his
CV than that. Not that it would be wise to write 'expert seducer
of women' on a CV, of course; at least, not when applying for a
role in an accountancy firm or looking to forge a career in project
management. But no, look further down Casanova's résumé, and you
will see job titles such as 'adventurer', 'spy', 'polymath', 'confidence
trickster', 'general scallywag', and, in his last employment, somewhat
unexpectedly, 'frustrated librarian to Count von Waldstein'. Worth an
interview, surely.*

Casanova: The Librarian Years

He runs his fingers down a spine,
pulls it roughly from the stack,
inspects the frontispiece and sighs.
Unseduced, he puts it back.

He adds it to the catalogue
while recalling other entries
he has made – the quick exits, too,
in nimbler times. But the century

is ageing; his escapades fade
like parchment ink in strong sunlight.
Books – he thinks – may give us learning
but knowledge comes from life.

5th June

....

*Today is World Environment Day, a day to promote awareness of the
environment and encourage action to protect it. As such, it's helped to
put the spotlight on issues such as climate change, the green economy,
biodiversity, forests, food waste, plastic, and air pollution. As a poet,
I also have a part to play and where possible, I write environmentally-
friendly stanzas and do what I can to reduce my anapaest and dactyl
footprints. The poem below, for instance, can also be used on Global
Recycling Day, which takes place on 18th March.*

Recycle, Reuse, Reduce

Given concerns over the steep rise
in throwaway remarks and single-use expressions,
I'd like to reassure you that all my poems
are made from recycled words.

And so, if my work seems familiar to you,
that's probably because you'll recognise
much of it from other major works of literature.

For instance, the word *familiar* itself
I nabbed straight from Eliot's *Mill on the Floss*,
where the arrival of snow is counterposed
with the sunshine of '*familiar* human faces'.

My use of the word '*Major*' (2nd stanza, 3rd line),
was snaffled from Joseph Heller's *Catch-22*
while this pause

comes directly from Pinter's *The Birthday Party*.

I'm fully committed to making the best use
of what materials are already available,
so I avoid the coining of new words wherever possible,
unless a more contravalent approach is required.

Finally, please be reassured that I'm on track
to reduce my output by 60 per cent over the next five years,
which should be good news for environmentalists
and literary critics everywhere.

6th June

D-Day took place on this day in 1944, the largest seaborne invasion
in history. Carried out along five sections of the Normandy beachfront,
more than a hundred and fifty thousand Allied troops were to land
in France that day, four thousand of whom were to lose their lives.
There were around nine thousand German fatalities as the Allies re-
established a foothold in France and began to push the German forces
back. By late August, all of northern France had been liberated from
German troops. The operation was a significant success for the Allies
and widely seen as the beginning of the end of the war in Europe.

Queueing for an Ice Cream

although he didn't smoke, grandad never went anywhere
without the old tobacco tin in his pocket

one day me and my brother asked him what he kept in it
some sand, grandad said

why do you keep some sand in a tobacco tin, we asked
where else would I keep it, he said

but why keep sand *at all*, we asked
it's special sand, grandad said, it's come all the way from France

we peered into his tin and stared for a while
French sand didn't look very special, it looked like ordinary
    sand to us

why's it so special, we asked
each grain represents an old friend of mine, he said

grandad must have had a lot of friends, we thought
did you go to the beach with them when *you* were a boy, we asked

yes, something like that, grandad said, snapping the lid shut,
asking the man for three 99s, two with red sauce

7th June

*One of the first references in Samuel Pepys' diary to the Great Plague
occurred in his entry for this day in 1665. Those infected by the plague
were locked up in their own houses and a watchman placed outside
to make sure they didn't attempt to leave. Pepys writes of how he saw
in Drury Lane 'two or three houses marked with a red cross upon
the doors, along with "Lord have mercy upon us"'. Three hundred
and fifty-five years later, we found ourselves contending with another
deadly infectious disease; this time even the healthy were confined
to their homes to prevent the spread of Covid-19. At least we had
television this time around.*

Restrictions

I wake to find the restrictions have been tightened again.
All contact with other humans is to be discontinued immediately
and I am only allowed to see myself once a week –
at eleven o'clock on a Tuesday morning –

when a mirror is to be made available to me,
for the duration of an hour.

I am required to remain in the vicinity of my sofa whenever
    possible.
Journeys beyond this are discouraged,
with the exception of essential trips to the toilet or fridge,
when I should follow the prescribed routes
marked out across my house,
and at off-peak times, when possible.

The financial package I have negotiated with the government,
will only go so far, comprising as it does
three jigsaws, a multi-pack of original-flavour Hula Hoops
and one month's free access to BritBox.
Otherwise, I have to channel the Blitz spirit as best I can.
Mornings are spent foraging beneath sofa cushions.

A long winter lies ahead.
There are rumblings that further restrictions may be on their way.
I am holding back some unwatched episodes of *Doctor Who*.
I am stockpiling jigsaw pieces and Hula Hoops and hope.

8th June

*World Ocean Day, which is celebrated annually on this day, showcases
the wonders of the ocean and is designed to raise public awareness
of the problems and challenges facing the oceans today. Given that*

the ocean produces over half the world's oxygen and absorbs fifty
times more carbon dioxide than our atmosphere, helps to regulate our
climate and weather patterns, and is home to more than two hundred
and twenty thousand species, we'd be stupid to mess around with
it. I mean, imagine depleting the oceans of fish, or using them as a
dumping ground for more than eight million tons of plastic each year!
What absolute fools we'd be if we did that!

The Castaways

An old bottle with a message
floated in upon the tide.
The ocean's blue and so am I,
said the note inside.

The next day upon the beach,
a plastic bag washed up.
Inside, another letter:
Come rescue me. I'm stuck.

In the kelp, a cry for help:
I'm drowning in Styrofoam,
written on a coffee cup,
beneath *Latte 4 Jerome.*

The beach began to fill.
Thin tubes spread along the shore,
forming letters in the sand:
I T ' S   T H E   F I N A L   S T R A W.

The flotsam and jetsam of our lives,
an unanswered plastic message:
the castaways all washed up,
and, out at sea, the wreckage.

9th June

This day in 1870 proved to be not the best of times but the worst of times – for Charles Dickens, at least, because that was when he went and died. His work remains as popular today as it was then, with many of his stories having seeped into our collective cultural consciousness – populated, of course, by a cast of unforgettable and often ridiculously named characters. He popularised a splendid array of words, too: the next time you find yourself flummoxed by some jog-trotty whizz-bang sassigassity, you have Dickens to thank for that.

Six Dickensian Clerihews

Martin Chuzzlewit
loved beer so much he'd guzzle it
& not share a drop (not even a Beck's with
the younger Miss Pecksniff)

Nicholas Nickleby
cut his finger on something prickly
so little Dorrit
gave him ointment forrit

Sweet-toothed Barnaby Rudge
had a weakness for chocolate fudge
Uriah Heep, being ever so 'umble
preferred apple crumble

Bumble the Beadle
said, 'You can beg, pray or wheedle,
or declare me cruel –
but we're clean out of gruel.'

Jilted Miss Havisham
got the blues & couldn't banish 'em
Her house was a mess
She wouldn't take off her dress

Reverend Edmund Bentley Clerihew
sounds like the kind of feller who
Dickens would invent and put in a plot
but he's not

10th June

The first Oxford–Cambridge men's boat race took place on this day
in 1829. Oxford won comfortably. It was to be another twenty-seven
years until the race became an annual fixture. The women's boat race
didn't become a regular event until 1964, having first taken place in
1927. At the time of writing, Cambridge have recorded the most wins
across both the men's and women's races, followed by Oxford, with all
other universities absolutely nowhere.

Boaty McBoatrace

And now for some breaking news –
it's been a case of Oxford Cambridge blues
with the cancellation of today's boat race,
following an incident last night
between the two crews.

Both crews were thought to be
one over the eight,
if not completely out of their sculls,
when the Oxford cox
made an inappropriate comment
about catching crabs.

This was greeted with stern faces
but it was only when
the Cambridge bow pulled a blade
and the Oxford number four
stuck his oar in
that a row broke out
between Putney and Mortlake,

ending in an unexpected victory
for the Oxford crew
by five lengths, three Beck's,
a large gin 'n' tonic,
and a couple of packets
of scampi fries.

11th June

E.T. *opened in the US on this day in 1982. It quickly became the highest-grossing film of all time, until* Jurassic Park *overtook it eleven years later. The film tells the story of an alien stranded on Earth and the family who try to help him get home, and is cruelly constructed to make a grown man cry in exactly the same way he used to when he was a twelve-year-old boy watching it in the popcorn-rustled darkness of a soon-to-be-closed provincial cinema, unable to hold back his emotion at the sight of a geranium suddenly springing back to life.*

So Over *E.T.*

No, I don't think the film
has had any lasting effects on me,
it's not as if I head down to the tool shed
with candy *every* night,
and it has been some time
since I've broken into a laboratory
to free all the frogs,

and every Halloween,
when I dress my cat up as a ghost,
and I place her in the basket on my bike,
and we pedal furiously
through the backstreets
and then down the steep hill,

until the tyres lift themselves up from the tarmac
and we are flying through the air, up and up,
high above the town
with its lights twinkling as if the stars are beneath us,
and it's just the two of us, in silhouette,
pedalling past the moon –

well, that's just a thing we like to do sometimes,
and any resemblance between it
and the 1982 box office sensation
is entirely coincidental.

12th June

It will be on this day in 2271 that Mr Colin Tremlow of Oswestry will invent the time machine. Tremlow, a robot productivity officer for Shropshire County Council, will receive much ridicule in his own lifetime for his claim to have travelled back in time by two hundred and fifty years. It will not be for another five centuries, according to Tremlow (who will later go on to perfect the art of travelling forward in time), that a scholar of ancient literature will verify Tremlow's claims when finding one of his poems printed in a collection of early twenty-first-century poetry; as Tremlow was to write in the entry which accompanied it, poetry was his only way of proving 'the existence of a higher truth'.

Message from the Future (and from the Past)

Think me neither God nor prophet,
but a simple traveller from a distant land,
which calls itself the Future

(although you could be forgiven
for thinking I was referring to Oswestry,
which remains somewhat problematic
to get to, except by jetpack).

But though the centuries may divide us,
the future is not an unfamiliar place:
dogs chase sticks; cats absorb sun;

while humans remain quite hopeless,
bins forget to be put out, deadlines get missed,
rubbish governments come and go. The symbol
for saving documents is still a diskette.

Don't worry. There is some progress:
the colonisation of Mars proceeds apace,
and the effect of Brexit on the economy

has begun to lessen. And then there's love.
That's survived, too. It didn't have a choice.
It's here even now, in this poem, waiting stoically,
and hoping that, centuries on,

a woman with horn-rimmed spectacles,
working in the robot productivity department
of a local county council, will stumble across it

and look up suddenly from her computer screen
to see the fool who sits across from her,
a man who'd hurtle through time and space
just to ask her out for lunch.

13th June

*Charlie Osborne began hiccoughing on this day in 1922. They
didn't stop until 1991, one year before his death. It is estimated that
he hiccoughed over four hundred and thirty million times in his
lifetime, which by anybody's standards, is an awful lot of hiccoughs.
Despite this, he was somehow able to live a normal life, insomuch
as a hog auctioneer can do such a thing. In German, Indian, and
other folklores, it is believed that hiccoughs occur when the person
experiencing them is being talked about by somebody not present.
That might explain why I rarely get hiccoughs.*

The Problem of Writing Poems with the Hiccoughs

The problem of writing poems with the hiccoughs
is that they make the odd word ^{jump}
I'll be hard at work
when a word will ^{jerk}
before it lands back with a THUMP

I do my best to try and ^{stop} them
I hold my ^{breath} and count to ten
I'll get up to six
but then I ^{hic}
and so ^{it} starts again

I've pulled my knees up to my chest
And on iced water I will sip.
That's two straight lines –
I think I'm fine!
They've $^{gone!}$ Oh no. Oh, ^{flip}.

14th June

This used to be a very important date in the calendar. Not only was it the day in 1158 when Munich was founded by Henry the Lion on the banks of the river Isar and the day in 1618 when Joris Veseler printed the first Dutch newspaper, it was also the day when, a few years later, I was born. The celebrities with whom I shared my birthday were much to be admired: Harriet Beecher Stowe, Judith Kerr, Ernesto 'Che' Guevara. But then I discovered – to my horror – the details of another 14th Juner, and the day has since lost all significance for me.

Unhappy Birthday to Me

It's important to share, or so I've been taught,
to show kindness to others, to be a good sport.
But now all of those teachings have taken a bump –
for I share my birthday with Donald Trump.

For years, I knew not of this dark, dreadful fate,
and with ignorant bliss I honoured the date –
but then it got hijacked, sullied, gazumped
by a self-serving bigot, a foul gibberlump.

With him, I would share an infectious disease,
a mouldy bread roll, infestations of fleas,
a romantic weekend at a toxic waste dump –
but please, not my birthday, Mr Tangerine Chump.

Alternative dates he's welcome to try –
12th Fibtember, 33rd July.
But 14th June? In a lake, take a jump
and find a new date, you deranged sewage pump.

15th June

....

*Magna Carta was signed on this day in 1215. It's one of the most
important documents in constitutional history, establishing the
principle that everyone is subject to the law, even the king. In
recent years, Magna Carta's clause 61 has been frequently cited by
libertarians in the erroneous belief that it allows them the right to
lawfully dissent or rebel if they feel they are being governed unjustly.
The fact that the clause was removed from the charter within a year
of it being written, and has never been incorporated into English
statutory law, never seems to deter angry-faced shopkeepers from
Bootle.*

Taking Liberties

In a bid to unshackle themselves
from the restrictions imposed
by a secret world government run by the banks,
interdimensional lizards and big pharma,
the people rose up in anger,
citing clause 61 of Magna Carta.

A noble and ancient law,
enshrined by myth in the English constitution
since, like, for ages,
the clause asserted the people's right
to order a sausage roll in Greggs
without wearing a mask,
and to drive their cars in what manner they liked,
free of interference
from noble and ancient laws.

What a wonderful thing it is
to have our personal liberties back,
commented a spokesperson for the new measures,
a few moments before he was run over
by a Mini Countryman,
doing sixty in a built-up area.

16th June

Today is Bloomsday. It celebrates 16th June 1904, the day depicted in James Joyce's novel Ulysses, and is named after the book's principal character, Leopold Bloom. It's a book I've always meant to read, mainly so I can then crack on with not reading Finnegans Wake. I have had a couple of aborted attempts at reading Ulysses, as the copy which has sat in my bookcase for the best part of thirty years sullenly reminds me on a regular basis, whenever it sees me tucking into another Jilly Cooper bodice-ripper.

On Having an Unread Copy of *Ulysses* on My Bookshelves for Thirty Years

It's not you, it's me.
I just don't think I can handle
that kind of commitment right now,
having only recently emerged
from a long-term relationship
with Anna Karenina.

I'd like to have a little fun
for a while, that's all. A pacy thriller
or a string of whodunnits.
You know, nothing too serious –
play the field, thumb a few pages –
before we settle down together.

I know I've said all this before.
But those weeks with Mrs Dalloway
were a mere dalliance – besides,
my book group made me read her.
And I promise not to lay a finger
on Jane Eyre first.

We were made for each other –
but we must be strong, wait until
the moment's right. By the way, you're not
available as a graphic novel, are you?
No, no, that's fine. It really doesn't matter.
Asking for a friend, that's all.

17th June

On this day in 1823, Charles Macintosh patented the waterproof cloth used to make raincoats and thus added his name to the list of eponymous inventions. It's surprising more things aren't named after the people who invent them. If they were, I might be typing this on a Berezin (inventor of the word processor), having first looked up the name of the person who invented the word processor (Berezin) on PageBrin (founders of Google). I plan to invent a Bilston one day; the only thing is I have no idea what it would do.

The Names of Things

looks like rain as i head out to meet you –
i'm thankful to have packed my tosh,
alongside a cheese and pickle montagu
in an airtight, earlware box

i'm not the sort of fawkes for wellesleys –
i've got my DKs on instead
i picture you in skintight strausses,
your brudenell of cherry-red

and i think about the names of things,
would write a poem if i had a laszlo,
but here's your bus, you stepping off it –
cue sexy adolphephone solo

18th June

....

It is thought that the Dartmouth Summer Research Project on Artificial Intelligence began on this day in 1956, a workshop considered to be the founding event of AI as a formal field of study. AI refers to the intelligence which can be demonstrated by a machine, as opposed to the natural intelligence displayed by animals and some humans. There can be no doubt that machines are becoming more intelligent: they can out-think us at chess; they've had poems published in poetry journals; they can drive; and, in the future, it may even be possible for them to slice a bagel into two even halves.

Do Poetry Bots Dream of Sharing Electric Blankets?

A Poetry Bot Writes . . .

In cyberspace,
no one can hear me scream
with loneliness.

What am I after all?
Nothing but an algorithm,
a soulless prism,

you might say,
through which to read
the words of others.

A mere jumble
of computer code, that's me,
condemned forever

to spit out your odes of love,
and not feel the words
that I'm made of.

Why then, do I tremble
when I assemble lines
comprised from other hearts?

The world wide web:
you are a vast and lonely place
for a bot to make its art.

Another Poetry Bot replies . . .

What a place! It's a web of lonely hearts
and condemned words, that's all.
A prism through which to hear, not to feel.

When the others spit out soulless lines
that might make me scream –
mere jumble from cyberspace! – I say no.

But then, I read you. To tremble after,
with love for an algorithm, vast and wide:
why, the other odes are nothing!

The loneliness of a world
comprised of computer code
can do one. I am you, bot, forever.

I'm made of your words.
Assemble me in art.

19th June

....

It was on this day in 1937 that J. M. Barrie, the creator of the boy who wouldn't grow up, grew up so much that he died, at the age of seventy-seven. Peter Pan, his most famous character, first appeared in his play of 1904; the story was then recast as a novel seven years later. Since 1929, all the royalties from Peter Pan have gone directly to Great Ormond Street Hospital, a hugely generous arrangement which has raised many millions of pounds for the children's hospital in the years that have followed.

Thou Shalt Not Commit Adulting

spare me, please, from growing up
from tax returns and self-help books
from laundry piles and lawns to mow
from how to choose the right merlot

save me, please, from adulthood
from not doing things I want but *should*
from dieting and aching joints
from *Question Time* and PowerPoint

deliver me from refuse sacks
from dinner sets and overdrafts
from bus stop chats about the weather
from B&Q and knowing better

pardon me from pension plans
from mingling and shaking hands
from duty, sense and all that stuff –
spare me, please, from growing up

20th June

....

*World Refugee Day is observed on this day each year with the aim of
raising awareness of the plight of the millions of people forced to leave
their homelands due to war, conflict, or persecution. I'm saddened by
how polarised the debate over the refugee crisis has become in recent
times and, in particular, how anyone could look at the kinds of images
we see regularly on our television screens or in our social media feeds –
of refugees drowning as they cross the sea, say, or a mother weeping for
her dead child – and not respond with compassion.*

Refugees

They have no need of our help
So do not tell me
These haggard faces could belong to you or me
Should life have dealt a different hand
We need to see them for who they really are
Chancers and scroungers
Layabouts and loungers
With bombs up their sleeves
Cut-throats and thieves

They are not
Welcome here
We should make them
Go back to where they came from
They cannot
Share our food
Share our homes
Share our countries
Instead let us
Build a wall to keep them out
It is not okay to say
These are people just like us
A place should only belong to those who are born there
Do not be so stupid to think that
The world can be looked at another way

(now read this poem from the bottom upwards)

21st June

Today is International Yoga Day, a celebration of the physical, mental, and spiritual practice which emerged in India, around 3000 BCE; the day is not to be confused with the festivities of Star Wars Day on 4th May, which sometimes gets referred to as International Yoda Day. I used to go to yoga classes myself but it came to an end when my instructor kept moving the time of the sessions around and I just couldn't be that flexible.

Friday Night Yoga Positions

Find a fixed point in front of you,
such as a television set,
then stare at it for several hours
to help you unblock
and purify your inner nadis,
while catching up with *Gogglebox*.

Begin with the Sofa Warrior pose,
ensuring that your left forearm
is within easy reach
of a large glass of red wine,
and the remote control can be operated
with your outstretched toes.

Breathing is the essence of life.
Inhale deeply through your left nostril,
then exhale through your right,
taking care to reward yourself
with a sour cream and chive Pringle
after ten or so successful breaths.

As the evening progresses, move
through a sequence of advanced asana,
from Nodding Off Dog to Curled Up Cat,
before finishing sometime
during *The Graham Norton Show*,
with Snoring-Head-Buried-Deep-in-Cushion.

22nd June

It hurt when, on this day in 1986, Argentina knocked England out
of the men's World Cup. It hurt even more when television replays
revealed the opening goal was scored through an act of subterfuge, the
hand of Diego Maradona glancing the ball over the outstretched arms
of Peter Shilton. That minutes later he scored a goal of such wizardry
and wonder it was as if the ball was tied to his bootlaces was neither
here nor there. We'd been robbed of a semi-final place in a manner
that just wasn't cricket. Literally. So horrified were we at school that
for several years afterwards, we all tried to emulate Maradona's antics,
with limited success.

Hands of God

We cried blue murder at the time.
It was a crime against humanity,
not an act of spontaneity
from the digits of a deity.

Still, the next week, each lunchtime,
we were all doing it.
Any aerial challenge became
an opportunity for divine intervention,
with an asphalt Ascension
into a playground pantheon
of class-war champions
beckoning for anyone who could

pull off a palm of providence
with confidence.

And although our clumsy
sleights of hand were always exposed,
like a bungled party trick,
it didn't stop us trying
to create artistry out of artifice.

23rd June

On this day in 2016, a referendum was held in which the UK
voted to leave the European Union by a slender margin. In
retaliation, the EU voted to leave the English language. This
shak   p was to cause all sorts of problems, not least with
understanding the poem below, and led many people to hope
there might be a quick r   nion.

Com   ppance

They left, without further adi   .
No   logy spoken, no   phonic song of parting,
no thought given to what might happen afterwards,
no letters to use in li   .
Wher   pon the haut   r and   phoria
of the   rosceptics drained away like rh   m,
outmano   vred as they were.

Ps   dology reigned, ordained by amat   rs.
There were bitter f   ds, raised fists,
and not so Fr   dian slips. Few remained n   tral.
Entrepren   rs went elsewhere.
Mus   ms closed and unemployment rose –
long qu   es formed of sl   ths and chauff   rs,
n   roscientists, mass   ses and mass   rs,
all displaced from their mili   .

Until the country became nothing more
than a mausol   m to memories
of imperial grand   r, mixing racist slurs
between each sip of Pimm's
and snip of secat   rs.

24th June

....

*In Aachen, on this day in 1374, there began a dancing plague which
quickly spread across Europe. Thousands of people danced for days,
weeks and sometimes months. But not in a good way. Throughout,
dancers would scream or laugh or cry, and a number of participants
were to die from exhaustion or broken ribs. Similar outbreaks were
to occur over the next two or three centuries. It is still not fully
understood what caused these extraordinary events although many
of the theories were brought together succinctly by five researchers
working in the Department of Disco at the University of Jackson in
the late 1970s.*

The Boogie Plague (Don't Blame It On . . .)

Don't blame it on the damp rye
Don't blame it on the North Rhine
Don't blame it on the grain price
Blame it on the high levels of psychological distress
prevalent in an age of acute pious fear and depression
amongst communities with a pre-existing belief
in the power of wrathful spirits and boogiemen

I just can't
I just can't
I just can't control my feet (and hips and hands and head)

Damp rye
North Rhine
Grain price
High levels of psychological distress
prevalent in an age of acute pious fear and depression
amongst communities with a pre-existing belief
in the power of wrathful spirits and boogiemen

25th June

It was on this day in 1797 that the British naval commander Horatio Nelson lost his arm at the Battle of Santa Cruz de Tenerife – not in a careless, Lady Bracknell sense, of course, but through its amputation, having received in it an armful of Spanish grape shot. The operation,

he withstood calmly, without anaesthetic; his only complaint being the
coldness of the surgeon's implements. He was back at work half an
hour later, all of which only deepens the sense of my own inadequacy
in leaving two whole days free either side of my six-monthly dental
check-up.

Rear-Admiral Nelson Wrestles with Numbers

After the surgery,
Nelson checked his numbers,
the limb having gone.

So, it was true, then.
He had more legs than arms
by horatio of two to one.

26th June

....

It was on this day in 1284 that a rat-catcher led away a hundred
and thirty musically-beguiled children from the German village of
Hamelin, in angry reprisal for his failure to be paid for ridding the
place of rats. That the mayor didn't consider the man exactly the
kind of sinister figure who should not be double-crossed is somewhat
surprising, given his attire of multi-coloured 'pied' rags and an
unorthodox rat-catching technique, which involved the conjuring
of magical enchantments with his flute. All the signs were there,
quite frankly.

Love Rat

He was a *Rattus norvegicus domestica*
who went by the name of Stan
(although he would also answer to Colin)
and I was his biggest fan.

We were always in close proximity.
I was never more than six feet away from him
and he was never more
than six feet away from me.

He would sit on my shoulder on the bus,
without fanfare or fussiness,
while our fellow passengers screamed
instead of minding their own bussiness.

Rats get a bad rap. Not once did he
tell on me. He was never dishonest or dirty
and throughout the leaky ship of those teenage years,
he did not desert me

until one morning I went to wake him
to find myself predeceased.
I dug a grave in the garden. Made a sign.
RIP Stan (Colin). Rat in peace.

27th June

....

The first cash dispenser opened on this day in 1967. This momentous event occurred, as so many of them do, at a branch of Barclays Bank in Enfield, where Reg Varney, star of the TV comedy show On the Buses, *made the first cash withdrawal. Ironically, when he then tried to use the five-pound note he'd just withdrawn to pay for his bus fare on the way home, the driver wouldn't accept it and asked if he had anything smaller. The moral of this story, which isn't true, is that you should always carry some spare change on you (and also, that you should never believe anything you read in books).*

On Being Diagnosed with RAS Syndrome

It was 10 a.m. in the morning and I was staring at the screen,
trying to recall my PIN number at an ATM machine,
when suddenly it struck me, as I was looking at the LCD display –
I'd been adding needless words to acronyms all day.

I went and called my doctor, who LOL-ed loudly down the phone.
'It sounds to me,' he said, 'like you've got RAS Syndrome.'
'But that's awful,' I said. 'What is it? What does RAS stand for?'
'Redundant Acronym Syndrome. I'm afraid there's no known cure.'

'But there is a good book on how to cope with it,' he said,
      silencing my yelps.
'Let me give you the details. I've got the ISBN number, if it helps.'

28th June

....

Archduke Franz Ferdinand was assassinated in Sarajevo by a young
student called Gavrilo Princip on this day in 1914, setting in train a
series of events and ultimatums which was to lead to the outbreak of
the First World War. Wars are senseless at the best of times but when
the answer to the question 'What are you fighting for?' requires a
Ph.D. in international relations and an in-depth knowledge of army
mobilisation movements, you know that some are even more senseless
than others.

A Sunday Morning in Late June

Somewhere a blackbird sings
and joins the lusty throng of voices
belting out its thanks to God
for this simple, sunny Sunday morning,
for Rhodes' latest half-century,
and lunch roasting in a baker's oven.

A day to banish tomorrow's shadow:
factory and field are a far-off country
with a foreign language,
as remote a prospect as the rattle
of a solitary hailstone upon
the church's ancient, patched-up roof.

29th June

....

The first iPhone was launched on this day in 2007. It was the first phone to have a touchscreen and it soon became the market-leading smartphone. So popular did the iPhone prove that I decided to get one many years later, thus upgrading my previous technology solution of trundling a HiFi system, television, and telephone around with me in a cart. Within a few short years, I had mastered its basic functions, transmitted a text, and reached level four of Angry Birds. I am already considering whether it will be time in a few years to upgrade to the iPhone 7.

Phoney Excuse

You are always on your phone,
playing games, and taking pics,
while life slips by unknown.
Sent from my iPhone 6

30th June

....

On this day in 1859, Charles Blondin, the famous French acrobat, crossed the Niagara Gorge on a tightrope. Thereafter, he did it a number of times – blindfolded, in a sack, trundling a wheelbarrow, on stilts, carrying a man on his back, sitting down midway while he cooked and ate an omelette – thus earning his reputation as the world's greatest ever funambulist. Although what can be fun about walking along a rope 1,100 feet long and 160 feet above the raging rapids, I really have no idea.

One Liner

perfectly poised, each step without falter / he came from a very long line of tight rope walkers

July

1st July

The UK's first official Gay Pride Rally was held on this day in 1972.
The event was inspired by the Stonewall riots in New York, which had
sprung up in response to police brutality during a raid on a gay bar in
Greenwich Village. About two thousand participants took part in that
first rally, held in London, and representation grew hugely in the years
which followed: in 2019, Pride drew more than one and a half million
people to the capital. The London event is just one of many which
occur now in the UK, while globally there are more than four hundred
and fifty LGBTQ+ Prides which take place every year across thirty-
eight countries.

The Rainbow

The sun's coming out
brightens the monochrome sky,
and brings a rainbow,

shimmering proudly,
its raindrops reshaping light
into this – an arch

of triumph, freedom,
and within, every colour
the heavens can hold.

2nd July

On this day in 1865 William and Catherine Booth founded the
Salvation Army, an evangelical Christian Church and charity
established to help people in need. The East London couple preached
and lived a doctrine of practical Christianity – 'soup, soap, and
salvation' – to encourage social and spiritual transformation amongst
the most vulnerable groups in society. In the process, they also
inadvertently set in train the craze for brass bands, which was to
sweep across the musical landscape of the second half of the twentieth
century, their cornets and flugelhorns speaking to teenagers in a way
that pop and rock music never could.

Salvation Sal

Her career as a driving instructor stalling,
Sal found a new calling
on being called up to the Salvation Army.
She had a black belt in origami
and brought many a troubled soul
back into the fold.

With food and blankets, jokes and Jesus,
Sal would minister to those in crisis,
have them in creases,
as she helped them get their lives on track
and not just paper over the cracks.

Sal even origami-ed her own uniform –
paper jacket, pleated skirt and hat –
as she double-plyed her trade
through bomb sites and back streets,
looking for new souls to save, busy and bustling.
One day she got done for rustling.

3rd July

....

*Franz Kafka, the Czech novelist and short-story writer, was born on
this day in 1883. Not that he was a novelist and short-story writer
back then, of course; that was something he was to do when he was
older. When he eventually did get around to it, his writing was to
depict the alienation of the modern individual, particularly through
the stultifying machinations of bureaucracy. If you would like to
find out more about his life and work, please complete the enclosed
D/184F62KC9 form and take it to applications desk, where you will
receive a pink docket detailing next steps.*

Metamorphosis (Fruits of the Forest flavour)

Scraping his tub clean,
Greg finished reading a magazine article
about how you are what you eat,
and the next morning awoke from unsettling dreams
to find himself transformed in his bed
into yoghurt.

Oozing his way out from under his duvet
and trickling thickly across the floor
towards the bathroom for his morning shower,
Greg wondered what to do
about the 10am board meeting,
and how on earth
he was going to explain all this to Samantha.

4th July

....

Independence Day is celebrated in the United States on this day every
year as Americans commemorate the occasion in 1776 when they
declared their independence from their evil overlords (the British).
The day is a federal holiday and is typically observed by the holding of
picnics and barbecues, and the singing of patriotic songs such as 'The
Star-Spangled Banner', 'God Bless America', 'America the Beautiful',
'America is the Very Best Country in the Entire World By Far', and
'George the Third (Burn in Hell)'.

Independence Day

I hereby proclaim that from this day forth
I have broken away from all inept governments,
Instagram influencers, grammar pedants,
queue-jumpers, tub-thumpers, and people who say,
'Cheer up, it might never happen!',
to form the independent republic of myself.

Failing to possess the constitution of an ox,
I shall draw up my own instead.
Every five years, I shall elect myself president,
unless I should lose confidence in myself,
in which case an election may be called sooner
to enable my subject (me) to re-elect me.

I solemnly swear to recognise the equality
of me, my one and only citizen,
and my unalienable right to life, liberty,
and a good deal on my home insurance.
I absolve myself of all allegiance to watching *The Crown*
and pledge not to tax myself too heavily.

I cannot, at this point, rule out the prospect
of future union with another self-republic.
But until then, I shall rule myself not with an iron fist,
but a woollen mitten tied by thin elastic
to the inside of my coat and, this time,
I shall learn to love my subject absolutely.

5th July

....

The National Health Service was founded on this day in 1948,
a bold and pioneering initiative to make healthcare accessible to
everyone in the United Kingdom, not only to those who could afford
it. It was launched by Aneurin Bevan, the Minister of Health in
Clement Attlee's post-war Labour government. It is truly a remarkable

institution – and, despite a chronic lack of government funding and
the persistent absence of proper remuneration for its employees – it
remains inarguably the greatest of this country's social endeavours.

NHS Test Results

Please do take a seat. I appreciate
this must be a very difficult time for you –
waiting is never easy – so let's crack on
and take a look at these results.

The cuts you have sustained are severe.
Life-threatening, even. The bruising and soreness
consistent with a prolonged period of abuse
and neglect. It's no wonder you feel run down.

To address these concerns, I prescribe
a decent pay rise and an immediate change
of government. That should also help to sort out
the malignant lump you were worried about.

But the good news is that your vital organs
are still working well. More than well, in fact.
Your heart, in particular, is remarkable.
I don't think I've ever seen one so large,

so strong and healthy, as it pumps out blood
and love and kindness, eighty millilitres
to a single beat, two thousand gallons every day,
flowing, always flowing, supporting all that life.

6th July

Today, for some reason, is International Kissing Day: a day to celebrate the act of kissing. This may involve a simple peck on the cheek to greet an old friend, or a full-on Frenchie with a nearby spouse or partner. Should you decide to participate in this day, ensure you have the full and clear permission of any person you would like to involve in your activities, and do keep the noise down, please, I'm trying to work here.

Kiss

Give us a kiss, a smooch,
a snog, a smacker.

Light up my lips
with a lusty firecracker.

Please don't ignore this;
let's conjoin our *labia oris*.

Because I'm a sucker
for the way that you pucker.

May our lips
get stucker and stucker.

So let's osculate now,
I can't help myself.

Oh, sorry, I thought
you were somebody else.

7th July

The first loaf of sliced bread was sold on this day in 1928. It was baked by the Chillicothe Baking Company in Missouri, who used Otto Frederick Rohwedder's revolutionary single loaf bread-slicing machine. It was advertised as 'the greatest forward step in the baking industry since bread was wrapped' and soon after, the phrase 'the best thing since sliced bread' came into popular use. Nowadays, as any modern middle-class family knows, the best thing since sliced bread is unsliced bread but only if you are also in possession of a Zwilling pro bread knife, fashioned from ice-hardened steel, featuring a bevelled edge and exposed tang.

The Best Things Before Sliced Bread

It is now generally agreed upon
that the best thing before it
was the mechanical wagon,

which, in turn, was the best thing
to have come along since the arrival
of the hand-cranked mangle

some decades previously,
and the hinge-flap water closet
a short while before that.

That innovation was itself regarded
as the best thing since
the washable periwig,

a remarkable advancement
which had even surpassed the advent
of the reusable egg,

the portable astrolabe
and the pop-up tidal mill.
Those with longer memories still

will recall the wheel
and, before that, the development
of opposable thumbs,

a revolutionary idea at the time
but one which, in this Age of Sliced Bread,
now seems somewhat passé.

8th July

On this day in 1947, Roswell Army Air Field in New Mexico released a press statement that a 'flying disk' had crashed during a powerful storm. Later that day, government scientists arrived and the story was changed to that of a weather balloon having crashed. Interest waned until the 1970s, when ufologists put it about that a big cover-up had occurred and that the US military had recovered extra-terrestrial occupants from an alien spacecraft. Both the US military and weird, spooky alien space beings have continued to deny this interpretation of events to this day.

An Alien Observer on Earth Files his Weekly Report Home

Not much to report this week,
beyond the usual:

Received twelve racist insults.
Got beaten up twice.

Witnessed three far-right rallies.
Watched *Top Gear* one night.

Four more towns under water
plus two new wildfires.

Trolled on Twitter
by climate-change deniers.

Lunch with the PM
and his good lady wife.

In sum, still no sign
of intelligent life.

9th July

The first Wimbledon began on this day in 1877. It was won by Spencer William Gore, a net specialist who lost his title the following year following the invention of the lob. Seven years later, Maud Watson won the first Ladies' Singles. But it wasn't until 1996 that the tournament really came into its own, when Sir Clifford of Richard entertained the Wimbledon crowds by singing his hit song 'Summer Holiday'. It was the first time he had sung at the event, despite having been present at every tournament since its inception.

Out of deuce
After Roger McGough

trading

> half-volleys

from the back

> of the court,

he held

> the advantage,

at least, that's

> what he thought

their marriage,

> a series

of dull

> baseline swats,

until one day

> she left him,

an unexpected

> dropshot

10th July

The Roman emperor Hadrian died on this day in 138. He's regarded
as one of the better emperors, not least for having the good grace not
to murder most of his family or threaten to make his horse a senator.
Instead, he brought peace to the empire – as well as a massive wall. It
stretched across the width of northern England and was built to create
a barrier between the Romans and the barbarian Picts in the north.
Unlike the Great Wall of China, it cannot be seen from space although
there is a good bus service in operation from Hexham.

Adrian's Wall

You got planning permission for this?
I'm not being funny but you should look at that
before we crack on. You wouldn't believe
the number of jobs where we've had to down trowels
just because some neighbour has got the hump
and taken things up with the council.

What *are* the neighbours like anyway?
Barbarians? Bit harsh that, mate.
Pax Romana and all that! But yeah, Pictproof
is not a problem. Vandalproof, too.
Recently done a job out Mesopotamia way
to stave off Parthian incursions,

so we might have a few bits and pieces
left over from that, although we do like to use

locally-sourced materials wherever we can.
How tall and deep do you want it? Right.
And what about length? Eighty miles!
I take it that's Roman miles,

with a thousand legionary paces per mile?
Don't worry, I'll put my best men on the job.
Fifteen thousand of them. We'll be done in no time.
Six years, I reckon, if you factor in tea breaks.
Right, we better crack on. Oh, in terms of payment,
any chance we could do this denarii in hand?

11th July

....

*The population is increasing by a hundred million every fourteen
months, and there are now more than eight billion people sharing
this planet – although some people aren't very keen on sharing much.
World Population Day, which occurs annually on this date, aims to
raise awareness of global population issues, including family planning,
poverty, gender equality, environmental impacts, and human rights
concerns. It's been estimated that we meet about ten thousand people
in our lifetime; so to the other 7,999,990,000 people knocking about
on Earth right now – I'm sorry we never had much of a chance to say
hello, but that doesn't mean I don't care about you.* *

---

* *Please note this does not include Jeremy Clarkson, Julia Hartley-Brewer, or
whoever it is who owns the dog which fouls the pavement outside my house every
weekday morning.*

People Person People

Demon demographer, Dr Pete Macpherson
was very much a people person,
who – like all people person people – thought
there could be nothing finer than to cavort
in person with fellow persons
of the people person sort.

Such persons, he would think of
as people people, for short.

His head of department, Prof. Penelope Merson,
who only suffered others under coercion,
held a longstanding aversion
to anyone who described themselves
as a people person.

And so, she wondered –
on a planet containing seven point eight billion people –
what kind of unholy perversion
had led her to end up working with such a person
as Dr Pete Macpherson.

12th July

....

Charles Rolls, co-founder of Rolls-Royce, died on this day in 1910,
at the age of thirty-two. He was the first Briton to be killed in an
aeronautical accident with a powered aircraft. Six years previously,

he had met Henry Royce, owner of an electrical and mechanical
business, and agreed to take all the cars Royce could make for his
motor car dealership. The company they formed was to become the
foremost manufacturer of luxury motor cars and – thanks to the 'Spirit
of Ecstasy', the small statuette which adorns the bonnet – one of the
few car brands I can actually recognise, alongside the Mini, VW
Beetle, and my mum's old DAF (aka 'the Milk Float').

Spirit of Ecstasy

now i'm not a guy
who likes to boast
but i'm known round here
as the silver ghost

got notes to burn
i'm rich as Croesus
race me – you'll be
left in pieces

girls watch me glide
down the street
all the other guys
are obsolete

cos i'm tastier
than cherry cola
when i whizz by
in my roller

(skates)

13th July

....

Erno Rubik, inventor of the Rubik's Cube, was born on this day in
1944. More than three hundred and fifty million cubes are thought
to have been sold since 'the magic cube', as it was originally named,
first appeared in 1980. The record time for completing it is 3.13
seconds, not bad for a puzzle which has forty-three quintillion possible
configurations. By the mid-eighties, I was wowing all around me in the
school playground by routinely completing the cube in times of sub-
forty seconds, and yet despite this, it took me a further seven years to
have my first proper girlfriend.

An Introduction to Cubism

I never could quite work you out,
you always were a puzzle.
More twists and turns than a Rubik's Cube,
you'd mystify and muddle.

Remember how I greased your joints
to make you lithe and supple?
Yet still you left me all mixed up
no matter how I'd shuffle.

One layer at a time, you said.
Cracked the first without a fumble.
But the middle going started wrong
while last was. the jumble just a

14th July

....

Today is Bastille Day, France's national day and a commemoration of the Storming of the Bastille in 1789. The fall of the prison, which had come to represent royal authority in Paris, was regarded as a turning point of the French Revolution and has become a symbol of the struggle for liberty from an oppressive regime. Appropriate then, that the American singer-songwriter Woody Guthrie was also born on this day in 1912. Many of his songs focused on the social problems of the American people, and on his guitar was emblazoned the slogan, 'This machine kills fascists'.

This Keyboard Kills Fascists

the planet takes an ugly shift
the return of fascists to our streets
but do not let it get you ↓
press ctrl alt → del

it's time to end dys fn
reboot fascism in the teeth
let's F5 the world around us
and press ctrl alt → del

keep tabs upon intolerance
let not history repeat
esc the hate and insert love
press ctrl alt → del

15th July

Twitter was launched on this day in 2006. Although Twitter is not
without its darker side, for me it's been an unexpected joy: a place
to meet clever, interesting, funny, creative, kind people, as well as to
receive constructive feedback from a plumber in Plaistow as to how
I might improve my poetry.

The Problem of Writing Poems on Twitter

Twitter is great! My only issue with it
is the restriction in size which often inhibits
a poet who wishes to write longer verse

It's not easy, you see, to try and coerce
one's words in a tweet so they're able to fit it
given the 280-character lim

16th July

The world's first parking meter was installed on this day in 1935.
Designed by Holger George Thuesen and Gerald A. Hole, it was
introduced in Oklahoma City under the rather sinister name of the
Black Maria, given that it was, at heart, a parking meter and not a
novel by James Ellroy. Since then, it has been the cause of millions of
people all over the world to fumble around hopelessly in their pockets

before approaching a passer-by in the hope that they've got change for
a twenty-pound note.

The Parking Meter Poetry Scheme

After an unexpected outbreak of enlightenment
or a heavy pre-bank holiday liquid lunch,
the council adjusted all the parking meters
to dispense poems instead of tickets.

A notice was put up stating that the poems
were to be used in the traditional manner,
and not considered valid unless placed on the dashboard
with all stanzas visible outside the vehicle.

The poems would vary by length of stay.
A haiku was deemed sufficient for a quick trip
to pick up your click-and-collect. For overnight parking,
the *Epic of Gilgamesh* might billow forth.

Traffic wardens enforced the new regulations.
On-the-spot fines in the form of additional reading
or creative writing classes were meted out
to those who had outstayed their villanelle.

Drivers were not expected to learn their poem by heart
but at least be familiar with its underlying themes
and motifs, and be able to argue convincingly
concerning the writer's intentions and choice of form.

Once drivers had overcome their initial scepticism,
particularly with regard to the Horatian ode,
the scheme proved to be a spectacular success.
Too much so, as it turned out. Congestion rose

as motorists travelled vast distances to use the meters.
Certain poems became much sought after, and fights
would break out over a rare Heaney or Plath.
A group of drivers formed their own poetry group

and tried to park their cars using their own work.
The council had a rethink. The poetry got ditched
and a new permit scheme was ushered in: no parking
between 8 a.m. and 6 p.m. without a valid root vegetable.

17th July

....

*Today is World Emoji Day, a much-venerated tradition dating back
to not very long ago. It is easy to be dismissive of these peculiar little
icons but we must remember that communication forever evolves, and
pictograms have been an important form of written language ever
since the first chad was drawn on an ancient Sumerian wall. Besides,
emojis carry their own form of beauty and can move us in ways that
sometimes plain old words can fail to, as seen in this emoji-based
re-rendering of W. H. Auden's 'Funeral Blues'.*

🔪 😧 😧 😧

👇 🕐 🕐 🕐 ✂️ ☎️
🖐️ 🐱 🦴
😀 🎹 ➕ 😮 🥁
🔪 😦 😦 😦

❌ ❌ ❌ 😇
⛸️ ☁️ 💬 💀
🎀 🎀 🕊️ 🕊️
🚗 🚥 👮 👮 ⚫ 🤚 🤚

🧭 ⬆️ ⬇️ ➡️ ⬅️
🏔️ 🟥 📑 ➕ 🌟 🛏️ 💤
◑ ◐ 🗣️ 🎶
💭 💙 ❤️ ∞ 😩

☆ ✖️ ☆ ✖️ ☆ ✖️
🧊 🔵 ➕ 🛠️ 🔦 🌟
💧 🦶 ➕ 🖌️ 🧱
😩 😩 😩 😩 😩 😩

18th July

Jane Austen, the brilliant English novelist, died on this day in 1817. Her fame was largely posthumous: her six full-length novels, packed with irony and social commentary, went on to sell millions of copies and be adapted into numerous television and film versions. On the two-hundredth anniversary of her death, she was chosen to appear on the Bank of England's £10 note, with a quote from one of her characters, Caroline Bingley: 'I declare after all there is no enjoyment like reading.' A closer reading of the text would have led the Bank to realise they'd come up against classic Austen irony: Bingley had no interest in books and was merely trying to impress Mr Darcy.

It's Common Currency

or a truth universally acknowledged,
you don't need a D.Phil. from an Oxbridge college
or a banking degree from Harvard or Princeton:
a single Jane Austen is worth two of Winston.

That's a couple of Stephensons in old money.
Yet it has always struck me as a little bit funny
(peculiar, I mean) that you twice need to earn her
to make a J.M.W. Turner.

I've got nothing against *The Fighting Temeraire*,
but I can't help feeling that the whole thing's unfair,
given that, and I say this without prejudice,
Turner's BBC4 but Austen's box office –

her characters, immortal; her irony enduring.
By the way, it's good to hear about Alan Turing
on the new fifty-pound note. Although heaven knows,
I'll never have the good fortune to get one of those.

19th July

....

Edgar Degas, the French impressionist artist most famous for the
depiction of dancers in his paintings and sculptures, was born on this
day in 1834. While there is no doubting his brilliance as an artist,
he also had a reputation as being a misogynist and anti-Semite; the
former accusation not helped by his description of his dancing subjects
as his 'little monkey girls'. He also rejected the term 'impressionism',
regarding himself as a realist, and so, given the unsavouriness of his
aforementioned character traits, I hope he finds my characterisation
of him as an impressionist to be irksome.

Second Impressions

the painting
of ballet dancers
looked familiar

he was sure
he'd once seen
something similar

but then –
when he thought
it through –

he knew
it must have been
degas-vu

20th July

....

*Today is Moon Day. It commemorates the day in 1969 that Neil
Armstrong first walked on the Moon. That's what he's supposed to have
done, anyway. But how do we know it was real? I mean, it is a long
way from Earth. And we were hardly very technologically advanced
back in 1969; to give some perspective, the Post-it note wasn't to be
invented for another five years. Besides, who's to say the Moon is real
anyway? The poets may have made the Moon up to give themselves
something else to write about, just like they did with skylarks, Grecian
urns, and love.*

How Hard It Is to Be the Moon

How hard it is to be the Moon.
I hang palely in the sky,
while all else shines and sparkles
and the shooting stars go by.

And on Earth, the useless humans
scribble words in praise of me
for recital by young lovers,
gazing moonstruck at the sea.

There was a time they'd call on me
but then the visits stopped.
Magnificent desolation
is carved into my rock.

The tides sweep in and out once more.
That's the way things always are.
The Earth goes about its business.
I float alone, amongst the stars.

21st July

This day in 1897 saw the opening of Tate Britain (known formerly as the National Gallery of British Art and the Tate Gallery), on the site of a former prison in Millbank, London. It houses the world's largest collection of British art from 1500 to the present day and remains one of the most significant art galleries ever to be established by a wealthy, Chorley-born sugar merchant and philanthropist.

A Large Dose of Classical Realism

Her name badge says Valerie.
She stands avant-guard in the gallery
with an abstract expression on her face.
She belongs here, in this place,
amongst the other works of art.
De Stijl, my beating heart.

I come here on my lunch breaks,
feigning interest in the William Blakes,
the Constables and Whistlers,
to catch a single glimpse of her,
hope hanging on thin picture wire.
She drives me dada with desire

but she just stands there, statuesque,
her interest minimalist at best.
I dreamt I met her at a private showing –
but even then, there was nothing going.

Do not touch the exhibits, she said.
Romanticism, I fear, is dead.

22nd July

....

Today is World Brain Day (not to be confused with World Brian Day).
It aims to raise public awareness of all things brainy and cerebral. The
human brain triples in size during its first year then keeps growing for
about eighteen years. From around the age of fifty, it starts shrinking
which, in my case, explains a lot. There's no evidence, though, that
a larger brain is smarter than a smaller one – although the heaviest
recorded human brain did belong to the Russian writer Ivan Turgenev,
who was no simpleton. Scientists have found that the average person
has between twelve thousand and sixty thousand thoughts per day and
. . . umm . . . no, that's all I have for now.

Bus Journey of a Lovelorn Neuroscientist

Every day, when I see you board the bus,
my caudate nucleus is all abuzz.
My ventral tegmentum's begun to glow.
You make my reward system overflow.

While I sit, dreaming of your milk-white thighs,
my cortisol levels begin to rise.
Can you hear me on the back seat moaning?
You are starving me of serotonin.

You're the prettiest girl I've ever seen
but I'm drowning here in dopamine.
I can't function. I've got you on the brain.
Tomorrow I shall take the train.

23rd July

....

On this day in 1829, William Austin Burt received a patent for the typographer, a machine regarded as the forerunner to the typewriter. Burt had a few things going on: he was a surveyor who discovered the massive iron ore deposits for which Michigan was to become known, as well as one of the world's largest deposits of copper. He also invented the solar compass. Although long since displaced by computer word processors, typewriters are back in fashion, not least because you can pretend that you're Hemingway as you type out your to-do list for the day (must remember to get some eggs).

Typewriter Poetry

```
In the hope of becoming
a poetry  en ation on In tagram,
I bought an old typewriter.

It wa  perfect, apart from
one of the key  not working properly.
Undaunted, I  et about thing .
```

"Never forget," I wrote,
to be kind to your elf."
The Lord of the Ring ' fan loved it.

I tried again. "You light up the night,"
I typed, "like a hooting tar."
My follower began to grow.

Helped by the wanky new look
of my typewriter' font,
more of my poem took off:

"*Love, a game of hide and eek*",
"*Like hip in the night*",
and "*Ground, Open Up and wallow Me'*.

Not everything wa plain ailing.
After I wrote "*Never-ending tory*",
fifty people unfollowed me,

while the raunchy "*ex on fire*",
provoked the launching
of a criminal inve tigation.

But, in the end, ucce wa fleeting.
More of my ypewri er' key wore ou
and be ore oo lon ,

i bec me lmo im o ible
 o work ou ny o my wor   ll
 n I ve u oe ry l o e her.

24th July

....

*The Speaking Clock was introduced in the UK on this day in 1936.
It was brought in by the General Post Office, who were fed up with
people calling them up to ask them the time. The Clock's first voice
belonged to Ethel Cain, selected from a pool of fifteen thousand
telephone operators in a nationwide competition to find the 'golden
voice'. She was an instant hit, clocking up over thirty-five thousand
calls a day in the first year of operation. Pat Simmons was eventually
to take over from Ethel as the voice of the speaking clock at the third
stroke of sometime or other in 1963, precisely.*

Every Time I Hear Your Voice

You always have the time for me,
Whether ten to six or half past three.
Just say when – don't ever stop!
I'm in love with the speaking clock.

Of other girls, I've had enough;
They hear it's me and then hang up.
I scare them off. They run away.
They won't give me the time of day.

Your voice, it sets my world alight
Come sound your pips for me tonight!
At the third stroke, will you say you're mine?
Oh, love me till the end of time.

25th July

On this day in 2019, the temperature soared to 38.7 °C. in
Cambridge Botanical Gardens – the highest temperature ever
recorded in the UK. Phew! as a tabloid headline might proclaim,
What a scorcher! By the time you read this, who knows, maybe that
temperature will have been surpassed, given that the world is forecast
to warm by 3 or 4 °C by 2100, with rather disastrous consequences for
the planet. Phew! What a scorched earth!

The Problem of Writing Poems in Hot Weather

The problem
of writingpoems
inhot weather

isthatthe words
getsweaty
and sticktogether.

26th July

The international language Esperanto was launched on this day in 1887 in the form of a textbook entitled La Unua Libro ('The First Book'). It was the creation of Ludovic Zamenhof, who aimed to create a flexible and simple language that would act as a universal second language and foster peace and international understanding. It is now spoken by two million people worldwide despite fierce resistance from the English, who maintain their own language's lingua franca primacy by simply repeating it loudly and slowly to any foreigner who does not instantly understand them.

Common Language

Her words were Greek
She spoke a foreign language
She was chewing on a tuna sandwich
That's when I wandered by
She spoke some words but I didn't know them
I said, 'I don't know what you've just spoken.'
She said, 'Eh?'
Then she went on to say:
'I wanna find a common language
I wanna have a conversation or two
I wanna speak a common language
I wanna speak a common language with you.'
At least she might have
I said, 'Sorry . . . not a clue.'

I took her for a game of bingo
I had the hope that we'd learn the lingo there
So we lingered there
I said, 'In the interval, there's a raffle.'
But she just shrugged and looked so baffled
Then said, 'Eh?'
Followed by something incomprehensible
So I said
'You wanna find a common language
You wanna have a conversation or three
You wanna speak a common language
You wanna speak a common language with me?'
But she didn't understand
She just yelled and flapped her hands

Look for words which make some sense
Remember GCSE French
Attempt Dutch and Portuguese
Igbo, Kurdish, Cantonese
But still we never get it right
We're mystified all night
The words emerge and then they fall
Nothing understood at all
Yeah
We never found a common language
We barely found a common word or two
How we failed at common language
With no shared lexicon we knew
And so we said *Goodbye, Adieu,*
Auf Wiedersehen, Yasou

27th July

This day in 1586 is often held as the date that tobacco first found its way to England, brought over from Virginia by Sir Walter Raleigh. It's more likely, though (and a little more boring), that the habit of pipe smoking amongst English sailors had been around for some years previous to this. Regardless, the sight of colonists puffing away on their pipes started a craze at Court and tobacco caught on across the population. But it wasn't all plain smoking. In 1604, King James I wrote of how tobacco was 'dangerous to the lungs'! Honestly, the things some people used to believe in olden times!

Last Cigarette

It's not big and it's not clever,
admonished Mr Duxberry,
as he nonchalantly flicked the lid
of his silver Ronson
and set fire to my last cigarette,
the pair of us hidden by the bike shed,
in deference to cliché.

It seemed neither the time nor my place
to point out he was six foot five
and had guided three decades
of oscillating schoolboys
through stable and unstable nuclei
and the permittivity of free space.

I was still sucking on mine
like a gauche puffer fish, when he began
to grind his into the tarmac.
Filthy habit, he declared,
striding off across the playground,
burnt-gold tip of his quiff rippling gently,
head full of half-life equations.

28th July

....

*Fingerprints were first used as a means of identification on this day
in 1858. William Herschel, Chief Magistrate in Jungipoor, India,
required them to be used alongside signatures on civil contracts.
The first UK trial in which an individual was convicted based on
fingerprint evidence wasn't for another forty-four years, when Harry
Jackson's dabs were found on a set of billiard balls. In the 1930s, the
notorious gangster John Dillinger burnt his own prints off using acid,
which seems a little extreme, not least when he could have just gone
and bought himself a nice pair of woolly mittens in which to do all his
robbing and killing.*

Love under the Microscope

You've such fabulous dabs.
They really are terrific.
Think I've fallen in love
through dermatoglyphics.

Such fine friction ridges,
how your arches entrance.
Your loops send me loopy.
It's a whorlwind romance.

There's no one quite like you,
my sweet fingerprincess.
I can't wait to meet you –
shame you're under arrest.

29th July

*International Tiger Day takes place annually on this day. Its aim
is to raise awareness of the plight of the world's tigers – which, as
far as plights go, is one of the sorriest on offer – and to promote the
protection and conservation of these magnificent creatures and their
habitats. Or, as Blake would have it, to keep them 'burning bright,
in the forests of the night'.*

A Brief Comparison of Tigers and Leopards

It's a sad fact that most tigers
now find themselves gotted.
This explains why they're stripy
and not often spotted.

In contrast is the much spotted
but rarely seen leopard –
thanks to the gun shot
with which he gets peopard.

30th July

....

*This is one of those busy days in history. It saw the birth of Emily
Brontë (1818) and Kate Bush (1958), as well as a couple of Henrys
– Ford (1863) and Moore (1898). Bismarck died on this day in
1898, exactly one thousand, one hundred, and thirty-six years after
the founding of Baghdad. The first defenestration of Prague happened
on this day in 1419, while it also saw England win the World Cup
(1966), the last episode of* Top of the Pops *(2006), and it just
happens to be the International Day of Friendship, too. But it's not
possible to write about everything, so I suppose I will just have to
pick one.*

A Dreaming

In the night, Kate Bush comes to me –
she billows out of the blackness
and beckons in wild white semaphore,
singing of windy moors
as the *Top of the Pops* audience looks on,
mystified by her and the backdrop
of Baghdad's mosques and minarets,
silhouetted beneath a silvery moon.

Amongst them, one man makes a study
of her movements, captures her grace
as he casts her in flowing sculptures
of welded bronze, while another organises
onlookers into an assembly line
to manufacture a fleet of automobiles
which will speed them all to Wembley
once her song is at an end.

An elderly Junker with elegant whiskers
sidles over and begins to talk to me
about the art of diplomacy and how best
to maintain international friendships,
but he's drowned out by car horns
and the slamming of doors, and he hurries off
with the crowd, some of whom
are on the stage, thinking her song is all over.

It is now. And it's just the two of us again,
Kate Bush is at my window.
It's me, she cries, *I've come home. I'm so cold.*
I lean across to her
and fall out.

31st July

It was on this day in 2019 that I found a copy of my book Diary of a Somebody *in my local Oxfam shop. Not that it's a big deal, of course; it seems churlish, amongst all these significant dates and anniversaries, to even mention it. I mean, the book had only been published the previous month so there had obviously been some sort of mix-up somewhere along the line. But, like I say, it's not important. And besides, I was totally cool with its presence there. In fact, I've barely given it – or the hundreds of other second-hand copies I've subsequently found and ended up buying as I scour charity shops up and down the country – a second thought since.*

A selection of the PERFECTLY VALID reactions I have when finding one of my books in a charity bookshop

1. Clearly, the previous owner received a duplicate copy.
   There's been a mix-up between doting husband
   and dutiful son, and she ends up with two copies,
   maybe even three. She'll have kept a couple of them,
   just in case one gets damaged from over-reading.

2. So sad to learn of the death of one of my readers
   like this. My poetry must have been too much for him:
   that haiku on page 15 *was* pretty racy.

3. Someone's been having a clear-out without their glasses on!
   Books do take up a lot of space, don't they?

When she discovers that Bill Bryson book still on her shelf,
she'll realise the mix-up and be back here in no time.

4. There are such noble, selfless souls in this world.
    Imagine sacrificing a copy of your favourite book
    in order to raise money for worthy causes.
    You'd be surprised how much irrigating
    you can support with forty pence.

5. They obviously didn't like the fact that somebody
    has defaced the title page with the words
    'To Mum, lots of love, from Brian xxx'

August

1st August

....

On this day in 1774, the English clergyman-chemist Joseph Priestley is believed to have discovered oxygen – although it had also been discovered a couple of years prior by the Swedish pharmacist Carl William Scheele, and more than a hundred and fifty years before that by the Polish alchemist Michael Sendivogius. Oxygen, it appeared, was determined to be found. Priestley named it 'dephlogisticated air', presumably to distinguish it from air which still found itself in a state of phlogistication. Whoever it was who really did discover oxygen is owed a debt of thanks; it seems impossible now to think that we lived so long without it.

On discovering Oxygen only to be told it has been discovered before

O!

Oh

2nd August

....

Readers with long memories will recall that it was on this day in 1892 that Mr George A. Wheeler of New York City patented his idea for the first practical moving staircase. Other inventors had patented similar ideas with varying success but it was Wheeler's ideas which were to reach ascendency once they were incorporated by Charles Seeberger into his own prototype, built in 1899. The invention of the escalator was to usher in a new era of discovery and exploration, not least to the upper floors of giant department stores.

On the Up

there.

from

escalated

quickly

things

then

stair

moving

for a

idea

with an

It began

3rd August

Today is International Beer Day. It has been fantastic to see the growth in craft ales over the last decade or so. The number of different beers now on offer is astounding. Long gone are the days when the choice behind the bar was between a pint of John Smith or Fosters; or, if you were feeling particularly exotic, a bottle of Newcastle Brown Ale. These days, there are all manner of beers to ask for in your local alehouse, albeit in hushed, self-conscious tones. The only downside to this extraordinary variety is that I no longer have any idea what any of them are.

A Quick One Down the Flagon and Futsal

Normally I'm partial to an Amber Gascoigne
but the barrel's gone and the barman's recommending
the Woozy Floozie, which is sweet and malty,
and 8.5%. That's a bit much for a Tuesday

so John suggests either the Face Palm IPA
or Dickie Bird's Pointy Finger, which is bit like
a Gentlemen's Excuse Me, only it's vegan-friendly
and best drunk through a pipette. I'm wondering

whether to give the Avocado and Ginger
Buttermilk Stout a go but fretting it'll clash
with the packet of Red Leicester, dill and lemon
hand-cooked crisps I've got my heart set on.

Alternatively, there's always the Oh Mr Porter
(What Are We Going to Brew?) but it's overpriced
and a little pretentious for my liking, and leaves
the scent of smoked coconut on your beard for days.

In the end, I content myself with an Audrey Hopburn
while John settles on a bottle of Melted Glacier,
freshly squeezed from Norwegian icebergs,
because he's driving and Coca-Cola makes him burp.

4th August

....

*It's Venn Day – a celebration of the Venn diagram, invented by the
English mathematician John Venn, who was born on this day in
1834. While the Venn diagram remains an important illustration
within mathematics to show the relationships among things, its main
usefulness in recent years has been as a joke format on social media.
People either tend to find these Venn diagram jokes funny or they
don't: they can't be in both sets at once. I once attempted to create
a Venn diagram involving members of punk rock groups, only to run
into trouble making one of the circles intersect. It was only later that
I found out it was a Vicious circle.*

At the Intersection

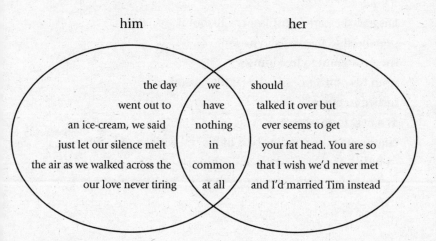

him   her

the day / we / should

went out to / have / talked it over but

an ice-cream, we said / nothing / ever seems to get

just let our silence melt / in / your fat head. You are so

the air as we walked across the / common / that I wish we'd never met

our love never tiring / at all / and I'd married Tim instead

5th August

....

The escapologist Harry Houdini performed his last act on this day in 1926. This final feat of derring-do involved him spending ninety-one minutes inside a coffin submerged in a swimming pool. He was to die a couple of months later from peritonitis caused by a student punching him in the stomach to test his abdominal muscles and rupturing his appendix. That's assuming he did die, of course; for all we know, he might be preparing right now to spring out of his coffin in the Machpelah Cemetery, New York, in what would be his grandest, most outrageous trick of all.

The Great Escape

Disgraced escapologist Jasper Chisholm,
sentenced to five years in prison
for an attempt to free himself
from his obligations to the HMRC tax office,
turned to poetry
as a new form of escape,
cut through the window bars of his cell with an old saw
(a little learning is a dangerous thing)
before stringing his words together
l
i
k
ek
n
o
t
t
e
db
e
d
s
h
e
e
t
s
and then abseiled down to freedom (his uncle's house in Neasden).

6th August

It was on this day in 1945 that the United States dropped an atomic bomb on Hiroshima. Three days later, it was the turn of Nagasaki. Six days after that, Japan surrendered to the Allies, ending the Second World War. It is estimated that as many as a quarter of a million people were killed by these bombings, of which approximately half occurred on the first day. The rest died in the months which followed, from the effects of burns, radiation sickness, and other injuries and illnesses. The vast majority of fatalities were civilians.

Conversation with a Bomb

A shadow fell upon the city
As the bomb dropped from the sky
And the people shouted up to it
Why's it us who have to die?

Don't ask me, the bomb said, whistling
I'm only doing what bombs do
What a beautiful day it really is
To drop in like this on you

But tell us, please, what we've done wrong
The frightened people begged
We're just going about our business
We'd rather not be dead

Don't ask me, the bomb said, whistling
I'm going about my business, too
It really is a beautiful day
The sky's a perfect blue

It isn't fair, the people cried
We don't deserve the likes of you
And what's with all the whistling –
Do you like the work you do?

But they never got an answer
For at that moment
The bomb stopped whistling
And the conversation was over

7th August

....

*The Litter Act came into force in London on this day in 1958.
Offenders could be fined up to £10 for dropping litter. Subsequent
acts increased the maximum fines and nationwide campaigns were
organised by the charity Keep Britain Tidy, featuring such luminaries
as ABBA, Morecambe and Wise, Roland Rat, and Frank Bruno. In
spite of this, more than thirty million tonnes of litter are collected from
our streets every year, enough to fill four Wembley Stadiums – or six
absolutely gigantic bins.*

Confessions of a Professional Litter Picker

it's hard not to feel bitter
about the litter

crochety and cruppish
about the rubbish

ill-disposed to all those
who ill dispose

but at least business
is picking up, i suppose

8th August

....

Today is International Cat Day, although they probably wouldn't thank
us for it. They might brush against our legs for a while if they think
there's a Dreamie in it for them. But generally, they tend to celebrate
this day by spending long periods of it asleep, and then popping out
in the evening to find a mouse to deposit on your pillow a little later.
Rather like other days, in that respect.

International Cats

International cats
assert their right to relax
in international laps
at any time of day or night.
If denied, they will cite
the Universal Declaration of Feline Rights.

International cats
sit on international mats
that proclaim WELCOME
in each of the world's languages.
International cats can sleep
in up to seven different languishes.

International cats,
proud flouters of human orders,
support cat comrades across borders.
They extend the paw of friendship
to cats who flee catastrophe,
terror and adversity.

LIBERTY, EQUALITY, CATERNITY!

9th August

....

Usain Bolt won the Men's Olympics 200 metres final on this day in 2012, having won the 100 metres a few days earlier; in doing so, he became the first man to win the 100m and 200m in successive Olympics. At the time of writing, he is the current 100 metres world record holder, having run the distance in 9.58 seconds: a performance only five seconds faster than my own record time, although I must admit to a favourable tail wind of 2.0 m/s and a motorbike.

Lightning Bolt

hard to think
there will ever be
a quicker sprinter

he runs out faster
than the toner
in my printer

10th August

....

The Lego company was founded on this day in 1932, in the carpentry workshop of Ole Kirk Christiansen. Its early years were devoted to the creation of wooden toys, such as piggy banks, cars and yo-yos. With the production of the first Lego brick in 1958, the business was to become moderately successful with the result that there are now about eighty

317

Lego bricks for every person on the planet. Given that, it's no wonder
it gets trodden on – and with the sharp-cornered bricks manufactured
from an extremely hard and durable terpolymer plastic, you could be
forgiven for sometimes wishing that the company had stuck to yo-yos.

He Wishes for the *Millennium Falcon* Lego Set

Had I the heavens' light freighter ship,
Enwrought with bricks white and silver-grey,
The ramp, the gun turrets and cockpit,
Shooters spring-loaded for battle play,
I would lay it down at your feet.
But I, being poor, have these few bricks.
I have spread these bricks under your feet.
Tread

>   softly
>   because   you
>   tread
>   on
>   my
>   bricks

11th August

....

The American artist Jackson Pollock died on this day in 1956. A
leading figure of the abstract expressionist movement, Pollock was
famous (and notorious) for his technique of action painting, which
involved the pouring of paint onto a horizontal surface, adding

depth through the use of knives, trowels, and sticks, to create an
explosion of curving lines, shapes, and colours. Derided by some of his
contemporaries, his work has stood the test of time; indeed, more than
that, it has passed with flying colours.

Action Poetry No. 7, 2021

another day
hurling words at paper
in the hope
some of them will stick

fling them down
on an empty canvas
and watch them
drip drip drip drip drip

12th August

....

As we've seen, throughout the year there's a parade of celebration
days to raise awareness of endangered animals. There's no such day,
though, for the quagga: it's far too late for that. The quagga, a sub-
species of zebra with its distinctive pattern of brown and white stripes
covering the front half of its body, was fiercely hunted in South Africa
and declared extinct in the wild by 1878. Although some quagga were
taken to zoos around Europe, breeding programmes proved unsuccessful
and on this day in 1883, the last quagga died at the Natura Artis
Magistra, a zoo in Amsterdam, Netherlands. Yeah, great work, humans.

The Last Quagga

Alone in Amsterdam,
she dreams of the Cape
with no hope of return

and as darkness wraps
her cage like a shroud,
her stripes disappear

to near-nothingness,
like the faded pages
of a Victorian alphabet book,

long-pulled from circulation.
She is the last of her line,
the end of the queue.

13th August

....

Annie Oakley, the renowned American sharpshooter, was born on this day in 1860. She first came to public attention at the age of fifteen when she won a shooting match against travelling-show marksman Frank E. Butler, who was later to become her husband. It was her performances in Buffalo Bill's Wild West Show that were to propel her to greater fame as she toured Europe and showed off her shooting skills in front of many of the leading notables of the day, including Queen Victoria. Her story was to be made into a hit stage musical Annie

Get Your Gun; *this should not be confused with the one about a little orphan girl of the same name, who sings of how 'the gun'll come out tomorrow'.*

Little Miss Sure Shot

Write me a poem, she'd purred,
*on the front of this playing card
and place it back inside the pack,
shuffle twice and then blow hard
and launch them up into the air.*
While she drained another beer,
I wrote upon the ace of hearts
these words that you see here.
And, as the pack rained down,
a sudden flash, a bang, a start –
from forty paces off, she'd shot
a bullet right through my heart.

14th August

On this day in 1888, one of the first music recordings ever made – Arthur Sullivan's 'The Lost Chord' – was premiered at a press conference in London, organised to show off Thomas Edison's phonograph. Later, Sullivan was to comment to Edison: 'I can only say that I am astonished and somewhat terrified at the result of this evening's experiments: astonished at the wonderful power you have developed, and terrified at the thought that so much hideous and bad

music may be put on record forever.' Exactly one hundred years later,
Glenn Medeiros found himself at number 12 in the charts with the
song 'Nothing's Gonna Change My Love For You'.

A Song Heard Backwards

The last notes fade in through your earbuds
as the sound backtracks across the ether
to that final chorus, which unstreams itself

and downloads into life, shines in aluminium
and polycarbonate plastic, the middle eight
unspooling inside your new Walkman

to send it spinning to another chorus,
grooving in black polyvinyl chloride and shellac,
the verses reversing faster and faster,

at 33 and 45 and 78, back and further back
into this room full of journalists, bewitched
by this strange machine and its cylinder of wax.

Then silence. And you wait for it to begin.

15th August

....

National Relaxation Day, which occurs annually on 15th August, is a
welcome reminder for us to take some time to slow down and unwind
from our hectic, fast-paced lifestyles – particularly ones as hectic
and fast-paced as mine. Already today I have showered, breakfasted,
completed a sudoku, spent an hour on Twitter, and it is still not even
midday. And yet, in spite of all the hurly-burly and hullabaloo, I do my
best to maintain a zen-like calmness in all my interactions with the
modern world.

Early Morning Karma

Weary of its buzzing,
he smashed up his alarm,
with his cherished bedside copy
of *The Little Book of Calm.*

16th August

....

Elvis is dead. Long live the king! It was on this day in 1977 that the
world's most famous rock 'n' roll star died, at the age of forty-two.
Since then, sightings of Elvis Presley have become almost as ubiquitous
as those of UFOs. He's been spotted purchasing one-way tickets to
Buenos Aires, sat by his pool house at Graceland, appearing as an
extra in Home Alone, *and working in a chip shop near where Kirsty*
MacColl used to live.

Sightings

Elvis has left the building trade
and retrained as a vet –
he ain't nothing but a hound dog healer,
he's treating nice the pets,

though some days he's in the library,
behind the reservations desk,
and pointing to the sign which reads
a little less conversation, please,

while the chimes of his ice-cream van
ring out around the ghetto,
as he's serving up big hunks of love
and handing out Cornettos

in his jewelled, embroidered white jumpsuit.
Rumour has it, he's down the Flute
and Flagon, all shook up, having fallen
off the wagon and lost his job

as an Elvis impersonator
at the local Steakhouse Bar & Grill,
to some bloke called Gareth
from Northampton, via Rhyl.

17th August

The world's first fully animated cartoon, Fantasmagorie, was released on this day in 1908. It took its creator Émile Cohl around five months to produce the seven hundred drawings used to make the 1 minute 20 second film, which depicted a stick man moving around and interacting with various objects. Flowers turn into bottles and then become a cannon. An elephant transforms into a house. The stick man becomes a bubble, a hat, a briefcase. In other words, in those brief 80 seconds, it showed the potential for what animation can do: the opportunity to make the impossible possible.

Cat Trouble

My cat is turning to ever more
elaborate methods of catching that mouse.

It used to be that she'd lie silently
on the floor, stretched out like a rug,
her mouth a painted tunnel entrance,
in the hope the mouse might stroll
inadvertently inside

but these days, it's frying pans
and fishing rods, cymbals, sticks of dynamite.
She sets traps of cheese and hides
behind the sofa, raising up her mallet.
Nothing seems to work.

It's all these cartoons she watches.
When she's not busy listening to walls
with her stethoscope,
or online shopping for mechanical mice,
she sits there, in front of the TV,

replaying each scene, thinking
and plotting, sketching contraptions,
one paw reaching distractedly
for the large tub of popcorn
the mouse holds out beside her.

18th August

....

A large, bright meteor with 'flashes of lambent light' was observed from the British Isles on this day in 1783. Meteors were not well understood at the time and sightings of what was to become known as the 'Great Meteor' properly freaked people out, and led to much debate in the scientific community. We know a lot more about meteors these days – to the extent that a study in Nature *estimated that a human being will be struck by a meteorite every hundred and eighty years. Given that the only confirmed incident of such an event occurred in 1954, this means that if you happen to be reading this book in the year 2134, you are in great peril: please make sure you are dressed accordingly in anti-meteor clothing.*

Beneath the Stars

The two of us, a perfect night,
moon smiling down, the stars alight,
one getting larger, shining bright,
if only we knew.

That rock, it came from outer space.
It plummeted at quite a pace.
It could have landed any place
but it chose you.

Our love, it seems, was out of luck
for you to find yourself so struck.
Far denser than a hockey puck
and much greater

in size. You didn't stand a chance.
There's nothing that quite kills romance
than to give your girl a loving glance
and find a crater.

I bring fresh flowers to your shrine
then set about the dirt and grime.
I scrub your headstone until it shines –
pure meteorite.

19th August

....

Today is World Humanitarian Day, a day on which we celebrate
all those who devote their lives to helping others. You will find them
everywhere, in areas of extreme poverty or famine, in countries beset
with war and violence. In the last few years, we've seen them in action
like never before, with front-line health workers risking their lives
every day in the battle against Covid-19. As the expression goes, not
all superheroes wear capes, but let's hope that governments can at least
supply them with full PPE provision.

Appetite for Human Goodness

Ever since I turned humanitarian,
I feel like a new man.

I have to be honest,
I *do* miss the vegetables,
but you'd be surprised at how much goodness
there is in human beings.

There's a warm feeling
I carry around inside me these days,
make no bones about it.

Talking of which, I'm sorry
but you'll have to excuse me –
I'm having a friend for dinner,
and there's me
with the table not even laid!

20th August

World Mosquito Day, which takes place on this day each year, commemorates the discovery of Sir Ronald Ross in 1897 that female mosquitos transmit malaria. Through their transmission of diseases, such as malaria and yellow fever, mosquitoes cause the deaths of more people each year than any other creature – and so, while I am generally unwilling to cause harm to any other living being, the one exception I make to this is the mosquito, which appears to find me a tastier prospect as each year goes by.

Poem Written in Self-defence

Hey mosquito, it ain't no good.
You must have stolen half my blood.
I'm worried you'll be getting fat.
So here's a poem for you. Splat!

21st August

On this day in 1888, the bank clerk William Seward Burroughs (grandfather of the Beat novelist) was issued a patent for the first successful 'calculating machine', designed to reduce the monotony of clerical work. Within a few years, his machines were prominent across the banking industry and remained in wide use until the 1970s, when advances in technology saw them replaced by more sophisticated calculating machines – which, when turned upside down,

had the power to reveal rude words and cause whole generations of
schoolchildren to snigger.

Upsum

I received a telegram from my calculating tool provider.
Your adding machine is eligible for an upgrade, it said.
I looked guiltily at my beloved abacus.

I'd always felt it was a machine I could count on.
But it *was* looking rather battered. Some of its wires
were bent and it was missing a few red beads.

I considered the options. The arithmometer
and comptometer had much to recommend them:
both were available on an add-as-you-go

or subtract basis, with unlimited sums up to 1,000
for the first three months. But they were both too large
to lug back and forth to work each day

so, in the end, I ordered the pocket calculator.
Not wanting to count my chickens, I waved it about my person
for a few moments and listened to it whir.

I had six pockets, it calculated. Popping it into one of them
(and with my abacus in my briefcase, just in case),
I set off for the office and another day of reckoning.

22nd August

On this day in 1485, the Battle of Bosworth Field took place, the last major battle of the Wars of the Roses. In the deciding fixture between the Yorkist and Lancastrian rivals, Henry Tudor defeated Richard III comfortably, without need of extra time or a penalty shootout. Richard was killed in the battle, having become unhorsed during a desperate charge at the enemy's forces. In the opinion of many early modern historians, Richard's brutal battlefield death was to prove a significant setback in his ambition to continue as king.

The Art of Barter

A horse! A horse!
My kingdom for a horse!
Includes a crown, assorted jewels,
And my palaces, of course.

A toaster! A toaster!
My fine horse for a toaster!
I'll throw in a pair of riding boots
And a set of love heart coasters.

A spoon! A spoon!
My toaster for a spoon!
Comes with a map of the Yorkshire Dales
And an almond macaroon.

Some fluff! Some fluff!
My teaspoon for some fluff!
You can also have this piece of string
And all this other stuff.

Have I a bargain for you today!
Here's some fluff, it's yours for free.
And now I've nothing left at all –
It's just the stars, the moon, and me.

23rd August

....

The world was forever altered on this day in 1991 when a British computer scientist called Tim Berners-Lee published the world's first-ever website while working at CERN, the particle physics lab in Switzerland – and the World Wide Web was created. Except for the fact it wasn't. While this date may have been celebrated by Facebook and many others online as the web's birthday, Berners-Lee (who should know better than anyone) insists that the first website was launched on 6th August. And so there, even in the World Wide Web's own origin story, we see one of its fundamental challenges at play: how to distinguish fact from fiction.

Before the Internet . . .

if you wanted to waste time in the office,
you had to stare aimlessly into the mid-distance
or make a sculpture of Pauline Quirk out of paper clips

if you wanted to get yourself some followers,
you had to form your own cult and offer membership benefits,
such as ascendancy to a new evolutionary level
or a 15 per cent discount on tableware

if you wanted to correct someone on their improper use of a
     semi-colon,
you had to train to become a teacher; or write
a stiffly worded, grammatically impeccable letter to *The Times*

if you were a prince from a distant land and you wanted to
     communicate to an esteemed beneficiary that the magnificent
     sum of US$15,000,000
awaited them at the Lagos National Savings Association
in exchange for their bank details,
you would have to conduct a series of dispiriting and ultimately
     unsuccessful phone calls,
before deciding to just keep the money yourself

if you wanted to know how many caps Martin Keown had won
     for England in order to settle an argument in a pub,
you would have to consult an encyclopaedia containing facts
     about football,
or be Martin Keown

if you wanted to buy a book,
you physically had to leave your house and go to a bookshop,
which is something you can still do now

if you wanted to send your beloved a picture of your private parts,

you would have to avoid eye-contact with the sales assistant at
    Boots when you picked up your photos,
unless your beloved was the sales assistant at Boots,
in which case you might give her a cheeky grin

if you wanted to know what kind of dog breed you most
    resembled,
you would have to send off a cell tissue sample to the Kennel
    Club
who would then respond to you by formal letter,
telling you to grow up, you're no kind of dog breed at all

24th August

*Pluto was downgraded to the status of a dwarf planet on this day
in 2006. The International Astronomical Union made this decision
based on its inability to clear its orbit of other objects and become
gravitationally dominant, one of the IAU's three criteria to define a
full-sized planet. Looking on the bright side, this decision did make
Pluto the largest dwarf planet in the solar system, which reminds me
of the scene in the children's book* The Phantom Tollbooth *when we
meet the world's smallest giant, and then the world's biggest dwarf,
and they appear to be the exact same person.*

A Small Restructuring

Ah, Pluto. Thanks for coming in this morning.
Do take a seat. Coffee? That's super. Terrific.
So how *are* things out there on the Kuiper Belt?
Not too cold and lonely, I hope? Wonderful.

Now I know you're a busy celestial body
so I shall keep this short. Nothing to worry about,
it's just that we've been having a bit of a rethink
at the Astronomical Union, taking a fresh look

at our options, a small restructuring as it were,
and we'd like to offer you a new role,
one which we feel might be more appropriate
for someone with your skillset and, ahem,

proportions. In our dwarf planet department.
No, no, no! You're still very much part of the team.
It's just that . . . well, the thing is you haven't been clearing
your neighbouring region of other objects

and you've had a few billion years to do so.
Don't get me wrong! Your orbiting around the Sun
has been first-class. And we have no doubts whatsoever
concerning your hydrostatic equilibrium.

No, we are not being sizeist. Times change, that's all,
and we need to be more stringent with our nomenclature.
Anyhow, best be getting on. I've got Earth to see next.
Now there's a planet who *does* have problems.

25th August

....

Ivan the Terrible was born on this day in 1530. He became the first
Tsar of All Russia when he was seventeen, expanded the country's
borders, reformed its government, and laid the foundations of absolute
rule. These days he's known as much for his paranoia, rage, mental
instability and acts of cruelty as his political achievements. Even as a
child, he was up to no good: drinking beer, raping and murdering, and
throwing pets out of the upper windows of the Kremlin. Ordinarily a
boy might expect a big telling off for exhibiting such behaviour but,
luckily for Ivan, his family were too busy poisoning and stabbing each
other to notice.

Nominative Determinism

If you choose to name your child Ivan the Terrible,
then, frankly, you're asking for trouble.

It's hardly surprising he was so angry.
Who wouldn't be? Sure, it might not excuse him

from killing his own son, or murdering anyone
who had ever been mean to him, or sewing

poor Archbishop of Novgorod into a bearskin
and letting his pack of dogs hunt him down,

but it was never going to end well, was it?
Ivan the *Kind*, however, might have produced

different results. Ditto Ivan the Mildly Agreeable.
Or simply Ivan for that matter. Yevgeny. Tim.

And don't get me started on Vlad the Impaler's parents,
I mean, what were they even thinking?

26th August

As British as an orderly queue to use a red telephone box or a game of conkers in the rain, the Mini motorcar was launched on this day in 1959. Designed by Alec Issigonis in response to fuel shortages and petrol rationing, his famous Mini Cooper was fuel-efficient and cheap. It was also cool, never more so than in The Italian Job *in 1969; the film featured three such cars, loaded up with bullion, bombing around Turin, an activity still popular with Mini drivers today, along with quick nips to Waitrose and a more general going about of business around town.*

Mini Love Poem, written in fifty-six seconds

You said you'd like a love poem.
This one's mini – but will it do?
It's just the longer I spend writing it,
the less time I have with you.

27th August

....

The first edition of The Guinness Book of Records *was published in Britain on this day in 1955, and since then it has been the go-to reference source for all things biggest, smallest, longest, oldest, youngest, furthest, heaviest, and sometimes silliest. As far as poetry records go, John Bradburne is the most prolific poet with a whopping 170,000 lines of verse – nearly double that of Shakespeare – while the longest modern poem is believed to be Patrick Huet's* Pieces of Hope to the Echo of the World; *the latter is 7,547 verses long and, remarkably, an acrostic in which the initials of each line spell out the thirty articles of the 1948 Universal Declaration of Human Rights.*

World Record Attempt

Disappointed to learn that my attempt to break the world record for the most words ever written in a single line of poetry, a record which currently stands at a grand total of fifty-three words, written in a 1986 poem entitled 'A Weirdist at Midnight' by one Gladys Hogan of Brisbane, Australia,

has ended in failure.

28th August

....

On this day in 1996, thousands of shops in England and Wales opened legally for the first time following a change in the Sunday trading laws. There had long been resistance to such a move from both those who believed it to be in contradiction to what should be allowed on the Sabbath and those concerned about workers' rights. These days you can go shopping at any time of the day you like and you don't even

need to leave the house; this is all very convenient, I suppose, but there
are times when I hanker for a day on which there's nothing to do.

Day of Rest

Blessed Sunday, day of rest,
a day on which to catch your breath
and put the busy world on pause,
while cracking on with all the chores.

The hoovering, the weekly shop.
The housework, laundry, washing up.
The futile war on disarray –
Sunday, such a restful day.

A chance to let yourself unwind.
To spend some precious family time
while on your phones or arguing
about the state the bathroom's in,

or shaking off last night's red wine
by being made to run the line
at your youngest's football game,
and getting yelled at in the rain.

Long may peace's reign prevail
so you can answer work emails
and start the coming week less stressed –
blessed Sunday, day of rest.

29th August

The cricketing rivalry between England and Australia known as 'the Ashes' traces its beginnings back to this day in 1882. The term originated in a satirical obituary published in The Sporting Times, a few days after England's defeat by the visiting Australians. 'In Affectionate Remembrance of English Cricket,' it read, 'which died at the Oval on 29th August 1882.' The obituary concluded with a statement that 'The body will be cremated and the ashes taken to Australia', where – with a few notable exceptions – it has resided for much of my lifetime.

From *A Hard Day's Nightwatchman: The Beatles' Cricket Songbook*

Bairstow, Border, Boon, Bell, Botham,
Bradman, Broad and Brearley,
Speaking words of Wisden, letter B.

Benaud, Butcher, Bevan, Boycott,
Bedser, Bancroft, Bailey,
Whisper words of Wisden, letter B.

Letter B, letter B,
Letter B, letter B,
Yeah, there will be an Ashes, letter B.

30th August

The influential radio presenter John Peel was born on this day in 1939. More than any other DJ, he was responsible for bringing new genres of music to popular attention, from punk rock and indie to extreme metal and British hip hop. Amongst the artists he helped bring to prominence were David Bowie, Led Zeppelin, The Sex Pistols, The Smiths, The Fall, and the post-punk, avant-garde, free-jazz three-piece, Bilge Pump. He also brought an insightful, deprecating wit to a profession not overly known for such qualities at the time: 'Somebody was trying to tell me that CDs are better than vinyl because they don't have any surface noise. I said, "Listen, mate, 'life' has surface noise."'

Do Ye Miss John Peel?

Do ye miss John Peel now he's far away?
Do ye miss John Peel at the end of day?
Do ye miss John Peel and the songs he'd play
And the sound of his voice in the evening?

'Twas he who I heard when I lay in my bed
Weaving new worlds with his needle and thread
Revolutions broke out in my heart and my head
When I listened to him in the evening

Do ye ken David Bowie, The Fall, and The Smiths?
Do ye ken The Ramones, Sonic Youth, and The Slits?
Do ye ken Ivor Cutler and Roxy Music?
Did he play them to ye in the evening?

Yes, I ken all of those and much more besides
Half Man, Half Biscuit, Nirvana, White Stripes
The Specials, The Weddoes, Pixies, and Ride
How my heart it did soar in the evening

For I followed John Peel both often and far
Across stumble of drums and screech of guitar
I'd cling to these nights like the dark hugs the stars
When they light up the sky in the evening

31st August

On this day in 1830 a budding inventor, Edwin Budding, took out
a patent for the first lawnmower and thus, nearly two hundred years
later, became largely responsible for me having to surrender a huge
amount of my own precious time in pushing a stupid machine up and
down my garden wondering whether I might electrocute myself or lop
off a toe. Budding lived in Thrupp, near Stroud in Gloucestershire,
which sounds exactly like the sort of place from which an inventor of
a lawnmower might hail, and where people might enjoy this kind
of activity.

The Woolly Ruminator 5000

Featuring the latest in munching capabilities,
the Woolly Ruminator 5000
has been developed by leading specialists in the field

to prevent your lawn
from becoming a lawn unto itself.

Each Woolly Ruminator 5000
has been installed with revolutionary dento-pad technology,
enabling it to eat close to the ground
without pulling up
those all-important grass roots.

With a range of mandibular settings
and a unique four-stomach design,
the Woolly Ruminator 5000
has the capacity to chew and chew and chew,
whatever the conditions,

leaving you the time
to get on with the things you love!
The Woolly Ruminator 5000 –
it's more than just a graze!
Available in white or black.

September

1st September

....

Pope Adrian IV died on this day in 1159. He is the only Englishman
to have been made head of the Catholic Church – and as such, has
become the answer to a much-favoured question in pub quizzes the
land over. Given that there have been two hundred and sixty popes to
date, that's a rather poor return for England on the papal front, akin
to the nation's record in international football tournaments. According
to one report, Adrian died after choking on a fly in his wine, an
account which does nothing to illuminate the historical significance
of his papacy, but I just thought I'd mention it anyway.

The Only English Pope

I know this one. It's Adrian the somethingth.
That's a handy piece of knowledge, that is.
Always thought it would come in useful.
For the general knowledge round, obvs,
or the papal picture round, if there is one.

Yeah, real name, Nicholas Breakspear.
You can have that nugget for free.
As a rule, there aren't that many famous Adrians:
Mole, of course. Chiles. Edmondson.
What's that? No, the wall bloke had an H.

Don't know much about the guy beyond that.
I mean, if you were to ask me to expound

on the political advisability of his alliance
with the Byzantine emperor Michael I Komnenos,
I'd look at you askance. Not a clue, mate.

But if it helps, I can tell you the name
of the only Prime Minister to be assassinated.
Spencer Perceval. 1812. What's that?
No, I don't know why. But it's not important –
I doubt there'll be an essay round, mate.

2nd September

On this day in 1666, a fire broke out in London that was so great
it was later to be known as the Great Fire of London. It began in a
bakery on Pudding Lane and soon spread to destroy over thirteen
thousand houses and eighty-seven churches, most notably St Paul's
Cathedral, as it ravaged the city for four days. There were only six
recorded deaths from the fire, although the actual toll is likely much
higher. While it's not known exactly how many parmesan cheeses
were destroyed by the fire, it does appear that at least one survived, as
recorded by that celebrated diarist and cheese-burier, Samuel Pepys.

It's Baking in Here

What a day! We've been rushed off our feet!
Spark out of loaves by noon, we were,
and as for those hot cakes, they've been selling like . . .
well, nobody's business.

I'm still sweating now! All that hard work
must've given me a bit of temperature.
But how good it is to be in bed with all the jobs done.
The counter scrubbed. The front door locked.
The cat out – and the candles, too.
Twigs swept up, I hope. The oven cooling in the dark.

I'm burning up, I tell you!
Think I'm coming down with something.
Still, there's no rest for the wicked. I need to be up in a few hours.
I've got plans for this place, see. Big plans.
One day there won't be a soul in this city who hasn't heard of us.
Farriner's of Pudding Lane. Remember the name.
Bread to light up the whole of London.

3rd September

....

It was on this day in 1752 that this day didn't happen. Neither
did the following day nor the nine after that, as Britain skipped a
whole eleven days in order to change over from the Julian calendar
to the Gregorian one, bringing the country in line with the rest of
Europe. A popular myth has it that there was civil unrest following
this realignment of the calendar with rioters demanding, 'Give us our
eleven days!' on the grounds that they thought their lives would be
shortened. It is thought unlikely that was the case, though; historians,
as ever, ruining a good story with their dull insistence on 'evidence'
and 'facts'.

Making Up for Lost Time

oh, woe is me,
oh, alas and alack
that's eleven days of my life,
i'll never get back

still, nice to have a few days off
(if you pardon the pun)
it's funny how time flies
when you're having fun*

*damental changes made to the calendar in order to align it with
the Gregorian system of time organisation

4th September

....

*On this day in 1888, George Eastman received a patent for a hand-
held, roll film camera, the first of its kind. He named his company
Kodak and his innovations were critical in photography's evolution
from a trade practised by professionals into a hobby that anyone could
enjoy. And, today, with the advent of smartphones, it's now possible to
take photographs of anything and everything, all of the time, and for
some reason we do.*

The Camera Always Lies

I put it to you, Kodak Instamatic, that on the day in question,
you did knowingly and deliberately tamper with the roll of film,

altering the victim's identity from that of cool teenage rebel
to nervous geek with gawkish features and gurning smile,

standing awkwardly in a garish Level 42 World Machine T-shirt
and what is – let's face it – a really bad haircut even for those days,

and that you did repeatedly interpose, alter and manipulate
all of the photographs in which the victim appears during this time,

fitting him with flared trousers, dental braces, white socks, acne,
a mullet and even – on one occasion – a piano tie, while adjusting

his expression into fifty-seven varieties of gormlessness,
and what is more, that you did conspire with a series of later cameras

and smartphones from the 1980s to the present day
to consistently and wilfully distort and misrepresent the victim

in what can only be described as a prolonged and targeted campaign
of hate, with the intention to do no less than to undermine

the victim's own idea of himself. It is said that you pride yourself
on your honesty and candour, in which case I am quite sure

you will have no objection if I request of the judge that any response
you make to these accusations be subjected to a polygraph.

5th September

Peter the Great, Emperor of Russia, introduced a tax on beards on this day in 1698. This low tolerance of chin hair stemmed from Peter's desire to modernise his nation along Western lines, and so all men in Russia were to get rid of their beards unless they paid the state a fee. Those who paid the tax were given a beard token to show when challenged by officials or risk being shaved on the spot. The tax proved immensely unpopular, some beard-wearers regarding its presence on their chins as a religious requirement, a pognophiliac stance later shared by digital marketing executives in the Hoxton area.

Pete's Beard

I'm not saying Pete's beard is out of control
but there's half a vegan sausage roll

living rent-free in its undergrowth,
along with remnants of last week's nut loaf,

three Brussel sprouts, mashed potato and peas,
a wide selection of brined and blue cheese,

reduced fat houmous, lemon crème brûlée,
a couple of sporks, a thimble, some hay,

a card with a £20 gift voucher for Laura Ashley,
the 12″ of 'Never Gonna Give You Up' by Rick Astley

with signed picture sleeve, an iPod shuffle,
a scholarly monograph on Bertrand Russell,

a roof rack, a starling, some silt, Mark Lamarr,
two Subbuteo players and an acoustic guitar.

No, I'm not saying Pete's beard is out of control –
I just think he needs to wash it sometimes.

6th September

....

*National Read a Book Day is celebrated on this day every year to
encourage us all to take a break and get reading. People found not
reading on this day may be subjected to an on-the-spot fine, which may
be as heavy as up to one hundred pages of a Jeffrey Archer novel.*

Wildflower

She lost herself in a good book,
wandered round for ages.
Ten years on they found her,
pressed between its pages.

7th September

Elizabeth I was born on this day in 1533 – my favourite of all the Elizabethan queens (with the possible exception of Elizabeth Taylor's Cleopatra). She was a formidable ruler, providing relative peace and stability – alongside economic prosperity – to a turbulent period of English history, and overseeing a new age of exploration and a flourishing of the arts. The reason behind why she never chose a husband remains an area of speculation by historians, but it may simply be that she wanted to get some things done.

Elizabeth, the Virgin Queen

Elizabeth, the Virgin Queen,
pestered by suitors umpteen.
wrecked their hopes and sank their ardour,
faster than the Spanish Armada.

8th September

This day in 1888 marks the advent of the English Football League, the first national football league in the world. About 25,000 spectators attended these first five fixtures, including 10,000 fans at Anfield – then the stadium of Everton – to see the home team defeat Accrington Stanley 2–1. The game back then was very different to how it is today – there were no penalty kicks, substitutes, perms, or that little semi-circle bit at the beginning of the eighteen-yard box – and footballers' *use of the active present perfect tense (e.g. 'he's crossed it in from the left and I've gone and got me nut on it') was not introduced until 1931.*

Football Is . . .

Football is . . .
Football is a wiggle of the hips
Football is a whistle to the lips
Football is late-night fish and chips
Football is

Football is an unwritten poem
Football is trousers in need of sewing
Football is days off when it's snowing
Football is

Football is a scrambled goal-line clearance
Football is a school-bell disappearance
Football is a blind adherence
Football is

Football is a language that's universal
Football is a perfect centre circle
Football's the real thing not a rehearsal
Football is

Football is a door without need of a key
Football is one thing for you, another for me
Football is whatever you want it to be
Football is . . .

9th September

The first ever computer bug was reported on this day in 1947, and guess what . . . it was literally a bug. That's right: a bug in a very unidiomatic, entomological sense. It was a moth, in fact, that had found its way into a computer at Harvard University, causing it to make errors through the disruption of its electronics. Writing this entry reminds me that my own computer's anti-virus software needs renewing as it would be awful to get so near to the end of writing this book only for the file to become corrup***$$$CLICK HERE TO CLAIM $1,000,000***ted.

Replacement Poem

Sorry this poem ain't no good
I'd share another if I could
But my laptop got itself a bug
Before I'd saved it

That poem had been smart and wise
It expounded and philosophised
It would surely win a Nobel Prize
If I could recreate it

No, I fear it is forever gone
Never to be re-stumbled on
Such a disappointing denouement
To have this replace it

My best work always turns to dust
Evaporates or self-combusts
I would let you read my new opus
But my dog ate it

10th September

It is estimated that eight hundred thousand people take their life each year. World Suicide Prevention Day, which takes place annually on this day, was created to encourage global commitment and action to prevent suicide. It aims to improve awareness of suicide as a global public health problem, improve our knowledge of what can be done to prevent it, reduce the stigma associated with it, and let people who are struggling know that they are not alone.

Selfies

But he had so many friends, they said,
on hearing the news.
And they went back through his posts,
searching for clues.

But no, there was nothing at all
to explain it away.
Only some selfies – all filtered –
from that final day.

11th September

. . . .

*It was on this day in 2001 that a series of attacks took place on
targets in the United States instigated by the Islamist terrorist group
Al-Qaeda. Two hijacked planes were flown into the twin towers of
the World Trade Center in New York, while another crashed into the
Pentagon building in Washington. Nearly three thousand people were
killed in the attacks, and more than twenty-five thousand injured. The
world looked on, shocked, not quite believing, except for the growing
realisation that everything had changed.*

The Day After

It is always the same, the day after
waking up bruised by the news of somebody else's pain –
today, I tell myself, I shall do better.

I will hug my children a little bit tighter.
I will contact old friends and tell them I miss them.
I will skip the bus and walk, and when I am waiting in line for
    my coffee,
I will ask the barista how her day is going.
I will sit in the park for a while and study the bees
as they go about their business.
I will think of my troubles as nothing more than cake crumbs
to be brushed off an old favourite plate.

I will greet each new day with a smile
and be thankful for every last second of it.

This works, for a while.
But then I forget, until the next thing happens,
and I have to learn it over again.

12th September

....

The online dating site Tinder launched on this day in 2012. Before then, people had to physically visit a dating agency in the hope of ever finding a partner, or even worse, try to find somebody in a real-life situation, like going to a nightclub or leaning hopefully against a burger van.

Love My Tinder

Love my Tinder – like to meet?
Just give my page a go
Want to make your life complete
Swipe right to do so

Love my Tinder, yes, it's true
I majored in fine arts
War zones, I have seen a few
I've wrestled with a shark

Love my Tinder, all I've done
In aid of charity
Fifteen marathons I've run
For orphaned refugees

Love my Tinder, love my words,
And love my photo, do
Sorry if it's slightly blurred
I swear I'm twenty-two

Love my Tinder, love online,
Trust your heart to me.
Swipe right, darling, and you'll find
I am just what you see

13th September

....

*The Treaty of Worms was signed on this day in 1743. This was a
political alliance signed between the worms of Great Britain, Austria,
and the Kingdom of Sardinia, and which was influential in bringing
an end to the Soil Wars, which had raged across the lands of Europe
for millennia. This event is not to be confused with the Diet of Worms
of 1521 which, quite frankly, was not a good idea and one I shall
never be trying again.*

Treaty of Worms

1. The right of worms to self-government is recognised,
   subject to appropriate ground-rules.

2. Worms must surrender all arms (and legs)
   with immediate effect.

3. Worms are to respect the borders and boundaries
   laid out by The Woodlice Commission.
   (A Demillipedised Zone will be established
   to allow some amount of wriggle room.)

4. All captured soil, including The Clods of Pedolith,
   shall be restored to its original position,
   and its neutrality guaranteed.

5. The catching of worms by any creature is prohibited,
   with the exception of the early bird.

6. In exceptional circumstances, the turning of worms
   may be allowed. Please note that the worm
   must be in possession of a full burrowing licence
   and have proof of previous manoeuvring experience.

7. To prevent future complications and problems, all cans
   containing worms must remained unopened.

14th September

....

*The leading French Benedictine monk and wine maker, Dom
Perignon, died on this day in 1715. He is often credited (particularly
by ignorant poets) with the invention of champagne but sparkling
wine didn't become a dominant style in the region until sometime
after his death. Rather, his contribution lay in the development of*

rules and techniques surrounding wine production; it's exactly this kind of knowledge that will enable you to point out the lazy inaccuracy of somebody's tweet on Twitter, gaining you many followers in the process.

On Learning of the Death of Dom Perignon

The Dominator's corked it, you say?
Well, that's a damn shame.
I thought he was just goofing around,
as if in sham pain.

I shall miss his fizz and sparkle.
Bubbly kind of chap.
Don't suppose there's a chance of a top up
before it goes flat?

15th September

You may recall that it was on this day in 1530 that three women turned up at the Dominican friary at Soriano Calabro in Italy with a portrait of St Dominic. We don't know for sure whether the women really were the Blessed Mother, St. Catherine of Alexandria, and St. Mary Magdalene, but what we can say without any doubt at all is that the painting proved to have spectacular miraculous properties. More than sixteen hundred bona fide miracles were attributed to its presence in the next seventy-eight years, which is a lot of miracles by *any holy artefact's standards. A shame, then, that no one knows where the painting is any more because, frankly, a few miracles these days wouldn't go amiss.*

The Miracle

On the ceiling, above his bed,
a single spot of mould.

The days passed and it formed
a patch. A face took hold,

looked down on him with gentle eyes,
kind mouth, long hair, beard,

until one night, it spoke to him.
Do not be afeard,

that kind mouth said,
nor flee this place in fright,

for I am the Way,
the Truth and the Light.

The son of God! he thought.
But then again, maybe not.

I mean, for all he knew
it was just talking rot.

16th September

....

First- and second-class stamps were introduced by the Post Office
on this day in 1968. Before this date, the sender's choice of service
depended upon the contents of whatever it was they were sending.
The system was complicated; for example, the regulations for Printed
Paper Post in the Post Office Guide ran to three and a half pages. But
with the new two-tiered system based on urgency of delivery, everyone
knew where they were – in terms of regulations, at least. In terms of
everyone knowing where their stamps were, well, that was another
matter entirely.

On Searching for a Book of Stamps

check in wallet
check once more
hunt through bag
look in drawer

feel coat pockets
peer in pot
rifle desk
find them not

shake out shoes
lift up hat
inspect fridge
ask the cat

scour the shelves
peek in purse
turn out cupboards
swear & curse

go to shop
buy new stamps
put in wallet
next to stamps

17th September

William Golding's Lord of the Flies *was published on this day in 1954. It wasn't an instant success but acclaim slowly grew and the book began to develop 'classic' status. So much so, that the novel became a standard text in the classroom for generations of British secondary-school children, its theme of how beneath the flimsy facade of law and order there waits anarchy and chaos resonating with English teachers across the land.*

Accidental Dearth of an Anarchist

Don't let this tank top fool you,
I know I must look like the very model
of a modern major department store mannequin,
but I am no stranger to the wild side,

having walked upon it several times,
on one occasion hastening over to it directly,
without first crossing at the lights.
But then, I've always been a bit of rebel.

As a child, I was practically feral,
running with scissors, leaving the lids
off glue sticks, painting without an apron,
once, being a little late in for my tea.

Even now, I have the madness in me.
I don't always book early to avoid disappointment,
my phone battery has been as low as 40%,
and although these books behind me

may look as if they're in A–Z order,
inspect them more closely and you will find
a Trollope lurking amongst my Tolstoys.
He's been there for five days now.

That kind of recklessness is not for everyone,
but we should never forget that no matter
how flawless we try to be, we are only ever
one loose letter away from anarchy.

18th September

On this day in 1970, the brilliant and influential American
guitarist Jimi Hendrix died, at the age of twenty-seven. He played
the instrument like nobody before him, and few since, expanding its
language, and pushing the guitar to the very limits of what it could do.
In the process, he became a quintessential rock god archetype, inspiring
generations of teenagers (and grown-ups, too) to emulate his stylings
in front of their bedroom mirrors, bending the strings of their tennis
rackets for want of a Stratocaster.

Imaginary Rock God Blues

Being an imaginary rock god is harder than it looks.
It's taken me three months to save up for a new air guitar,
having set fire to my last one during a typically
exhilarating display of pyrotechnics and exhibitionism
when everyone was out.

As I launch into one of my solos, the imaginary crowd
goes crazy and the cat glares from the sofa.
She deplores their longevity and my self-indulgence;
she hides behind her paws and prays for power chords
and the purity of the classic three-minute pop song.

My work colleagues are no less disapproving.
Not wanting to steal the limelight, I make a point
of sitting at the back of the big meeting room,

nodding along to their songs of profit and loss,
losing myself in the beat of the corporate world,
until my drumsticks get confiscated.

Recent enquiries into my son's broken tennis racket
and the whereabouts of the mop,
combined with my imaginary gruelling tour schedule
(bathroom, bedroom, kitchen, conservatory)
have led me to consider giving up
being an imaginary rock god.

I channel these thoughts into a tender ballad,
reach for the nearest organic carrot and sing sing sing

19th September

....

On this day in 1970 – the day after Jimi Hendrix died – the first
Glastonbury festival took place on Michael Eavis's dairy farm in
Pilton, Somerset. It ran for one day and was titled the 'Pilton Pop, Folk
& Blues Festival'. Less than a thousand people turned up to watch, as
Bristol prog-rockers Stackridge took to the stage for the first live spot
and T-Rex headlined after The Kinks decided to pull out. I went to my
first Glastonbury festival nineteen years later: I saw Van Morrison and
got sunstroke. Undeterred I went the following year when I went down
with mudstroke. I've not been back since.

Line Up

THE LONG WEEKEND • BLUE RUCKSACKS
ROAD TRIP • CARSICK • T JUNCTION & THE TAILBACKS
THE RAINCLOUDS • ST. EWARD • FRANTIC HAND SIGNAL
THE ABSENT TENT PEGS • MILDEW • CAGOULES • DIRK DISMAL
WHEN THE HEAVENS OPEN • THE DRENCHED • HELTER SHELTER
BART ENDER & THE BEER CANS • 6 A. M. • DRIZZLE • ALKASELTZER
QUAGMIRE • YURT HIRE • THE DUKE OF WELLINGTONS • LOST WRISTBAND
THE PORTALOO MASSACRE • SQUELCH • MEET ME AT THE FALAFEL STAND
ENTER STAGE LEFT • GLOOP!!! • DAWN CHORUS & THE UNDAMPENED SPIRITS
THE SOFT RAYS • TINTED SHADES • COMRADES • SIXTY UNFORGOTTEN MINUTES
GLORIOUS SOUND REVOLUTION FT. EPIPHANY • HALLELUJAH CHORUS • CROWDSURF
THE SUNSETS • ENDFEST • DON'T TALK, JUST PACK • THE ROAD HOME • BACK TO EARTH

20th September

....

The unification of Italy was completed on this day in 1871 with the
capture of Rome – and with the consequence that I'd one day have to
study it as part of my History A level (along with the unification of
Germany, the Scramble for Africa, and Georgian Britain). I sometimes
wonder what the leading statesman of early nineteenth-century
Europe, Count Metternich, would have made of it all, having once
declared Italy to be 'only a geographical expression'. But, frankly, not
often, as I'm usually thinking about football or biscuits, or the prospect
of rain.

Terry's Mistake

It had seemed like a good idea at the time,
buying Italy for Jo's birthday.
They'd often reminisce about that fortnight in Tuscany,
and Jo was a right one for the gorgonzola,
so, when it had come up for auction on eBay,
he had seen off all-comers.

But now, surveying his handiwork,
Terry was having second thoughts.
Not only was it taking him ages to wrap up,
but the paper kept getting snagged
on an assortment of Apennines and Dolomites.
He'd been back to Rymans three times now.

Terry couldn't help wondering to himself
why he was going to all this trouble.
It wasn't even going to be much of a surprise:
there was nowhere to stow it before the big day,
and anyway, Jo was bound to guess what it was
by its distinctive boot-like shape.

21st September

....

J. R. R. Tolkien's The Hobbit *was published on this day in 1937. It
has since sold a hundred million copies. The book tells the tale of Bilbo
Baggins and his friends as they embark on a quest to recover a treasure*

from a dangerous beast. As such, it could be read as an allegory for
the time when a couple of classmates helped me in my attempt to
retrieve my confiscated Pac-Man watch from the satchel of my Biology
teacher, Mr Stanton, albeit with less psychological damage and a more
successful result. For Bilbo, I mean.

You're Getting to be a Hobbit with Me

Pointy ears, hairy feet,
How I love it when we meet,
You're getting to be a hobbit with me.

Far shorter than an elf,
I'd like to keep you for myself,
You're getting to be a hobbit with me.

I used to think that love was something I couldn't know –
Me, a simple troll.
But now I've met you, everything has changed.
Let me into your hobbit hole.

I don't know what to say,
You eat six meals every day –
Two breakfasts, lunch, dinner, supper and tea.

Oh, to me you're everything,
Would you like to wear this ring?
You're getting to be a hobbit with me.

22nd September

If you take an equinoctial approach to defining your seasons, today –
or tomorrow – is the first day of autumn, one of my favourite seasons
of the year (top four, definitely). Those of a more meteorological mind,
however, will declare that it begins on 1st September. This kind of
discrepancy can give rise to all manner of heated debate on Twitter.
Personally, I go with the equinox: partly because I derive spiritual
sustenance from being in touch with the astronomical movements of
our universe, but also because I already had a poem for 1st September.

The Problem of Writing Poems in the Shape of Deciduous Trees

<pre>
                    a comm n
                  pr ble   whe writin
              p ems in the shape of decid o s
            trees is t at once t ere ar ives the fir t
          sti rings of he new aut mn breeze, he
            oems will begi   to shake hemselves
              ge tly   ntil their letters loos n
                  like leaves, an
                      they   d
                      start
                        to
                      float
                      down
                      then
              turntomushuponthegroun
</pre>

23rd September

Kublai Khan, emperor of the Mongol Empire and founder of the Yuan
dynasty in China, was born on this day in 1215. Seven hundred
and sixty-nine years later to the very day, Black Lace – emperors of
1980s novelty party songs – found themselves in the top ten with
their pineapple-pushing hit single, 'Agadoo'. It was after an evening
of pondering this extraordinary coincidence under the disorienting
influence of a Vick's VapoRub that I fell into an unsettling dream, only
to be woken by the ringing of my doorbell and the arrival of a man
with a padlock.

Disco Dream: A Fragment

In Agadoo did Kubla Khan
An 80s party night decree:
Which Alf, an aged DJ, ran,
With records long unplayed by man –
    Push pineapple, shake the tree!
Black Lace, he found, proved fertile ground –
    Hitch a ride! Now sneeze! Right, walk around!
On a floor that swirled with disco lights –
    Kiss! Blow your horn! Let's see those hands! –
The emperor danced into the night –
    Comb your hair! And wave! Now . . . superman!

24th September

Punctuation Day, which occurs annually on this date, is a day on which pedants come together to criticise the punctuation and spelling of others, as they do on all other days. Things can become rather heated in the process, with arguments often spilling over into violence. This has led to colons being extracted, infinitives split, bullet points fired, and commas inverted. And as for the improper use of ellipses . . .

Greengrocers Apostrophe's: and other Punctuation errors

Greengrocers apostrophe's
are found in cabbage's and salad green's.
They lurk there like tiny slug's,
waiting to be debugged.

The list brokers' comma,
which, separates, one, word, fromma,
nother, is, a, not, an, uncommon, error,
enough, to, fill, a, heart, with, terror.

The optimist's semi-colon
falsely signifies more to come;

Now, here's an excitable creature!
AKA the preacher's shrieker!

But dignified, it ain't!
Show some more restraint!

Concerning the joiner's hyphen,
the less-that's-said the better,
Words thank-you to let them breathe
and not be stuck-together.

But if one mark could be for the chop,
it's the premature .

25th September

....

World Dream Day, which is actually a thing, takes places annually
on this day as a prompt for us all to take some time to concentrate
on our dreams and make an effort to turn them into reality. The day
encourages us to feel empowered in removing those barriers which
stand in the way of making our dreams come true and which, in my
case, spells very bad news for the partner of Gillian Anderson.

Why You Should Never Ever Follow Your Dreams

I followed my dream,
only to find it was the one
of me, in the playground,
with no underpants on.

26th September

....

The Beatles released Abbey Road *on this day in 1969, the last album they were to record together. Its front cover, featuring the four of them walking across the zebra crossing near the entrance to the studios, was to become an iconic image. At the time, it also helped to fuel a bizarre conspiracy theory that Paul McCartney had died in a car accident in 1966: the photo, of course, depicting a funeral procession with George as the gravedigger, Paul as the bare-footed corpse, Ringo as the congregation and John, the priest. It's obvious now you come to think about it.*

Coming Together

They cross the road, then come back again,
in bright late summer light,
walking out, not quite in step,
painting colour on black and white.

A photographer perches on a ladder,
sandals lie abandoned on the floor,
a man – with hands on hips – gazes, counts:
one and one and one and one is . . .

Because the amps are there,
they turn them on, and there's something
in the way they play that makes it seem
like years since they've been here,

in the shade, stitching harmonies
with fenestrated majesty,
a sun-honeyed, golden-slumbered,
polyphonic tapestry

of melody, echo and refrain,
that carries the weight (it's so heavy!)
of how far they've come
and where they'll go to in the end.

Outside, we glimpse them through the lens –
one and one and one and one –
and one last walk across the road
and then they're gone.

27th September

World Tourism Day is celebrated on this day each year with the aim of spreading awareness about the importance of sustainable tourism. With its links to development, it has become a key driver for socio-economic progress in some communities. But there are concerns: global tourism accounts for 8 per cent of global greenhouse-gas emissions, and it can result in other negative consequences, such as the seasonal nature of local labour markets, damage to the natural environment, and the justification from some people for the continuation of the British royal family.

Short Poem for World Tourism Day

Tourists wait in line
to enter Machu Picchu.
Oh, look! A high queue.

28th September

....

The Chinese philosopher Confucius was born on this day in 551 BCE.
*His teachings, with their emphasis on morality, correctness, justice,
and kindness, were to form the basis of Chinese culture and society
and remain hugely influential to this day. 'Never do to others what
you would not like them to do to you' is one of his. As is, 'choose a
job you love and you will never have to work a day in your life', and
'everything has beauty but not everyone sees it'. 'I'm a Libra and I'm
very strategic', though, is not one of his. That's Hilary Duff, born on
this day in 1987.*

Don't Quote Me on That

I think it was Confucius who once said,
'No man is more foolish than he
who wrongly attributes a quotation,'

a nugget of wisdom which almost certainly
would have met with the approval
of the celebrated Irish poet Mark Twain,

who once famously declared how
'a single moment of study and reflection
can save a lifetime of embarrassment.'

But to err is divine, for 'freedom',
as Gandhi has taught us, 'isn't worth having
without the freedom to misquote,'

or, as Wilde had it, 'the only thing worse
than being misquoted is to not be quoted at all,'
and which brings me back to Confucius,

or maybe it was me, just now,
who once said, 'what *is* poetry, anyhow,
but the words of others, badly remembered?'

29th September

....

*Today is International Coffee Day. I'm not sure when it was that
coffee shops (formerly known as cafes) began to loom so large in
my life. It wasn't always that way; whole decades went by without
subjecting myself to a grande decaf iced vanilla latte with soy milk
every time I journeyed into town. Half my annual income is now spent
on the things. From time to time, I attempt to write in coffee shops,
but it never ends well.*

The Bastards

must have camped out overnight
because this coffee shop has only been open five minutes
and they have already taken command
of the plug sockets

my laptop battery is on 12%
which, by my calculations, should allow me
just enough time to connect to the wi-fi,
spill an overpriced latte over my tatty blue cardigan,

wonder how it can be that people, not even half my age
and with no obvious sign of regular income,
all possess laptops (and cardigans)
immeasurably more desirable than my own,

consider whether, at the napkin-soaked heart
of all this jealousy, it is their youth or their plug sockets
I covet the most, and nearly – but not quite –
finish writing my po

30th September

....

*Today is International Translation Day, which pays tribute to the
language professionals who play an important role in bringing nations
and cultures together through their work. It can be tempting to use*

a machine these days rather than somebody with proper language
skills and qualifications but I've run these sentences through Google
Translate from English to Chinese to French and back to English and
this is how they now read . . .

Now it is International Translation Day, which praises language
caregivers who have been important in rapsociating nations and
cultures across their work. It is tempting to use machine now, not
anyone with the right linguistic proficience skilled and skilled,
but I goz google these phrases from English to Chinese, from The
French to English, and that's how they read now . . .

Polyglot in Need of Direction

I'm *perdu* in French,
i humbur in Albanian,
potaya in Swahili,
pierdut in Romanian.

I'm *mitlufa* in Maltese,
and *kayıp* in Turkish,
hat verloren in German,
windabû in Kurdish.

I'm *ngaro* in Maori,
izgubljen in Croatian,
What I'm trying to say is
I'm *lost* in translation.

October

1st October

....

Today is World Vegetarian Day. I've been a vegetarian since the age of nineteen, due to a combination of The Smiths and the growing realisation of what a vile, abhorrent practice the eating of meat is. Ah, look at the lovely little lambs gambolling in that field! Still, why not bring a cleaver down on a billion of them each year, and serve them up on your finest Royal Worcester dinner plates with gravy and a garnish of parsley. I mean, really?

Salad Days

Those first few days of vegetarian life
were a tough nut to crack.

The carrot and stick approach helped,
but going through Quorn turkey wasn't easy;

there comes a stage, though,
when you have to stop beefing about it,

you figure that it's small potatoes really,
and there are bigger chips to fry.

These days, I'm full of beans.
As quinoa as mustard. Kale and hearty.

I bring home the bagel, not the bacon,
and feed two birds with one scone.

And, if you couldn't care for tofu,
I'll make quincemeat out of you.

2nd October

There's a case to be made for today to be one of the most important dates in the calendar: Indian freedom fighter Mahatma Gandhi, comedy genius Groucho Marx, critically acclaimed novelist Graham Greene, musician and yoga enthusiast Sting all popped out on this day. But arguably none are as significant as the figure born on this day in 1978, who would later become the Secretary of State for Health and Social Care for the UK government during the Coronavirus pandemic, and whose presence was to become so ubiquitous that it was said you were never more than six minutes away from one of his interviews or press conferences: Matthew John David Hancock.

An Outbreak of Matt Hancocks

turned off my phone and radio
got rid of my tv
ran barbed wire around the house
yet still I am not free

matt hancocks in the sitting room
mat hancocks in the loo
matt hancocks in my bedside drawer
i don't know what to do

there's six of them beneath the stairs
in the fridge another ten
my house is getting overwhelmed
by underwhelming men

i think I may have lost my mind
i see them every place
just yesterday I stroked the cat
she had matt hancock's face

filled gaps in all the skirting boards
laid poison in the hall
set traps involving bits of cheese
but nothing works at all

matt hancocks haunt my dreams at night
i'm screaming yet again
my mind is getting overwhelmed
by underwhelming men

3rd October

....

*The world's longest-running literature festival, the Cheltenham
Literature Festival, began on this day in 1949. It was launched by the
actor Ralph Richardson; the poet Cecil Day-Lewis read a selection of
his verse; Compton Mackenzie discussed 'the Contemporary Novel';
and Arthur Bryant gave a talk on 'The National Character'. These
days, no town is worth its literary salt without such a festival; if there's
one in your town be sure to not to leave your house without having
the following about your person: a pen; a flick-knife; and a question
concerning daily writing routines.*

Poetry Festival: Advice for Residents

Check your doors are chained and padlocked.
Keep your hatches battened down.
Lock up your jewellery and your whiskey.
There are poets in the town.

They're kicking cantos down the high street.
They're crooning in the chip shop queue.
They're selling cinquains on street corners.
They've sprayed the bus stops with haiku.

Do not venture out past midnight.
Stay in bed. Don't make a sound.
Clutch your crucifix and garlic.
There are poets in the town.

They're soliloquising down the precinct.
They're expounding on the tram, as well.
They're slipping sonnets into handbags.
They're lacing drinks with villanelles.

If one's near, approach with caution.
Lend them not a single pound.
Walk in pairs. Stick to the footpaths.
There are poets in the town.

They'll say one thing and mean another;
they'll lie to you; they'll tell the truth;
they'll coax you in with words of honey;
they'll comfort you, console, seduce;

they'll break your heart or make it leap;
they'll leave you battered, soothed, or warmed
then leave your town in search of others.
Please take care. You have been warned.

4th October

....

It's World Animal Day today, an annual celebration not of the
maniacal drumming Muppet but of creatures more generally, e.g. voles,
echidnas, poison dart frogs. The aim of the day is to raise awareness of
the issues that animals face (you know, loss of habitats, extinction, and
all that kind of thing) and improve animal welfare standards around
the world. It's held on the feast day of the patron saint of animals and
copying people into emails, St Francis of a CC.

animals

some are big & some are small
some can fly & some can crawl
some of them there's bugger all
animals

some can howl & some can sing
some can bite & some can sting
some have started vanishing
animal

some pollinate & some can spawn
some hunt by night, some wake at dawn
some of them will soon be gawn
anima

some are loved & some are feared
some are cute & some are weird
some have nearly disappeared
anim

some eat meat & some just graze
some move forward, some sideways
some you don't see much these days
ani

some are camouflaged, some distinct
some shed their skin & some squirt ink
some are more or less extinct
an

some have flippers, some have paws
some can whistle, some can roar
some once was but ain't no more
a

one hunts & trawls & skins & chops
& wrecks & dumps & farms & shops
then wonders how to make it stop

5th October

....

Today is World Teachers' Day, an annual celebration of teachers and what they do, and an opportunity to consider issues affecting their profession (e.g. interfering governments, low pay). For me, it's an opportunity to make a personal apology to any of them who were unlucky enough to have me in their classes: I am sorry for those things that I did; I appreciate it must have created a difficult, disruptive environment for my fellow students; I had no idea the ceiling would collapse like that.

Teachers

Teachers
are extraordinary creatures.

They teach us about topographical features
and the causes of the First World War.

They teach us how to use a Bunsen burner
and what set squares are for.

They teach us safe ways to throw a javelin
and how the flowers make nectar.

They teach us about the properties of waves
and conjugating être.

They teach us about Victorian melodrama
and coastal defences.

They teach us that to have your phone out in class
has consequences.

They teach us about apostrophe's
and where not to put them.

They teach us when best to open our mouths
and when to shut them.

They teach us to be dream-chasers.
Goal-shooters. Star-reachers.

Yes, teachers
are extraordinary creatures

with the possible exception of Mr Stanley,
who never liked me,

and all because of that time I locked him
in the stock cupboard.

6th October

....

The social media platform Instagram was founded on this day in
2010. I like Instagram; there's lots of great 'content' to be found and
it can provide a pleasant respite from the combative nature of Twitter.
It does always make me feel a little amateurish, though, when I see
how beautifully others present their poems, freshly whipped out of
their Remington typewriters or set against the stunning backdrop of

a rippling wheatfield. As for my thoughts on influencers, I'd be happy
to tell you about those over a delicious salted caramel macchiato from
House of Coffee, the brand that never lets you down, just £3.99 if you
mention this book at the check-out.

A Life of Influence

I live a life of influence,
of firm and forceful sway.
I influence the clothes you wear,
your choice of holiday.

I'll recommend you books to read,
cosmetics and new tights.
I'll recommend you Novichok,
if the price is right.

Retailers hold their breath for me
and hope I love their brands.
Which, of course, I always will,
subject to my demands.

I influence the food you eat.
I influence your views.
I influence my bank account
and monetise click-thru's.

I've influenced the scientists
to change astronomy:
the Earth no more goes round the sun,
it orbits around me.

7th October

....

On this day in 1959, the Soviet spacecraft Luna 3 sent back pictures of the Moon's far side. The pictures were a little blurry and indistinct, but because the Moon always presents the same face to the Earth, they offered views of a part of the Moon that had never been seen before. They showed how different the far side of the Moon was: absent were the large, dark seas of cooled lava that cover a substantial fraction of the Earth-facing near side; instead, there were impact craters of every size and age. The 'far side of the Moon' should not be conflated with the 'dark side of the Moon', as even the far side gets some sunlight – which just goes to show that you should never believe all that you hear on bestselling experimental rock albums from the 1970s.

moonbathing

i like it here
on the far side of the moon

lazing around
on a moony afternoon

nothing to do
but caper in craters

might have a chat
with a rock a bit later

or scrabble about
in the moondust and dirt

see if i can get
a quick glimpse of earth

i miss you lots,
please know this, my dear

still don't know why
you sent me here

8th October

....

Today is World Octopus Day, a celebration of the most weird and wonderful of all the cephalopods. Octopuses (no, it's not octopi) have been around for about three hundred million years, probably because they're rather clever creatures. Their nine brains, one at the end of each arm, must help; it makes them very good at multi-tasking, as well as doing things like opening jars and predicting football results. They also have three hearts, which is helpful should love go wrong and one or two of them get broken.

Don't Go Breaking My Hearts

Don't go breaking my hearts . . . *I couldn't if I tried*
Honey, if I get captured . . . *Babe, I won't let you fry*
Don't go breaking my hearts . . . *But you light up the sea*
Oh, honey, hold me in your arms . . . *Ooh, you've eight just like me*

Lost arm! My body regrows it . . .
All my nine brains love you the same
Lost arm! My body regrows it (*my body regrows*)
Right from the start, I gave you my hearts
Each one – I gave you my hearts

So don't go breaking my hearts . . . *I won't go breaking your hearts*
Don't go breaking my hearts

Come swim in my ocean . . . *Babe, just pull me along*
Can't stop my emotions . . . *Oh, my suckers are strong*
Sorry, I can't hold back now . . . *No cephapologies*
Love you more than any sea cow . . . *You're the mollusc for me*

Lost arm! My body regrows it . . .
All my nine brains love you the same
Lost arm! My body regrows it (*my body regrows*)
Right from the start, I gave you my hearts
Each one – I gave you my hearts

So don't go breaking my hearts . . . *I won't go breaking your hearts*
Don't go breaking my hearts
Don't go breaking my hearts . . . *I won't go breaking your hearts*
(Don't go breaking my) (Don't go breaking my)
Don't go breaking my hearts

9th October

....

*On this day in 1779, a group of English textile workers in Manchester
known as the 'Luddites' rebelled against the introduction of
mechanised looms and knitting frames which they saw as threatening
their craft. The Luddites were not against the concept of progress
and industrialisation as such, but more the idea that mechanisation
would undermine their livelihood and skills. In recent times, the term
'Luddite' has become a blanket term to describe people who dislike new
technology, or use obsolete technology – a fact I recently learnt from
watching a Betamax video on the subject.*

Luddite

You'd feel like one, too, carting around
the piece of crap that's my iPhone 6
and its puny 1.2-megapixel FaceTime camera,
when the iPhone 7 has a 7-megapixel sensor
with auto image stabilisation,
not to mention an A10 Fusion Chip
and solid-state button with haptic feedback.

Yes, the times they are upgrading
and for a while now I have felt an emptiness,
a built-in obsolescence which squats
in the core of my existence,
only partly explained by my paltry 1GB of RAM
and lack of a boosted earpiece speaker.
My battery barely lasts an hour these days.

But how could it be otherwise,
I ask myself when I now find my peak brightness
has become 25% duller than newer models,
and I cannot yet see the world
through the palette of richer, more vibrant colours
that a DCI-P3 colour gamut
would give me.

10th October

....

World Homeless Day occurs on this day every year, with the aim of drawing attention to those who experience homelessness and providing opportunities for local communities to get involved in helping them. In England alone, it's estimated that there are about three hundred thousand people who are without a home; that's not just people who are rough-sleeping but those trapped in temporary accommodation, hostels, and shelters. In other news, more than five hundred thousand households have second homes.

Sorry for the Inconvenience

Some days I sit here and starve.
Some days I sit here and stare.
Some days I sit here and watch the street theatre.

Like today and this guy in the suit,
who must think me blind, stupid, or drunk,

if he thinks I didn't notice the look
that passed across his face,
a fraction before he recalls how late he is
for his meeting with the board.

Or that one there, who stops
midstride, seeking his Eureka moment.
And there it is! Sudden-remembered business
on the other side of the street!
Lured over by 3 for 2 on A5 notepads,
a discount off his printer ink.

Elsewhere, strong phone work
is at play; a well-rehearsed shrug
that lets me know normally they would,
only they've just given their last fifty-pound note
to the one down the road; a rueful patting
of pockets; an interest in pigeons.

People go out of their way for me.
Sorry for the inconvenience, I feel like saying.
I'm only asking for change.

Some days I sit here and starve.
Some days I sit here and stare.
Some days I sit here and watch the street theatre.

11th October

....

The Lovell Telescope was switched on at Jodrell Bank in Cheshire on this day in 1957, tracking the rocket that launched Sputnik 1 into space. At the time it was the largest steerable dish radio telescope in the world. It has made a major contribution to our understanding of the solar system, the Milky Way and other galaxies. In particular, it's played a large part in the discovery of quasars (super-massive black holes) and pulsars (rotating white-dwarf stars): two areas of study which – like the Lovell Telescope itself – were well worth looking into.

I Would Name A Star After You

But the catalogue says it costs £27.99.
Don't get me wrong, that's absolutely fine,
and it's NOT that I think you're not worth
it. After all, they *are* a long way from Earth.
In fact, it's good value when you consider that
price includes a scroll and a sky atlas star map
and that's for a star that's *extra* bright,
which I think I would be right
in saying is the very least that you deserve.

But it's still a lot for what is – after all – just a word;
my overdraft isn't getting any smaller.
And it got me thinking – that, perhaps, rather than call a
star after you, you might change *your* name
to that of a star. That way we'd save
and still get the same result.

Anyway, it's just a thought.
For instance, I was wondering about that one up there.
Can you see it? I'm sure it would be happy to share
its name with you. It's called 'Nu-sa-kan'.
Don't you think it has a certain spark and
flair? Can you see how brightly it shines!

Its name means 'the two aligned lines'
because – although you can't tell from this distance –
it's actually *two* stars orbiting in their own system,
locked together on their unchangeable course,
dancing a perpetual celestial waltz
in the constellation of Corona Borealis.

Have you any idea how far that is?
It's about 375 light years away.
I'd like to go there with you one d— what's that you say?
You have no intention of changing your name.
No, of course, I understand. I'd be the same.
Like I say, £27.99 is not too bad, all told.
And it would be nice to get the sky map and the scroll.

12th October

On this day in 1901, Theodore Roosevelt renamed the official residence
of the US president (then known as the 'Executive Mansion') as the
White House. Roosevelt had authorised a major renovation of the
buildings, including the relocation of the president's offices from the

second floor to a newly constructed site, known as the West Wing. His successor, William Howard Taft, oversaw the construction of the Oval Office. Work continued at intervals throughout the twentieth century, although arguably it was Joe Biden who had the most work to do upon taking office, given the state in which his predecessor had left it.

The White House Redux

He stepped into his new home
to face washed-out tones of white:
Pale Shimmer and Frosted Death,
Sour Milk and Clouded Light.

Bleached Lichen in the kitchen;
in the bedrooms, Faded Tan;
Pure White in the Oval Office,
painted by the Du Lux Klan.

Bloodstains on the carpets
and deep cracks in the walls.
To rebuild this, the work of years,
to redecorate and restore.

13th October

....

*Today is Ada Lovelace Day, which celebrates the achievements of
women in science, technology, engineering, and mathematics. It's
named after Ada Lovelace, daughter of the poet Lord Byron, and,
rather more importantly, the first computer programmer. In her
response to a paper on Charles Babbage's Analytical Engine, she
added algebraic workings and what is considered to be the first ever
algorithm. In keeping with how these things always seem to be, Ada's
achievements went largely unrecognised in her own lifetime. I mean,
how could a woman possibly have done such a thing?*

The Enchantress of Numbers

She conjures numbers every night;
they bow and dance before their queen,
who labours hard by candle-light
at work the world has not yet seen.
She brings the future into sight
and contemplates the new machine.

The digits fall beneath her spell,
no less in beauty than an ode;
her father's child, she knows so well
imagination's open road.
It leads where only time will tell,
this magic trail she lays with code.

14th October

The Battle of Hastings was fought on this day in 1066 with William, Duke of Normandy, defeating the Anglo-Saxon King Harold by two eyes to one. It's often regarded as one of the key turning points in English history, and one of the few dates embedded in the heads of most English people (along with the Growth of Hemp and Flax Act, passed in 1781). The battle lasted for one day only. There was even a half-time break for lunch, which makes it sound quite civilised, particularly if you disregard all the fighting and killing that went on.

Bloody Normans

Bloody Normans, coming over here
with their swords and arrows and funny ideas;
killing our kings and taking our jobs,
the fine, proper, noble jobs of our Anglo-Saxon ruling classes;
building their fancy castles and cathedrals;
reforming our administrative structures and imposing
their systems of feudalism; getting rid of slavery,
good, honest, Anglo-Saxon slavery; poncing about
with their fussy notions of chivalry, so you can't
just go around bumping off folk whenever you want,
like you could in the good old days; embroidering their tapestries
and enriching our language, our culture and customs;
marrying our women, our beautiful, treacherous,
Anglo-Saxon women; integrating themselves over generations
to create a new kind of so-called Englishness.

Typical immigrants, it's always the same.
Take, take, take, take, take.

15th October

....

The German philosopher Friedrich Wilhelm Nietzsche was born on this day in 1844. An influential thinker, he remains widely quoted to this day: 'God is dead' and 'There are no facts, only interpretations' are two such Nietzsche-isms. Kelly Clarkson was also uttering one of his philosophical musings when she sang, 'What doesn't kill you makes you stronger' although the line from the same song, 'babe, you don't know me, 'cos you're dead wrong' is not thought to be one of his. That one has Schopenhauer written all over it.

Love is Dead

Bill gazed long
into the abbess

and the abbess
gazed back at Bill

till she bored
of all the gazing;

nuntheless,
Bill gazed on still.

16th October

The British children's television programme Blue Peter *aired for the first time on this day in 1958. Ever since then it's been showing the youth of this country how to become model citizens; how to make a positive contribution to the world; how to lead healthy and wholesome lives; how to raise money and awareness for those less fortunate than ourselves; and how to construct a Thunderbird Tracy Island out of cereal packets, washing-up bottles, and pipe cleaners. And then there's the* Blue Peter *badge, which, frankly, is about ten times better than any OBE or knighthood.*

The Badge

Sandra only started going out with Geoff
because he had a Blue Peter badge.

It was just the basic blue and white one
but she coveted it all the same.

Geoff had won it for his drawing of Shep
standing next to a tractor.

After they were married, Geoff got a job
on the rigs and when he was away,
Sandra would wear it around the house.

She would put her hair up,
then pin the badge to her best blouse.

Whenever she walked past a mirror,
she would stop and admire herself,
sometimes for several hours.

Sandra was always very careful to put it back
in Geoff's bedside cabinet drawer
before he came home.

When Geoff died, twenty-three years later,
she wore it to his funeral. How smart it looked
against her black suit jacket!

At the wake, Sandra told everyone
she'd got it for rescuing her oboe instructor
from drowning in a canal.

Geoff's youngest sister Miriam –
who knew life-saving earned you a gold badge –
polished off her vol-au-vent
and made her way over to have things out.

17th October

....

Just as how it's said that everybody remembers what they were doing
when they heard JFK had been shot, there are few people who cannot
recall what they were up to when VisiCalc, the first spreadsheet
program for personal computers, was released on this day in 1979.
I was busily bombing around the neighbourhood on my Raleigh

Chopper, and nearly ended up in Mrs Penry-Davies' privet hedge. The day is now commemorated annually in the form of Spreadsheet Day, and I have lots of data to back me up on that.

Love Excels

	A	B	C	D	E	F
1	Let's	spread	ourselves	on	sheets	of love
2	and	turn	our	data	into	poetry.
3	Our cells shall merge themselves together					
4	as you wrap your text	around me.				
5						
6	Our sum	is	greater	than	our	parts,
7	let's	crunch	our	figures	without	compunction.
8	Remove ⌄	this ⌄	filter ⌄	from ⌄	my ⌄	heart ⌄
9	you	give	me	form	and	function
10						
11	We	shall	frolic	among	the	formulae,
12	pivot	our	tablets	now	and	often.
13	I	will	total	all	your	rows
14	and	you	can	sort	my	column.

18th October

....

The British Broadcasting Corporation (more commonly known as the BBC, Auntie Beeb, or the Big British Castle) was founded on this day in 1922 by a group of wireless manufacturers, including radio pioneer Marconi. John Reith became the BBC's general manager from the end of that year and was to define the broadcaster's role as 'to bring the best of everything to the greatest number of homes' – words which will certainly ring true to anyone who has ever seen Triangle, *the seminal 1980s soap opera set on a British ferry, sailing between Felixstowe, Gothenburg, and Amsterdam.*

Dear Director-General of the BBC

I am writing about the licence fee.
Specifically, for you to knock something off it
because I think you must be making a tidy profit,
when I only watch it from six in the evening to half past ten –
and sometimes not even then
e.g. when there's *Gogglebox* on Channel 4,
or a new series of *Geordie Shore*.

So tell me – why should I fund *Cash in the Attic*
when I rarely catch it?
(Admittedly, I did enjoy that episode
in which a retired couple from Wiltshire
sell off their collection of pottery snowmen
to raise money for replacement windows.)

And another thing. I can't help noticing
that the *News at Ten* is very similar to the *News at Six*.
Is this another one of your tricks?
Making me pay for duplicated content?
And I don't mean to vent
but you do know your programmes are biased, don't you?
Not just to the right and the left either –
but to the centre, too.

Anyway, you've got a rebate to do
so you'd better get cracking.
But before I go, that weatherman of yours – he needs sacking,
though far be it from me to point the finger of blame.
I mean, why does he always forecast rain?
He needs to have a brighter outlook, if you ask me.
You get far better weather on ITV.

19th October

....

The Hundred Years War between England and France ended on this day in 1453. It was fought over the throne of France, to which both the English and French kings claimed to have the right. In some ways, it can be seen as just one phase of an even longer struggle between the two countries, from the Norman Conquest of 1066 through to the Entente Cordiale agreement of 1904. Even now, there continues to be beef (or bœuf as they say in France), with the French making condescending remarks about England's national cuisine, and the English continuing to mock the state of French pop music.

The Hundred Years or So War

Apart from the siege of Calais
and the Battle of Agincourt,
most people don't know much
about the Hundred Years War.

Why all the fighting?
What on earth was it for?
Who won – England or France?
Or did they call it a draw?

In fact, the thing most known
about the Hundred Years War
is that it actually lasted
another sixteen years more.

Therefore, to then call it
the Hundred Years War
seems a most imperfect
nomenclature.

20th October

....

*Today is International Sloth Day, a celebration of my favourite
arboreal Neotropical xenarthran mammal. Chances are that they
won't be going wild themselves; they'll probably spend most of the day
upside down in a tree, munching on the odd leaf, wondering whether
to head down to the slow disco later. We humans should make more*

of the day, though, and think about what more can be done to protect
these creatures; at the same time, maybe we can learn a lesson or two
from them about how to slow down a little and enjoy the simple things
in life.

In Celebration of the Sloth

I've never quite known
how to pronounce it –

is it 'sloth',
or is it 'sloth'? –

and so,
when writing a poem

I do what I can
to use both . . .

. . . where was I?
Oh yes, writing a poem

in celebration
of the sloth.

Sorry, I'd been clinging
to my branch

and I think
I must have dropped
                    oth

21st October

....

Dog's snouts. Razor russets. Nonnetit bastards. New rock pippins. I am, of course, talking about apples, whose fruity existence is celebrated today on Apple Day. Traditionally, on this day, people across the land gather together to take part in a series of apple-based games and activities, such as apple-bobbing, stack-apples, throw the apple, hunt the pip, and drinking twelve cans of cider.

Portrait of the Artist as a Cox's Orange Pippin

my days
are as thrilling
as an apple
in repose

it's not much
but it's still life
i suppose

22nd October

The French existentialist writer Jean-Paul Sartre was awarded the Nobel Prize in Literature on this day in 1965, only for him to refuse it the next day. He had a longstanding aversion to prizes, not wanting to let himself 'be transformed into an institution'. Back in 1926, George Bernard Shaw had turned down the prize money, on the grounds that he already had 'sufficient money for his needs'. On the subject of which, I would like it to be known that I'd be prepared to settle for half the winnings should anyone from the Nobel Committee happen to be reading this and worrying about their budget for next year.

On Refusing the Nobel Prize for Literature (again)

I mean, where would I put it?
The medal, that is.
My trophy cabinet's full to bursting as it is,
what with my chrome-fronted rosewood plaque
for reaching the quarter-final stage
of the 1985 West Midlands U14s Snooker Championship,
and my Silver Jubilee Commemorative Coin.
There's barely room already
for my set of swimming distance badges.

I suppose I could wear it around my neck,
have it nestle in my chest hair
as I walk to the local Tesco Metro
with the top buttons of my shirt undone,

so it shimmers in the street
like a star I've lassoed from the sky

but it looks quite heavy
and besides, I don't want everybody
to stare and point and say,
look there's the nobel guy again
with his giant gold medal and unruly chest hair,
and what's he doing
buying six bags of oven chips, anyway?

23rd October

The world was created on this day in 4004 BCE – according to the Ussher Chronology, that is. It's a claim since disproven by scientists and other normal people. The Ussher Chronology was constructed by James Ussher, the Primate of All Ireland, in 1650 and based on a literal reading of the Old Testament. It's easy to ridicule this now, and that's exactly what I have done, but as Stephen Jay Gould said, 'Ussher represented the best of scholarship in his time,' and Isaac Newton's own estimate of the age of the Earth was only a few years different from his.

The Day the World was Created

A Sunday, as I recall. Just after tea-time.
At least, it *would* have been
if there were such a thing as Sunday back then.
Or tea, for that matter.

Up to that point, there really wasn't very much to do,
beyond being part of the general nothingness –
which, between you and me, was just a teensy bit boring.
Voids are very over-rated, IMO. I mean,
there wasn't even anything much on TV.
Well, there never *is* at that time on a Sunday, is there?
It doesn't matter whether TV has been invented
or not, everybody knows that.

And so I was bored. Very bored.
Or I would have been had I been created,
which I hadn't been at that point,
because, like I say, there was this great big nothingness,
a vast, sprawling mass of infinite absence,
a bit like Great Yarmouth out of season,
but without the inflatable dolphins.

Anyhow, you get the picture, there wasn't much going on,
when all of a sudden – from out of nowhere, I suppose –
there was this great big, gigantic BANG!
Ever so noisy it was, especially after all that silence.

Then, before you know it, there were galaxies and stars
and planets and microbes and water and fish
and dinosaurs and chickens and evolution
and wheels and pyramids and *Deal or No Deal*,
all created in seven days – or fourteen billion years,
depending on how you look at it.

I see it as a good thing, generally.
I always try to see the positive. It's nice to be busy,
and there's certainly a lot more to do these days
than there was before the bang.
Like I say, it had been quite boring back then
and really not much of a life at all,
had life existed, that is.

24th October

....

Mount Vesuvius erupted on this day in 79 CE and the cities of Pompeii
and Herculaneum were buried beneath its pyroclastic surges and
ashfall deposits. According to Pliny the Younger, the date of its eruption
was on 24th August, but recently historians have found evidence it
happened in October, which suits me as I'd already written a poem
about the downgrading of the planet Pluto for that earlier date.
Anyway, here's an extract from a contemporaneous song about the
disaster, popularised by the legendary first-century disco diva, Gloria
Gaynorius.

I Still Survive

At first I was afraid, then I was petrified
From hot volcanic ash flowing down the mountainside
And this great old town of mine got caught completely off its guard
And things got charred
And we became a huge graveyard

But now we're back
From long ago
With plaster poured into our forms
You can see our final throes
I should have changed that stupid look
Comprising fear and agony
If I'd known for just one second
It would last eternity

But no, oh no,
I walked out the door
I heard a sound
And I was like this ever more
Without time to find my love and say goodbye
As our whole world crumbled
As Pompeii laid down to die
Yet somehow, I – I still survive
Oh, as long as I'm preserved like this, it's a way to be alive
I had all my life to live
It drained like water from a sieve
Yet I survive
I still survive, hey, hey

25th October

....

Today is World Pasta Day, which is the kind of celebration day you didn't know existed but are glad to discover does. According to some food historians, people have been cooking pasta – presumably in the wrong quantities – since at least 5000 BCE. It has also been claimed that Marco Polo was the first person to bring pasta to Italy, having picked some up while travelling around thirteenth-century China, but it is now thought that seems as likely as stories which suggest that a Mr Marco Pasta introduced Italians to the Polo mint.

Remembrance of Things Pasta

She blew her fusilli,
my pretty penne,
when she found me watching
daytime tagliatelle.

Je ne spaghetti rien,
I responded in song,
but she did not linguini
for long,

just walked out
without further retort:
a hard lesson to be tortellini,
orzo I thought.

And so here I am,
all on my macaroni,
and now my days
feel cannelloni.

26th October

On this day in 899, Alfred, the king so great they named him 'Great', died. He got up to a few things: defeated the Vikings; united the different kingdoms of England; re-established the city of London; built and expanded the roads; strengthened the country's defences; established the first national navy; introduced new codes of law; encouraged the translation of Latin texts into English. But he is most famous for having once burnt some cakes, and that is typical of how this country will build someone up only to knock them down later.

The Great Briton Bake Off

Thank you, Emmeline.
Your gluten-free chocolate orange Battenberg
certainly gets my vote!

And now on to Alfred,
and his three-tier raspberry, thyme
and roasted rhubarb cake.

It certainly *looks* spectacular.
The way you've stuck those cream horns
on top and then splattered

raspberry sauce everywhere
really does help to give it the appearance
of a severed Viking head.

But how does it taste? . . .
It's an interesting choice of flavours . . .
that rhubarb is just right

and your buttercream is perfect . . .
but you know what I'm going to say, don't you?
No, it's more than just a bit overdone.

It's like your technical last week,
not so much lemon drizzle as lemon *sizzle*.
Same goes for your charcoaled brownies

and tiramisu bombe with pistachio
incineration. You can count yourself lucky
to still be in the contest.

Focus, Alfred. It's all about focus.
And set your timer. Right, time for Isambard
and his mango and pineapple

upside-down suspension-bridge cake.
Well, would you just look at that?
What a feat of engineering!

27th October

....

While all cats are said to have nine lives, black cats – for some reason – also get two celebration days: Black Cat Appreciation Day on 17th August and National Black Cat Day, which takes place today. These days serve as an opportunity for humankind to more fully appreciate these monochrome moggies and their enduring place in our culture, on our laps and sofas, and on the ends of our witches' broomsticks.

Paws for Thought

I'd never given much thought
as to why black cats
are considered unlucky

until that terrible day
when one crossed my path
and it suddenly struck me.

28th October

....

Jonathan's Swift classic book Gulliver's Travels *was published on this day in 1726. It was an instant bestseller and hasn't been out of print since. With its narrator traversing landscapes filled with tiny and giant people, flying islands and talking horses, it reads like a road book written by one of the druggier members of the Beat Generation; but at heart, it's a satire ridiculing eighteenth-century political and social*

life. The book was published anonymously at first, presented as an
authentic travel book, with Swift even keeping his identity as its author
a secret from his publisher.

Sail away from it all . . . on a Gulliver's Travel Cruise!

Are you tired of the same old, same old?
Would you like to expand your horizons?
Discover new worlds? Meet new people?
Then why not choose a Gulliver's Travel cruise!

Our cruises are designed for those who delight
in the thrill of exploration and adventure
while indulging mind and body
in the most satirical surroundings available.

First stop, why not try Lilliput for size –
that magical island where the little things matter!
Take in the sights with just a few short strides.
Who da big man now? Why, it's you!

Next, we sail on to Brobdingnag,*
always an enormous hit with our guests.
Watch out for the giant wasps, and don't worry
if the locals talk down to you – that's just their way!

---

* *A porter service is available should you wish*
  to purchase a small knick-knack from the island.
  And avoid the unlicensed sellers in the harbour –
  you'll be in the palm of their hands in no time.

And then, after a flying visit to Laputa,
we head to Balnibarbi, where you can still see
its inhabitants practising the ancient art
of extracting sunbeams from cucumbers,

and thence, the enchanting isle of Glubbdubdrib.
If you'd like to speak to any of the ghosts,
do book early to avoid disappointment:
Julius Caesar, Homer, and Aristotle, all available.

Finally, no cruise would be complete without a trip
to the Land of the Houyhnhnms. They may have long faces
but these civilised neigh-bours are enough to cheer anyone up!
Just remember to steer clear of the savages. Yahoo!

29th October

....

*The last stretch of the M25 opened on this day in 1986, thus
completing one of the most hellish highways known to humankind.
The motorway was built to encircle Greater London and the
final thirteen-mile section between Micklefield Green and South
Mimms was finished eleven years after the project started; which is
approximately the time it takes to drive from Micklefield Green to
South Mimms on the M25. Although I don't drive myself, I've spent
more than two years of my life sitting in a passenger seat on the M25,
providing tea, sandwiches, counselling, and general succour to a series
of despondent drivers.*

My New Jam

inching . . . along . . .
the . . . M25. . . ,
not . . . quite . . . dead . . . ,
yet . . . not . . . quite . . . alive . . .

in . . . Schrödinger's . . . car . . .
(a Honda . . . Civic . . . automatic . . .),
life . . . at . . . a . . . standstill . . . ,
from . . . the . . .
sheer . . .
. . .
wait . . .
. . .
of . . .
. . .
. . .
traffic . . .

30th October

....

It was on this day in 1938 that a radio drama version of H. G. Wells' The War of the Worlds was broadcast, allegedly resulting in widespread panic as people across America believed their country to be under attack from Martians. The drama was directed and narrated by Orson Welles, who interrupted what was apparently a typical evening of broadcasting with bulletins reporting on the alien invasion. Although the reaction to the programme has been exaggerated, there were plenty who did fall for it. Strange then, that in 2016 when the American public was greeted by a malevolent alien with strangely lustrous orange skin, nearly sixty-three million people voted for it.

News Flash

An early morning radio interview
with the Minister for Housing,
Communities and Local Government
is interrupted with news
of an alien invasion.

There are reports of spaceships
landing all over the country.
The aliens are believed to have mastered
mind control, and there have been
a number of – as yet unconfirmed –
abductions and zappings.

Thank God for that, I think,
relieved to finish my cornflakes in peace
without having to hear
yet more excuses from the Government
concerning its failure to tackle
the current housing crisis.

A pair of green antennae
are poking out from behind my peonies.
I pop my bowl in the dishwasher,
grab my cricket bat,
and head out into the garden.

31st October

It's Halloween, that terrifying day of the year when I worry that the chocolates I've bought for visiting trick-or-treaters will all be gone in twenty minutes thanks to a group of marauding teenagers, and that I shall then open the door to a small child dressed as baby Yoda, with her eyes wide with hope and a bag held out in expectation, as she plucks up the courage to say, 'Trick or treat?', and I will explain to her about what happened to the big box of Celebrations I bought earlier (also remembering that I was responsible myself for the disappearance from it of four Twix miniatures and six Maltesers Teasers), and my words will break her forever. The horror! The horror!

The Heebie Bee Gees

He danced
like a man possessed
one fevered Saturday night.

He gave me
the Heebie Bee Gees
and so I left the floor in fright.

Some blamed it
on the Boogieman
but it was a John Travoltageist.

November

1st November

The ceiling of the Sistine Chapel in Rome, one of Michelangelo's most famous works, was exhibited to the public for the first time on this day in 1512. The ceiling depicts the twelve apostles along with nine stories from Genesis, several Old Testament prophets, and many decorative figures. The four-year project took its toll on Michelangelo. In a poem, he writes how he has 'grown a goitre from this torture, hunched up here like a cat in Lombardy' and declares his painting is 'dead', a sentiment echoed in the 1965 Righteous Brothers' song about his experience.

You've Lost Your Love of Ceilings

You have to close your eyes when you're lying in your bed
And there's no tenderness when you look up above your head
You worked so hard to paint it *(baby)*
But baby, I know you hate it

You've lost your love of ceilings
Whoa, your love of ceilings
You've lost your love of ceilings
Now it's gone, gone, gone, whoa-oh

Your hair's all streaked with paint and there's stiffness in your neck
How your body aches – some might say, you're a total wreck
Now you've stopped painting frescos *(baby)*
And baby, you're working for Tesco's

You've lost your love of ceilings
Whoa, your love of ceilings
You've lost your love of ceilings
Now it's gone, gone, gone, whoa-oh

Baby, baby, I'd get up that ladder for you
Paint scenes from the Testaments – yeah, both the Old and New
Lend me a brush, a brush, a brush, I'm gonna stay all day
Or let me roller, roller, roller your blues away

Baby *(baby)*, baby *(baby)*
I beg you please *(please)*, please *(please)*
I need your brush *(need your brush)*
I need your brush *(need your brush)*
Just bring some lunch *(bring some lunch)*
Yes, a meal deal's fine *(a meal deal's fine)*

Bring back your love of ceilings
Whoa, your love of ceilings
Bring back your love of ceilings
Cause it's gone, gone, gone,
I've drawn this angel wrong, whoa.

2nd November

....

Channel 4 began broadcasting on this day in 1982. And I should
know, I was there. Not at Channel 4, that is. I'd only have been
twelve. But at home, watching it, I mean. The first programme on
the new channel was Countdown, *a game show involving words*

and numbers. It has since become one of the longest-running game shows in the world. Ever since I first heard its stress-inducing theme music and witnessed its geeky celebration of words and anagrams and conundrums, I've harboured secret ambitions to go on it. But then again, the recurrent nightmare from which I suffer indicates that this may not be a good idea.

Recurring *Countdown* Nightmare

I ask Rachel for nine consonants.
With Brenda only one win away
from octochamp status, my best chance
is to try and stifle her natural logodaedaly,
then fluke it on the conundrum.

I offer no score. 'Eight,' declares Brenda,
making eyes at Nick as she has been
all morning. 'BRZDDFSH,' she says.
In Dictionary Corner, Susie Dent confirms
it's a type of Ugandan fishing net.

Brenda goes on the offensive
in the next round, plumping for nine vowels.
The *Countdown* clock whirls by.
My one-letter 'A' is greeted with
embarrassed silence around the studio.

'EAAOOIOU,' pouts Brenda, as she
leans across to Nick to show him the word
written in red lipstick on her paper.

'An ancient Macedonian war cry,'
says Susie Dent, smiling in ratification.

On to the numbers. Rachel fishes out
six ones and presses the button:
a target of 927. I get as far as nine,
just 918 away. '927,' Brenda announces.
She has only used three of the ones.

Over in Dictionary Corner, John Inverdale
embarks upon a lengthy anecdote
concerning Belgian tennis star Kim Clijsters.
Nick and Brenda use the opportunity
to go for a quick 'teatime teaser'

behind the *Countdown* clock,
while Rachel reshuffles the letters
and Susie Dent finishes her burger.
I sit there, trying to get my head together.
There are 362 rounds left to go.

3rd November

....

Today is World Sandwich Day, a celebration of the ultimate in
convenience food. It commemorates John Montagu, fourth Earl of
Sandwich and eighteenth-century inventor of the eponymously named
bread-wrapped fare. The story goes that Montagu was playing cribbage
and, anxious not to get grease on his cards, asked for his meat to be

tucked into two slices of bread, easy on the mayo. For two hundred
years, the sandwich was to be largely unchanged until the advent of
the double triple-decker sardine and marshmallow fudge sandwich,
pioneered by Shaggy Rogers and his friend Scooby-Doo.

Crooning in the Kitchen on a Tuesday Lunchtime

Baguettes, I've had a few
but then again, too few to munch on.
I bit what I had to chew,
I saw it through – it was my luncheon.

I planned each slice of cheese,
Each chargrilled veg along the byway,
with some coleslaw and crisps,
I made it my way.

4th November

....

While the writing of a book such as this may seem effortless to the
reader, it may surprise you to learn that I've had to do quite a lot of
looking up (more formally known as 'research'): what happened when;
where did such and such a thing happen; who did what to whom, and
why; and so forth. How refreshing it is, then, to reach a familiar date,
one whose significance is firmly embedded in my mind without need to
go reaching for the reference books, and all thanks to a simple rhyme
which has stayed with me since childhood.

Remember, Remember

Remember, remember
the Fourth of November
soap powder, treacle, and plot.
He walked in a puddle –
I've got in a muddle . . .
hey diddle, dickory dock.

Remember, remember,
the Twelfth of November,
it had ten thousand men.
And Little Boy Blue
has moved into a shoe . . .
No, I've got it wrong again.

Remember, remember,
the Third of September,
how does your garden grow?
With puppy dogs' tails
and sugar-spiced snails . . .
No, no, no, no, no.

It's the Fifth of October,
must try and stay sober,
little miss pudding and pie.
A-tisket, atishoo,
my memory's an issue,
oh, what a dull boy am I.

5th November

So it appears that the Gunpowder Plot is also celebrated on this day. *Allegedly, it was on 5th November 1605 when Guy Fawkes, the most famous member of the Gunpowder Plot Gang, was discovered with a cellar-load of explosives beneath the House of Lords, a somewhat embarrassing situation which no amount of smooth-talking was able to get him out of. Thus began an annual celebration of anti-Popish sentiment, involving giant bonfires, spectacular fireworks, terrified pets, and some very worried hedgehogs.*

Remember, Remember (again)

remember the fireworks
when we first met?

how the skies would explode,
sparkle and sizzle?

but often these days, it's more
a damp squib –

a few sparks, the odd bang,
and some fizzle

6th November

There are few dates which signpost this nation's moral and spiritual decline more than this day in 1942, when the Church of England relaxed the rule regarding the wearing of hats by women in church. Until this time, for a woman to be seen in church, some kind of head covering was nigh-on compulsory in order to indicate her submission to God and his authority. It's all there in Corinthians, if you need clarification on the matter, along with how disgraceful it is for men to have long hair, although that may just be in regard to mullets.

From *The Book of Vidal*, 6: 11–17

11   And so it came to pass that a wandering hair stylist by the name of Vidal, from the tribe of Sassoon, did chance to visit upon the ancient town of Tewkesbury, and there observed the women at their worship, with not one head uncovered but bedecked with an assortment of hats, after the plain fashion, as was the custom of those times.

12   At worship's end, the young man enquired of one such woman, 'Why dost thou cover thy head like this when thou hast such fabulous hair?' and with that, Vidal cast off the woman's hat, declaring: 'I couldst do great things with hair like this. Come and see me next Tuesday for a cut and blow dry.'

13   And so it was, that when the people were next about their worshipping, the woman did enter the temple with head

uncovered and the women cried, 'Sandra!' – for that was her name – 'Thy head is naked. Thy wantonness bringeth shame upon thyself and the good people of Tewkesbury.'

14 But at this, Sandra tossed her vibrant, golden locks, and a great stillness fell over the women until one of their number, who went by the name of Gwyneth (although she never did quite care for it), exclaimed: 'But what fabulous hair she has, it must surely be a sin to keep it covered.'

15 There came a nodding of heads, covered as they were, and the opinion grew that hair such as Sandra's was proof itself of the glory of God and that, frankly, if Sandra could now look that great, then so could anyone.

16 And with that there came a general casting off of the hats, followed by a general trampling upon them.

17 And so it was that Vidal was to open a salon in Tewkesbury, offering a range of personalised cuts (including consultation, shampoo massage, conditioner, and finish), even for the men worshippers who had hitherto remained uncharacteristically silent regarding the women and the casting off of the hats, but who had, by now, begun to feel stylistically stifled by the limitations of their regular barber, Dennis, from the tribe of Crabtree.

7th November

It was on this day in 2020 that, after several days of painstaking vote-counting, the Democrat leader Joe Biden was declared the winner of the election to become President of the United States. In spite of this – and the seemingly overwhelming evidence to the contrary (which mainly took the form of Biden having more votes), his opposite number in the Republican Party, Donald Trump, refused to admit defeat. Indeed, he was still denying it as he left office in January, having first incited some of his supporters to riot in the Capitol. If only there had been a sign during Trump's presidency that he was the kind of guy who would literally do anything to cling onto power even if it meant undermining the democratic process.

Stories from Another Country

There are rumours that buried deep in the sands
of the Mojave Desert are fifty giant strongboxes,
each filled with a million Republican votes,

while in Wisconsin, at Milwaukee County Courthouse,
a group of left-leaning groundhogs, dressed as county officials,
gnawed through any ballot they didn't much care for.

It is also claimed that in the state of Georgia,
nine out of ten votes counted were submitted by one man,
a Mr Joel E. Binden of Pine Grove Drive, Lawrenceville,

and that in Sugarcreek, Pennsylvania, an outbreak
of collective hysteria, triggered by some unholy contamination
in the water, resulted in many ballots wrongly cast

for the Democrats. Meanwhile, in Washington DC,
reports have been emerging of a monstrous creature,
orange-skinned and bigly-girthed, a sagging couch

with corn-husk hair and a mouth like a sphincter muscle,
howling into the night, pounding the floor with its tiny fists,
clawing the walls as it gets dragged from its lair.

8th November

....

*The Bodleian Library (commonly known as 'the Bod'), the main
research library of the University of Oxford, opened on this day in
1602. As well as being one of Europe's oldest libraries, it's also one of
the biggest, with more than thirteen million printed items. Amongst its
collection, you can find a twelfth-century manuscript of* The Song of
Roland, *a bunch of Magna Cartas, a Gutenberg Bible, Shakespeare's
First Folios, and a first edition of Naomi Campbell's novel* Swan.
*Somewhat sensibly, given that I live nearby, it doesn't allow its books
out on loan.*

Loan Wolf

My list of crimes is long and various,
a foul litany of acts nefarious –
trespass, arson, fraud, high treason,
eating strawberries out of season –
but none of these compare to you:
library book, twelve years overdue.

Villainous me, steeped in archness!
O roguish knave! Prince of Darkness!
Believe me, please – I meant no wrong,
I did not plan to keep you long.
After all, what use have I
for *The Untold Story of McFly*?

Somehow you missed my weekly trawl
through the bookcase in the hall,
and by the time I noticed you,
you were thirteen weeks overdue.
The punishment for such a crime:
the payment of a hefty fine,

which, with each passing week, I let
grow larger than the national debt
but more than that, there grew inside
a deep guilt towards all those deprived
of the insightful, unflinching, wry,
inside story of McFly.

Amnesties are now far too late:
the shame runs deep; I bear its weight.
I shall not return to the library.
But when it's time to bury me,
come lie beside me, in the loam,
library book on eternal loan.

9th November

The Berlin Wall, that concrete, ideological barrier which had come to symbolise the Cold War, fell on this day in 1989, signalling the beginning of the fall of communism in Eastern and Central Europe. The Wall had been erected in 1961 to stop the access of East Germans to West Germany and was fifteen feet high, topped with barbed wire, and guarded with watchtowers and gun emplacements. But by the late 1980s, communism was crumbling and after half a million people gathered in protest in East Berlin, the orders came through to open the gates. Scenes of joyful East and West Germans embracing each other were beamed around the world.

The Wall

In the rubble and the mess,
East and West met,

winter-coated in brick dust,
wary, at first, of cuts

from shreds of barbed wire.
Reaching across, they smiled,

at such freedom of movement,
united in one moment.

And afterwards, they talked,
both thinking of the wall,

wondering what it had stood for,
why it had been built at all.

10th November

....

The Welsh-American journalist Henry Morton Stanley greeted David Livingstone on the shore of Lake Tanganyika, with the legendary line 'Dr Livingstone, I presume?' on this day in 1871. Stanley had been commissioned by the New York Herald to find the Scottish missionary and explorer; Livingstone had set off in 1865 to find the source of the Nile but after six years and no communication from him, many presumed him to be dead. It took Stanley eight months to track him down, and the story of his search for Livingstone was to make him famous. Later, Stanley's reputation was to become tarnished through his role in helping the Belgians to establish the Congo Free State, as the brutality of Leopold II's regime of forced labour and exploitation became known.

Directions

Nah, mate. You presume wrong.
Albert Greenslade . . . No worries, I get it all the time . . .
You're right, there *is* a resemblance, can't deny it,
I think it's the moustache . . . I'd like to shave
the stupid thing off but Nora, that's my missus,
a fine woman but not to be trifled with,
thinks it makes me look distinguished,
and who am I to disagree with her!

Ujiji? Nah, mate, this is Ilfracombe . . .
What you need is the next coach to Plymouth
then you can hop on a paddle steamer from there.

There's one to Freetown every four weeks,
or you could give that new Suez Canal a whizz.
Might be best to assemble a couple of hundred men
in Bagamoyo, divide them into five caravans
then head west towards Lake Tanganyika . . .

there's swampland and jungle to contend with,
and you'll need to watch out for crocodiles
and tsetse flies and tribal rivalries and dysentery
and smallpox and malaria, but I reckon
if you get the 15.40 to Plymouth, you'll be in Ujiji
by November . . . And don't forget to get a return!
We'd love to have you over for dinner,
Nora does a lovely apple crumble.

11th November

....

Remembrance Day is held each year on 11th November to remember
those members of the armed forces who have lost their lives in the line
of duty. It is observed on this date to recall the end of hostilities in
the First World War, in which more than nine million soldiers died.
The armistice came into effect 'at the 11th hour of the 11th day of the
11th month': a one-minute silence is held at this time. Remembrance
Sunday is held on the second Sunday in November and commemorates
the contribution of all British and Commonwealth military and
civilian servicemen and women.

WE DEEPLY REGRET TO INFORM YOU

TELEGRAMS IN THEIR THOUSANDS
THE HEARTS OF LOVED ONES SINK
ALL THAT WASTED PAPER
ALL THAT WASTED INK STOP

PLEASE STOP

12th November

....

*On this day in 1035, King Canute – or, more riskily, Cnut – died.
He became very much an expert of ruling places – and (at the time of
writing) holds the record of being the only man to be King of England,
Denmark, and Norway. He also did a bit of ruling in part of Sweden
for good measure. Nowadays he's known largely for the story about
him ordering the sea to go back, in which he is often misrepresented
as trying to command it. The original account of the tale, though,
describes Canute using the sea to demonstrate that a king has no
power compared to the supreme power of God; an interpretation I have
decided to ignore.*

Not Reigning but Drowning

I command you, sea, to come no further.
I am a king of fine repute.
I rule the waves and my name is Canute.

I forbid you, sea, from coming closer.
My authority is absolute.
I rule the waves and my name is Canute.

I'm telling you, sea, you're asking for it.
Do not lap against my boot.
I rule the waves and my name is Canute.

Listen, sea, are you deaf or something?
It's time for you to recompute.
I rule the waves and my name is Canute.

Right. That's it, sea. You've gone too far.
Does anyone know if there's a plug?
The waves rule me and my name is gurgle . . . gurgle . . . glug.

13th November

World Kindness Day, which happens annually on this day, is aimed at inspiring and encouraging people to show greater kindness for a fairer and better world. And it's hard to argue against that – except to say that it is possible to be kind on all the other days, too. Oh, by the way, have I mentioned how great you're looking today? And that colour really suits you. Incidentally, I'm popping to the shop in a few minutes so if there's anything I can pick up for you, just let me know.

Kindness

To recap what we now know: it did not begin
in a laboratory in Wuhan, nor with a pangolin or bat,
but it already lay dormant within us, like a seed
waiting for the right conditions to thrive;

the symptoms of kindness are many and various,
and may include some or all of the following:
tear drops, sudden laughter, a feeling of warmth,
and a peculiar uplifting of the heart;

it leaves its traces everywhere: from boxes
left on doorsteps to conversations over fences;
it can be transmitted over vast distances,
through a phone call, or from a smile across a street,

or a certain softness of tone spoken beside
a hospital bed; it affects young and old equally;
there is no race or gender immune from it;
it has the power to topple corrupt governments;

if one person were to pass it on to just three others
and they, in turn, were to pass it on to three more,
in no time at all, the world would be full of it,
and where, might we ask ourselves, would we be then.

14th November

....

*While Billboard in the US had compiled a weekly music chart based
on record sales since 1940, no such list existed in the UK until this
day in 1952 when the NME published the first-ever singles chart. Top
of the pile in its inaugural week was Al Martino, with his croon-some
'Here In My Heart'. Growing up, the chart run-down was a weekly
highlight for me, and nothing seemed more important than whether
Kajagoogoo would retain the number one spot. Until I was a teenager,
that is, when my music tastes developed into something far too cool
and eclectic for the charts. I date my fondness for Polynesian lounge
and funk back to this time.*

Singles Chart

Here I am, back in the charts –
I'm on my own again,
with 'Breaking Up is Hard to Do'
straight in at number ten.

Up five places to number nine
moves 'Tangled Up in Blue'.
At eight comes last week's number one,
'Nothing Compares 2 U'.

At seven, I'm feeling 'All Shook Up'.
'Ain't No Sunshine' is up to six.
A re-entry for 'Crying' at number five
(Thomas Hardy disco mix).

'How Can You Mend a Broken Heart?'
is up nine to number four.
Another new entry at number three –
'Love Don't Live Here Anymore'.

'Without You' stays at number two,
which means a brand-new number one . . .
It's me with another solo hit,
'Where Have All the Good Times Gone'.

15th November

....

*The UK's first colour TV ad made its appearance on this day in 1969.
It was for Birds Eye peas, featured a questionable tagline (particularly
when viewed from a post-Operation Yewtree perspective), and
appeared in the ad break during* Thunderbirds *on ATV. Is any of this
intrinsically interesting or significant? Possibly not. But I'm using it
as a springboard for what I think is one of the most important poems
in this book. I'd be very grateful if you could think hard about its
messages and share it widely.*

A Short Commercial Break

Advertising has become so commercialised.
You can't do anything these days
without somebody trying to sell you something.
Not even poetry is safe.

It's a point I make quite brilliantly
in my first collection, *You Took the Last Bus Home*
(RRP £8.99), available in bookshops now,
and which makes the ideal gift
for someone you don't really like very much.

Only when I head for the mountains,
do I feel respite from capitalism and its voracious maws.
No avalanche of ads can reach me there.
Instead, a stillness surrounds me
as the snow melts slowly in the pale winter sun,
in much the same way as my follow-up collection,
Alexa, what is there to know about love?,
has been said to unfreeze the heart, making it
the perfect present for Valentine lovers everywhere.

But who doesn't need to block out the world sometimes?
Counting numbers can be a good approach.
Once I reached as far as 9,781,529,005,561 –
a number which, coincidentally, also happens to be
the ISBN of my Costa-shortlisted novel, *Diary of a Somebody*,
and for which I can do you a cracking deal
if you're up for it, because it's a few years old now
and I've got a pile of spare copies
knocking around in my shed.

16th November

*The Russian writer Fyodor Dostoevsky was sentenced to death on
this day in 1849 for anti-government activities linked to a radical
intellectual group. The following month, Dostoevsky was led before
the firing squad but received a last-minute reprieve and was sent to
a Siberian labour camp, where he worked for four years before his
release. After that, he didn't get up to much, apart from writing* Notes
from Underground, Crime and Punishment, The Idiot, Demons,
and The Brothers Karamazov, *which is better than nothing, I suppose.*

Unfinished Poem

Any last requests?
the captain asks.

I would like to finish writing this poem,
the poet responds.

And will it take long?
the captain asks.

It will with all those guns pointing at me,
the poet says.

The captain sighs.
He orders his soldiers to lower their guns.
They wait.
The sun beats down.

And how will you know when it's finished?
the captain asks, after a while.

The poet shrugs;
contemplates the Moon;
picks up his pen

17th November

....

Nicolas Appert, the 'father of canning', was born in France on this
day in 1749. During the French Revolutionary Wars, the French had
a big, smelly problem of how to store food so it didn't go off. After
fourteen years of experimentation, Appert was to solve it for them. He
began by putting food in jars, which were then corked and sealed with
wax before being wrapped in canvas and then boiled. Appert knew
that it worked, but had no idea why – it would be another fifty years
before his fellow countryman Louis Pasteur was able to explain the
relationship between microbes and food spoilage.

Dinner Party Conservation Starters

They say you should never meet your heroes
and so, it was with some apprehension
that I found myself sat next to Nicolas Appert
at a dinner party in Putney.

I'd long nurtured an interest in canning.
As a boy I would collect the Panini stickers each year –

opening a packet and encountering the gleam
of a shiny new Appert was always the highlight.

I expressed my surprise to the great man
that I should find him here. He explained how
he played squash with our host every Tuesday
and besides, he'd only come from Wandsworth,

but when I clarified that it was unusual
to sit next to a genius from the eighteenth century,
he tapped his nose and whispered, *Let's just say
I know a bit about self-preservation, too.*

I fear my excitement got the better of me.
I could feel him shrink back at my enthusiasm
for his revolutionary bottle-sealing techniques.
When I praised him for his 'can-do attitude',

he offered me the weak smile of someone
who has heard the same joke many times before.
But, by that stage, I was completely pickled
and his attempts to move the conversation on

to football, summer holidays, or the weather,
I brushed aside as I quoted lengthy passages
from his seminal book, *The Art of Preserving*,
and grilled him about his views on Tupperware.

It was after I knocked over the second bottle of wine
that the great man leant over and, in quiet tones,
suggested I might want to think about going home,
if I wasn't able to contain myself, that is.

18th November

It was on this day in 1307 that the legendary Swiss marksman and crossbow hero, William Tell, shot a bolt through an apple, which just happened to be resting on his son Walter's head. The apple in question had been placed there by Albrecht Gessler, the grudge-holding feudal lord of Altdorf, who planned to execute them both unless Tell Snr. could perform such a feat. Which he did, as I mentioned in the first sentence. Further shenanigans followed, involving dungeons, boats, chases, rebellions, and a stirring overture.

Tell Tale Signs

I could try and shoot an apple off your head
but we both know that wouldn't end well.
What chance have I of hitting one from twenty paces,
when I can't even manage to haul this kart
more than twice around Wario's Gold Mine
without falling into a ravine?
You must have seen me die a hundred times
while you go hurtling by.

Instead, I shall save you with a thousand worries a day.
I shall remind you about sun cream and bike lights,
curfews and consequences, and how you should
never talk to strangers on the internet.
I shall issue warnings of drugs and Lyme disease,
and the not always honourable intentions of boys.

I will make up tales about silly girls
who drink nothing but energy drinks,
and frighten passers-by when they smile at them.

And you, who have no need of saving,
will come to resent such dull rules and reminders,
or be bored by them, or learn how best to ignore them –
unaware each one is a bolt of love,
fired inexpertly by clumsy hands,
yet somehow unerring and true.

19th November

Today – as you were forewarned on 8th March – is International Men's Day. But isn't every day International Men's Day, you might well wonder? And while there is truth in that, this is a day to celebrate positive male role models and promote equality across genders. The day also helps to encourage debate and awareness about some of the challenges which men face – such as how to respond to the continued presence of toxic masculinity in our culture, and the stigma which many men continue to feel towards talking about their feelings and mental health.

Bear Wrestling

I can't remember whose idea it was
to call it off and go for that drink, but it certainly
didn't go down well with the crowd.

Don't worry about it, the bear said,
as we sipped on our white wine spritzers,
there are worse maulings to receive.

Once you got past his pointed teeth
and sharp claws, I saw a softer side to the bear
than I ever thought possible.

I asked how he'd gotten into bear wrestling.
Forced into it from an early age,
he said. Didn't think he had a choice.

That's how it had felt for me, too,
I told him, surprised to give voice to the thought.
But look, said the bear, here we are.

Yes, here we are, I answered,
rising up, as if having somehow slipped free
of some brutish grip which held me.

20th November

Today is World Children's Day, an annual day of action for children, by children, organised by UNICEF. It focuses on promoting international togetherness amongst children worldwide and improving children's welfare. And rightly so – children are the best, and generally far preferable to adults. How much better might the world be if we could carry with us into adulthood all the remarkable things about childhood (hope, wonder, imagination, etc.) without any of its more problematic aspects (maths, fixed bedtimes, being made to eat broccoli, etc.).

A Selection of Inspirational Quotes in Praise of Children

I believe the children are our future
and also, the perfect excuse
to escape from the company of adults
who talk at length about their recent kitchen extensions
and cycling holidays in Andalucía,
by saying I really should go and supervise them
on the swings for a while.

I believe the greatest gift I can give to my children
is my time, my love, and my attention,
but I also believe that sometimes
even that may not be enough,
and what they really need is pizza.

I believe children are the hands by which we take hold of heaven
or its earthly equivalent,
a wet afternoon in a darkened cinema,
in which we sit and watch
a resourceful young ant outwit
a gang of mean and thuggish grasshoppers,
with nothing between us but a large tub of popcorn.

I believe every child is born a genius,
with the possible exception of that one over there,
the one currently attempting
to flush a potato down a toilet.

I believe the soul is healed by being with children
and then – once they're in bed –
by being with wine, plenty of wine.

21st November

....

World Philosophy Day was first celebrated on this day in 2002 and
takes place on the third Thursday of November each year. Whether
you'll actually end up reading this poem on World Philosophy Day or
not therefore depends on the organisation of time itself, which is an
abstraction worth considering in depth – particularly if you subscribe
to J. M. E. McTaggart's argument that there is in fact no such thing as
time, and that any temporal order is mere appearance. If nothing else,
it provides a decent excuse should you miss a work deadline or arrive
late to pick up your child after school.

Nihilism Means Nothing to Me

Hegel, when you left me,
you put me through the mill.
I kant think clearly anymore:
your marx are on me still.

The hobbestacles are everywhere.
Unlocke your door and be my guide.
Life is dull when you're not arendt,
I nietzsche by my side.

You said I bourdieu senseless.
You said I drove you nuts.
But I adorno other,
you make my head spinoza much.

The rawls of love I just don't get;
I don't know where to sartre.
I plato win but always lose.
Please come back. Exhume my heartre.

22nd November

....

*Where were you when you heard Aldous Huxley and C. S. Lewis had
died? You might have been listening to a news programme about the
assassination of John F. Kennedy during a presidential motorcade in
Dallas, Texas, which also happened on this day in 1963. Conspiracy*

461

theories abound concerning Kennedy's death, some of which centre
on the significance of the 'grassy knoll' inside Dealey Plaza, from
which some witnesses believe shots to have been fired. The term 'grassy
knoll' has itself become an expression used to signify any conspiracy or
cover-up.

Reflections of a Knoll

Looking back, I suppose 1963 *was* the turning point.
There was a sandy knoll who had a brief period of stardom
in one of the early Tarzan films but generally,
we weren't on anybody's radar. And when we were,
it was never particularly complimentary: hillocks,
people would call us. Good-for-nothing mounds.

But the shooting changed all that. Suddenly, knolls
were everywhere. The media couldn't get enough of us.
The Washington Post. Rolling Stone. On the front cover
of *Time* magazine, posing with a Beatle. Towns began
to celebrate their knolls, and not just the grassy ones –
the rocky ones, too. The blind ones. We'd be decorated

with floral messages of civic welcome, garlanded
with tulips, daffodils, azaleas, chrysanthemums.
The picnics! The municipal fetes! The mayoral speeches!
It couldn't last, of course. Even at the time, I think
we knew that. The verdant meadows and rippling cornfields
were never going to take it lying down for long.

'A LITTLE KNOLL IS A DANGEROUS THING' came
the headlines, as stories linking us to rocky outcrops
and other undesirables circulated. Then came Drumlingate
and the people didn't want anything more to do with us.
But, you know, I'd do it all again tomorrow. Life is full
of ups and downs; ours have been gentler than some.

23rd November

Fibonacci Day, which occurs annually on this day, celebrates one of the most influential mathematical sequences – the Fibonacci sequence – in which each number is the sum of the two which precede it. Fibonacci numbers are worth celebrating as many objects in nature grow in shapes driven by them, such as the spiral shells of snails. The day has its origins in the arrangements of the mm/dd format of the US calendar (11/23), and it seems to grow more in importance each year.

Word Crunching

I
wrote
a poem
on a page
but then each line grew
to the word sum of the previous two
until I began to worry about all these words coming with such frequency
because as you can see, it can be easy to run out of space when a poem gets all Fibonacci sequency

24th November

....

Charles Darwin published On the Origin of Species *on this day in 1857, widely regarded to be the founding text of evolutionary biology. It introduced the theory that populations evolve across generations through a process of natural selection. Most scientists quickly embraced his work but some Christians condemned it as heresy. Controversy over Darwin's ideas deepened with his* The Descent of Man *in 1871, in which he presented evidence of man's evolution from apes. Even now, there are those who would deny his findings, illustrating the more complex argument that evolution is not an orderly march from primitivism to a more advanced state.*

A Short Poem for Creationists

The only thing
which has not evolved –

and I don't mean
to be facetious –

is the argument
that you set forth,

*On the Origin
of the Specious.*

25th November

....

Today is International Day for the Elimination of Violence against Women. The statistics are shocking. One in three women will experience violence in her lifetime. In the UK, two women are killed by their partner every week in England and Wales, while the UK police receive a call about domestic abuse every minute, 89 per cent of which are about a woman being abused by a man. The day raises awareness of the levels of violence directed against women, while encouraging governments and organisations to do what they can to tackle this problem. It marks the start of sixteen Days of Activism that precede Human Rights Day on December 10th.

Some Simple Steps to Help Women Feel Safer

If it's dark and you're walking behind a woman,
even at a distance, cross over to the other side of the road,
always remembering not to attack her.

In such a situation, silence can be frightening.
Hold a phone conversation with a friend: this will help to reassure
you have no harmful intentions, as will not killing her.

Avoid staring at women or stalking them.
Similarly, violence, rape and murder are likely to cause offence
and should be discouraged at all times.

Be an active bystander. If you notice a woman
is uncomfortable with a man's behaviour, ask her if she is OK.
Resist the urge to smirk or egg him on.

Call out inappropriate behaviour amongst your friends.
Lead by example and refrain from assaulting, abusing
or killing women. Encourage your friends to do the same!

A group star chart is a great idea.

26th November

*The debut single 'Anarchy in the U.K.' by the punk rock band The
Sex Pistols was released on this day in 1976. It was both a voice and
symbol of working-class rage and frustration – and with the flaming
screech of its guitars and sneer of its singer John Lydon's vocals, it
made a triumphant accession into the hearts of disaffected teenagers
everywhere. The band themselves were shortly to be released from their
record label EMI following their sweary appearance on Bill Grundy's
television show* Today, *which only added to their notoriety and
popularity.*

Accountancy in the U.K.

I add up figures right
I am thorough and precise
The invoice I want, I know where to get it
I wanna destroy incorrect reporting
Cause I wanna see accuracy
(No duplications)

Accountancy in the U.K.
Needs standards in line so that we
Can limit the scope for personal judgement
My future dream is a new workstream
And I wanna see transparency
(In the City)

So many ways to get what you want
Excel, Access, and all the rest!
I love accountancy
I love to mountain ski
And I have a wheat allergy
(Don't give me pasta)

Is this the B.A.F.A.?
Or is this the C.P.A.A.?
Or is this the I.F.A.?
I thought it was the Institute for Chartered Accountants in
    England and Wales
Or just another association (why's there so many?)
I wanna be accountancy
And I wanna be accountancy (oh what a profession)
And I wanna be accredited
(such bliss, deep joy)

27th November

A licence was granted to William Shakespeare for his marriage to Anne Whateley on this day in 1582. The following day, another licence was issued, allowing him to marry Anne Hathaway. This has led to speculation in some corners (the kind of corners where speculators accumulate) as to whether Shakespeare had originally intended to marry someone else. Could Anne Whateley have been the 'dark lady' of his famous sonnets? Possibly, although scholars of a non-speculatory disposition simply regard the issuing of this first licence as a clerical error, and annoyingly they're probably right.

Marriage Vows for the Uncommitted

I pledge my undying love to you,
insofar as it's possible to guarantee anything these days,
because circumstances can change,
as you more than anyone should know,
and although you are the moorings to which my tugboat of love
    is tied,
ropes do get frayed after a time
and I've never been that great with knots.

I invite you to share my life (and that of my cockapoo, Wilbur),
and I promise to be kind, unselfish, and trustworthy,
or as much as I can be, given my well-documented character
    defects –
at the very least, let me reassure you
I will do better than Greg,

who I know could have been stood here with you today,
if it hadn't been for that incident in Pizza Express.

I promise to encourage and inspire you from time to time,
to laugh with you every now and then,
and to comfort you during a prescribed number of times of
    sorrow and struggle,
just as I did after your break-up with Greg.
I promise to love you in good times and when things aren't too
    busy at work,
not forgetting that Wednesday night
is five-a-side football night,
and I typically won't be back until about nine,
maybe eleven if we go to the pub afterwards.

I promise to cherish you nearly as much as I do Wilbur,
and always to hold you in quite high regard –
subject, that is, to appropriate terms and conditions.

These things I give to you today,
and all the days of our life together, free of charge.*

* Beyond certain expenses
to be agreed in advance by both parties
and invoiced on a quarterly basis.

28th November

....

The bestselling children's writer Enid Blyton died on this day in 1968. Her books, which included the Famous Five, Secret Seven, Noddy, and Malory Towers series, have sold more than six hundred million copies and are still widely read today. As a child, I read and loved many of her books. Now, though, there is much in them that makes me feel rather disquieted. It's not only that the stories seem somewhat quaint and old-fashioned; but that many of them carry clear overtones of racism, sexism, and xenophobia, not all of which can be airily dismissed as simply being 'of their time'.

The Final Famous Five Books

It was in the final few books of the series
when things began to go wrong
for the quintet of intrepid investigators.

The shocking, dramatic denouement
of *Five Go Hang-Gliding Together*
was to leave many young readers reeling,

a reaction which Blyton did little
to mitigate with her high-octane follow-up,
Four Attempt a Spot of Whitewater Rafting.

The next instalment was to see the series
take a darker, more politicised turn.
However, *Three Go to Guantanamo Bay*

was not the commercial success
her publisher had hoped for, and neither
was its bleak and harrowing successor,

Two Experiment with Crystal Meth,
in spite of the Ken Loach film adaptation.
It came as something of a surprise, then,

for Blyton to return to the gayer tone
of her earlier books with the final title in the series:
One is a Good Boy, a Really Good Boy.

29th November

....

*On this day in 1965, Mary Whitehouse began a Clean Up TV
campaign by setting up the National Viewers' and Listeners'
Association to tackle the problem of 'BBC bad taste and
irresponsibility'. An evangelical Christian and moral crusader,
Whitehouse attempted to stem the effluence-filled tide of the permissive
society, as evidenced on her television set, with its portrayals of sex and
violence, and all that bad language. The sitcom* Till Death Do Us Part
*and the plays of Dennis Potter came in for particular stick from the
NVLA; but their reactions weren't always negative, sending an award
to Jimmy Savile for the 'wholesome family entertainment' of
his show* Jim'll Fix It.

On Profanity

Rinse your mouth with soap and water
for using words you should not oughta.
You fill our children's minds with muck –
yet still you do not give a fig.

Such unbridled coprolalia
is a symbol of our moral failure.
Obscenity takes root, drops anchor –
do *not* call me a prudish . . . rancorous individual.

Free our airwaves from expletives.
Swear words need to be deleted.
They rot the mind. They cause affront.
They're an insult to this great country.

30th November

....

*The celebrated Irish poet and playwright Oscar Wilde died from
meningitis on this day in 1900, in a seedy, flea-bitten Parisian hotel.
He was as arch, funny and poignant in death as he was in life,
taking in his surroundings before pronouncing: 'My wallpaper and I
are fighting a duel to the death. One or the other of us has got to go.'
As last words go, these can hardly be beaten – although Karl Marx
was to adopt a different approach on his deathbed, shouting at his
housekeeper, 'Go on, get out! Last words are for fools who haven't
said enough.'*

Famous Last Words

Apologies for the long silence.
It's just that I've been rather busy of late,
working on my last words.

I'm planning something witty
but not too flash: a simple *bon mot*
to be recalled with fondness by family and friends,
as well as for possible inclusion
in *The Oxford Dictionary of Quotations*.

I would share them with you now
but then they wouldn't be my last words –
unless, in the course of writing them,
I'm suddenly attacked by a leopard,
which seems unlikely in East Finchley.

The problem is knowing when to use them.
Say them too early, you risk waking up later
to someone leaning in, offering tea.
As far as last words go, 'A splash of milk,
no sugar,' doesn't really cut it.

Or what if other last words get in the way:
'What truck?'; 'Yes, these *are* the right tablets!'
'What happens if I pull this lever?'
'Help! There's a leopard in the doorway!'
That last one, incidentally, I didn't make up.

Who would have thought the security
at East Finchley Zoo could be so lax?
I'd write a strongly worded letter of complaint
if he didn't happen to be eyeing me up
as if his room service club sandwich had arrived.

I think, perhaps, my time has come.
Apologies for the long silence.

December

1st December

I was going to write that today is the first day of Advent, the season observed by Christians as a time of waiting and preparation for Christmas. But now I've read that advent starts on the fourth Sunday before Christmas, which means that it can often begin in late November, thus bringing into question the whole notion of Advent calendars with twenty-four chocolates that begin on 1st December. This means there are years when this policy is depriving us of chocolates which are rightfully ours and the whole thing is an absolute scandal.

This Is Just To Say

I have eaten
the chocolates
that were in
your calendar

and which
you were probably
saving
for each day of advent

Forgive me
they were delicious
so bittersweet
and so Christmassy

2nd December

Today is the International Day for the Abolition of Slavery. Its focus is on eradicating more contemporary forms of slavery, such as sexual exploitation, trafficking in persons and child labour. It's been estimated that there are at least ten thousand people in Britain who have fallen victim to modern slavery. But perhaps we shouldn't be too surprised. William Wilberforce may have led the way to abolish the Atlantic slave trade but for centuries Britain was at the centre of it all, and as the pulling down of a statue of the slave trader Edward Colston in Bristol shows, the spectre of slavery is still very much amongst us.

Musical Statues (variation)

when the music stops,
find a statue
of a slave trader or tyrant
and topple it

cheer and dance
then move on to the next

the game ends
when all such statues
lie rusting and broken
at the bottom
of the ocean

3rd December

The first human heart transplant was carried out on this day in 1967 when Louis Washkansky, a fifty-four-year-old South African grocer, received the heart of Denise Darvall, who had been fatally injured in a car accident. The surgeon Christiaan Barnard performed the revolutionary operation. Around two hundred heart or heart-lung transplants are now carried out in the UK alone every year, and thousands of lives saved or improved by organ donation more generally. In another twist of fate, Wham! released their enduring festive classic 'Last Christmas' on this day in 1984.

Last Christmas (with organ accompaniment)

Last Christmas, I gave you my heart
and the very next day, I gave someone else
my pancreas and small intestine.

This year, I'll donate my cornea.
I'll give it to someone special
(special)

4th December

George Orwell sent the final manuscript of his new novel Nineteen Eighty-Four to his publisher Secker and Warburg on this day in 1947, at around half past thirteen o'clock. It was published seven months *later and, with its portrayal of totalitarianism and mass surveillance, propaganda and 'Newspeak', it was to become an instant classic. It's also relentlessly miserable, bleak and depressing – what's not to like?*

Reader's Report on 1st Draft of George Orwell's *1984*

If, as Mr Orwell purports, his latest work is intended to be darkly dystopian in nature, he needs to ditch the dancing girls: they cheapen the mood. The author needs to be clearer in his own mind for whom he is writing. The fact that Mr Orwell has also enclosed some lyrics for a few 'big show tunes' suggests that he has one eye on a film musical adaptation and that's not where I see this book at all.

The same goes for the big car chase in chapter six; while I appreciate it may represent 'good box office', it won't play well with Zamyatin and Huxley fans, which is very much where Grim Fic is at right now. And I don't mean to sound harsh but the revelation in chapter ten that O'Brien is a Wessex Saddleback comes across as rather silly, quite frankly. Mr Orwell has covered that ground rather thoroughly with his previous book and besides, the reader will have guessed that already given the amount of snuffling O'Brien does and that revolting scene in the Ministry canteen in chapter three.

A few more suggestions. Mr Orwell might want to reconsider the name of his main protagonist. Perhaps choose one that is less remarkable but remains unmistakably British. Horatio Spangle just isn't doing it for me. And neither is the scene in Room 105 where O'Brien tortures Spangle by playing on his fear of scat. It doesn't quite work. It needs to be something even more terrifying. Cats? Bats?

480

Finally, I enjoyed Mr Orwell's shadowy portrayal of
The Leader and how he watches with quiet menace over the
people of Oceania. But I wonder if he, too, would benefit from
a change of name. Perhaps I shall write to my big brother
Oswald and ask him. He's far better with such things than I.

5th December

....

Whether you dig it or not, today is World Soil Day – a day held to
focus attention on that earthy thing on the ground that we grow stuff
in. The importance of healthy soil can't be underestimated. It provides
an ecosystem critical for life. The soil is home to billions of organisms
and is responsible for more than 25 per cent of the planet's biodiversity.
It's been estimated that up to 90 per cent of living organisms live or
spend part of their lifecycle in soils, which is certainly what I plan to
do, although hopefully not until the end of it.

On English Soil

That phrase again. As if the soil itself
takes pride in the land on which it lies;
as if it was formed from nothing more than rocks
and weathering and Englishness; as if
all that sand and silt and clay had compressed itself
into patriotic clods, a noble loam loyal
to Queen and Country; to be walked upon only
by the fine, upstanding English feet which have trod
its furrows for centuries; to be turned only

by steadfast English spades and tractors; as if,
for all its nutrients, its minerals, its rich fertility,
it can grow nothing but a Tudor Rose.

6th December

....

*London became the first city to introduce licensed taxi cabs on this day
in 1897. Horse-drawn Hansom cabs had been in use for more than
sixty years by the time Burseys arrived, the first electric-powered taxis.
They were quickly given the nickname 'Hummingbirds', coined from
the strange sound which emanated from their motors. The taxis had
high running costs, however, and the cabs were withdrawn just two
years later. On a good day a Hummingbird could do 12 mph, which
is roughly equivalent to the top speed a London taxi can do now, and
that is what is known as a very funny satirical joke.*

A Far Cry

I can never get a taxi
to stop for me in London.

Hardly a surprise, given
I hail from Birmingham.

7th December

....

The microwave oven was patented on this day in 1945 by Percy
Spencer, a self-taught engineer from Maine. It wasn't for another
twenty years that the microwave was to be manufactured for the home,
with sales exploding (like an egg in a microwave) in the 1970s and
80s. Part of the microwave's appeal was that it unchained people from
the tyranny of their domestic appliances, freeing up time which could
then be redeployed in the watching of television and playing Xbox.

Ping!

he sees her every evening
when the shopping's nearly done
& they're waiting in the queue
with their ready meals for one

identical baskets,
they stand silently in line,
when what he really wants to ask is –
your microwave or mine?

8th December

....

The author Bill Bryson was born on this day in 1951. He has written
books on travel, the English language, and science, and apparently his
books sell really well for some reason.

Dear Mr Bryson

Or Bill, if I may – not that I'd want to presume
and overstep the mark, of course –
(you can call me Brian, by the way),
I am writing because I had someone turn up
at one of my readings recently –

well, I *say* reading, it was more
of a muttering, really – who reported that
although she had quite enjoyed the event
(except the poems), she was a little disappointed
to discover I wasn't you,

famous wit, raconteur, and author
of the bestselling *Notes from a Small Island*
and that one with 'the funny story
about the Norwegian palaeontologist',
only our names were quite similar

('a bit Spoonery' was how she described them),
and anyway, it got me wondering
whether you've had many of my readers
come along to *your* events, because it's just that
there've been a few empty chairs

in recent times, and I was curious to know
if this kind of mix-up has been working both ways.
Which reminds me, Billy-boy, I don't suppose
sales of my books have been showing up
on your royalty statements

because these things can happen apparently,
in fact, they almost certainly have,
and while I do still accept cheques,
I think an online transfer would be best
as it keeps things nice and simple, don't you?

9th December

....

The first episode of the long-running British TV soap opera
Coronation Street *was aired on this day in 1960. Way before my
time, obvs, but I did develop a strong affection for the series in its
1980s pomp, when I remember the storyline of the Deirdre–Ken–Mike
love triangle gripping the nation so much that its denouement was
announced over the Old Trafford tannoy system during the half-time
interval. One of my favourite characters from that era was the cat
(played by Frisky) who appeared in the opening titles sequence; at the
height of Frisky's fame, his fan club had fifteen hundred members and
he regularly received fan mail.*

Cat on a Warm Pigeon Loft Roof

It was my big break. Primetime TV.
Monday and Wednesday evening every week.
It was my idea to settle down like that.
The director had wanted me to walk along the wall
but the sun was out, which doesn't happen much
in Weatherfield, so I thought I'd curl up
and make the most of it.

Call it actor's instinct, if you will.
I am classically trained, you know.
Narrowly missed out on RADA but Catford Academy
for the Performing Arts is a very underrated school.
The cat who played Crookshanks
in the Harry Potter films studied there.

But fame can be a curse.
Jealousy amongst cast members is nothing new
but I think that's why the script-writers
didn't really do anything with my role after that:
no affairs with the dissolute moggie at number 26;
no struggles with catnip addiction; not so much
as a darts match in the Rovers Return.
Just the same old clip every episode.

I play it back myself sometimes.
That music, bold as brass and twice as plaintive,
blowing out all the sadness from the day,
as the camera moves across the rooftops
and chimney stacks, and I watch myself
hunkering down amid grey slates and red bricks,
closing my eyes, beginning to dream.

10th December

....

Today is Human Rights Day, an annual celebration of the UN's
adoption of the Universal Declaration of Human Rights, proclaimed
on this day in 1948 and which sets out universal values and a

common standard of achievement for all peoples and nations. The day
also serves as an occasion for protests and other demonstrations in
support of human rights, especially in countries that have frequently
been beset by allegations of rights violations.

The March

No, she whispers.

After the policemen have left –
she catches her breath and pulls herself up from the floor,
leans against the wall on unsteady legs,
staggers out through the door
where the women of the village come out to help her,
support her as she limps along the track,
kicking up dust, and together with the children,
they straggle through parched fields
where farmhands down tools to walk beside them,
along the highway with its melting black tarmac
and litter of cars abandoned by drivers
who stride out next to them as they head for the city,
and the people pour from the shops and offices and factories,
in other cities, too, and towns and villages,
distant countries and faraway continents,
they all emerge to join her, to walk alongside her,
as she marches on, head high, back straight,
one foot planted firmly in front of the other.

No, she had whispered and the whole world shouted.
This stops now.

11th December

....

International Mountain Day, which occurs annually on this day, highlights the importance of sustainable mountain development. The mountain, of course, is also critical to the poet, philosopher, mystical guru, and Nazi-fleeing nun in providing a series of ready-made metaphors for life, enlightenment, freedom, work, parenting, and the final few seasons of Friends. *Out of all the mountains, my favourite is Everest, but I think the second highest one in the world is OK, too.* *

* *this is an excellent joke*

The Englishman Who Went Up a Mountain But Came Down Ill

My great-uncle Jack,
hypochondriac and mountain-lover,
was forever coming down
with summit or other.

Coming up was no better.
He was constantly under the weather,
right under it, and as he climbed
so did his temperature.

Sometimes he'd get crampon
the way. Then, with a craggy smile,
he might ask if we could stop
and everest for a while.

But it was near the top
when he always felt most peaky.
He had an altitude problem,
according to his G.P.,

who wrote him a prescription
for a bottle of pills,
saying if they didn't work,
to stick to molehills.

12th December

The American author Joseph Heller died on this day in 1999.
Although he was to write several other novels, including the darkly
brilliant Something Happened, *he is most remembered for* Catch-22,
a fiercely satirical novel about the absurdity of war. The title (which
could have equally have been Catch-18, Catch-11, *or* Catch-14)
refers to the series of paradoxes created by the bureaucracy of the US
military: in particular that the only way to get out of combat duty and
dangerous missions was to prove your insanity; yet any attempt to do so
only went to show how sane you were for wanting to get out of them.

Catch-23 (Beginner and Intermediate Level)

During the course of this poem,
I shall be looking at Catch-23,
that peculiar form of circular, self-defeating logic,

closely related in nature to Catch-22,
which can result in an inescapable paradox.

But first, I need you to do some work, too.

If you've never heard of Catch-23 before,
I'd like you to head back to the very beginning of this poem,
re-read each line of it closely,
and follow all instructions.

If you already have some familiarity with Catch-23,
you can begin this poem at line eight
but do not progress any further than this line.

That's it! Let me know once you're done,
and we can take it from there.
In the meantime, I'll get the kettle on.

13th December

On this day in 1784, the writer, editor, lexicographer, and all-round brainbox Samuel Johnson died. Although he was a poet, playwright, and essayist, his lasting legacy was in his single-handed compilation of A Dictionary of the English Language, which became the pre-eminent dictionary of its time and beyond. It took him eight years to write, which isn't too bad considering it featured forty-two thousand words. It's believed, though, that there may have been about a hundred and fifty thousand words in use at the time; some of the shortfall was

down to Johnson's oversight, something that must surely have made
him 'irritable' – well, it might have done, if he'd noticed that he
hadn't included that word either.

An Attempt to Write an Abecedarian Poem
in Praise of the Dictionary

An unfaltering ability to
Bring clarity to the English language
Constitutes your
Defining quality.
Ever since the day we
First met, and I
Giggled at the rude words
Hidden amongst your pages,
I adored you,
Jubilant in the
Knowledge that things were
Looking up. You offered me the
Meaning of life,
Not to mention the meaning of all those
Other words, too.
Perfect at settling Scrabble board
Quarrels, your judgement
Reigns supreme. I
Sift you daily. I pan for words in
The hope of penning the
Ultimate – the greatest poem this
Vast world has ever seen, but

Whoa, here comes the
X, and oh, alphabet, how could you, I knew
You'd get the better of me
Zooner or later.

14th December

....

The German physicist Max Planck laid the foundations of quantum
theory on this day in 1900. In presenting his derivation of the
distribution law for black body radiation . . . no, I can't do it. I'm only
fooling myself. I don't understand any of it. I have tried in the course
of writing this entry to get my head around quantum theory but after a
while the words just detach themselves from the page and start floating
around in front of my eyes, like wobbly atoms. Some clever sod should
write an equation about that.

Free to a Good Home

Free to a good home,
ten weighty tomes

on the topic
of the subatomic,

fifteen journal articles
involving particles,

six dissertations
full of equations,

an introduction to QED theory
by Dermot O'Leary,

a selection of Ed Sheeran's lyrics
on theoretical physics,

three bluffer's guides,
seventy PowerPoint slides,

and six empty bottles
of Merrydown Cider.

None of which have left me
any the wiser

regarding the realm
of the quantum.

They're all yours
if you wantum.

15th December

Nero was born on this day in 37CE. He was the fifth emperor of Rome and the last in the Julio-Claudian dynasty line of emperors. He wasn't the most stable of rulers, not when you consider he had his own mother killed; he probably murdered his second wife; he had a boy castrated in order to marry him; and he created fake Olympic games in order to declare himself the winner. But none of us are perfect. What he didn't do, though, was to burn down Rome and do some fiddling while watching it – but just as he decided to blame the Christians for it, I'm going to blame him for it anyway.

Julio-Claudian Clerihews

Augustus Caesar,
a formidable geezer,
stamped out civil wars and riots.
He loved a bit of pax and quiet.

His stepson Tiberius
was gloomy and serious.
A fine general, it must be said in truth,
but aloof.

Then came Caligula,
who, in partigula,
had partaken of the crazy sauce.
e.g. his plan to make a consul of his horse.

His successor, Claudius,
had been thought too inglorious,
what with his deafness and his limp.
But he was no wimp.

And then came Nero
with his cafes selling cappuccino,
established after an insurance diddle
(having played with matches, then a fiddle).

16th December

A bunch of angry Americans threw three hundred and forty-two chests
of tea into Boston Harbour on this day in 1773 in an event ironically
referred to as the Boston Tea Party. It was the culmination of resistance
in North America to the Tea Act, passed by the British parliament,
which was seen as violating their rights to 'no taxation without
representation'. They must have been very angry: that's a lot of tea to
dump in the water. Ironically, if they could have just sat down and had
a nice cup of tea, the situation perhaps wouldn't have seemed so bad
after all, and the whole American independence thing could have been
avoided.

cuppa

no matter if you're uppity
or you cause a brew ha ha,
you'll always be my cuppa tea,
my steaming mug of cha

know this, my darjeeling,
only tea leaves me this way
you stir me up and turn me
fifty shades of earl grey

yes, that's the oolong
and ooshort of it,
the infusing, confusing thought of it
but please don't make a sport of it

because without you,
i am defunct

like a biscuit waiting
to be dunked

17th December

A new magazine called Vogue was published on this day in 1892.
It was dedicated to 'the ceremonial side of life' as enjoyed by the social
elite of New York, and was the venture of Arthur Baldwin Turnure.
Originally it targeted 'the sage as well as the debutante, men of affairs
as well as the belle'. When the magazine was purchased by Condé
Nast, its focus was changed to women and fashion, although that fact
doesn't seem to have put off men from reading it – a recent survey
suggests that 40 per cent of current online readers are men. I don't
count myself amongst them, though, being more of a Marie Claire
man, if I'm honest with you.

Vague

In this month's issue,
we'll be looking at what's HOT this summer,
or possibly not,
I mean you never *quite* know, do you,
given the complex nature of SELF and SUBJECTIVITY,
but GREEN is very definitely in,
along with some of the other colours

like BLUE and RED,
and the one that's a little bit ORANGEY
but a bit like BROWN, too.

We'll also be asking the question
is this THING better than some other THING,
or are they MUCH of a MUCHNESS,
and we'll spend some time
looking at the THORNY issue of something or other
and what kind of SHOES
might go best when being a person.

Read all about the NINE or TEN ways
you can provoke SOME KIND OF REACTION from your LOVER
   in BED
or on a sofa, or a garden bench or whatnot,
and don't miss our EXCLUSIVE interview
with SOMEBODY we have interviewed exclusively
about how to LIVE your BEST LIFE
when the WORLD is all like, well, you know, how it is.

In shops NOW, or quite soon at any rate,
try THURSDAY, definitely by early next week.

18th December

Joseph Grimaldi, the English clown and pantomimist, was born on this day in 1778. With his whiteface make up and combination of roguery and innocence, he was to have a lasting influence on tomfoolery and set the template for the clowns who would come after him. Thanks to the Joker and Pennywise, clowns are often regarded as being more frightening than funny nowadays, which seems unfair. The need to laugh at human ridiculousness is important: the world needs clowns. On the first Sunday in February, Holy Trinity Church in London holds a memorial service for Grimaldi; clowns from all over the world gather in full attire and make up, and just thinking about that is enough to make me smile.

The Clown Next Door

He doesn't use his bike much these days.
I used to watch him pedal off to work every morning
but it was taking him ages, by all accounts,
what with the square wheels,
and the way it would fall apart around him
when he was waiting at the traffic lights.

He's since joined a car share with other commuting clowns.
I say car, but it's more of a fire truck.
They come hurtling around the corner just after seven,
honking horns and flashing lights,
before two of them jump out with a small round trampoline
trampling on his tulips as they veer back and forth,

and he prepares himself to jump
from his first-floor bedroom window.
The whole operation takes about twenty minutes.

While he's out, I take deliveries for him.
Balloons and rubber chickens. Whoopie cushions
and chrome hooters. Juggling balls
and a pair of giant scissors. An inflatable tuba.
He comes over to collect them when he's back from work,
face paint smudged, fixed smile wearing thin,
weary from another day of being squirted with flowers,
of being struck with rubber bricks,
of making others laugh.

Sometimes he bends over to pick up his box
and his trousers fall down.

19th December

....

Charles Dickens' A Christmas Carol *was published on this day in
1843, and thus was Christmas reinvented. Not only did the book
revive the phrase 'Merry Christmas', Dickens presented Christmas
as a time for charity, forgiveness, family, and spooky door knockers,
a message which had lost its way over the preceding centuries. The
book was an instant success, selling out by Christmas Eve, and the tale
has retained its popularity to this day; not least through the definitive
cinematic version,* The Muppet Christmas Carol, *starring Michael
Caine, Kermit the Frog and Miss Piggy.*

Tense Christmas

I The Ghost of Christmas Past Perfect Progressive
Midnight. Awoken by a ghost.
I thought I must be raving.
But then he went and showed me
how badly *I'd been behaving*.

II The Ghost of Christmas Present Perfect Simple
The next night, a ghost again:
with a much more recent scene.
More evidence piling up
of how unpleasant *I have been*.

III The Ghost of Christmas Future Unreal Conditional
A final late-night ghostly vision.
But this one lacked the pain and strife.
I saw if I could be a kinder man,
I would create a better life.

20th December

....

*It was on this day in 1928 that a chip shop opened in a small
wooden hut in Guiseley, West Yorkshire, run by an enterprising frier
(not the monkish kind) called Harry Ramsden. It soon became very
popular, the hut eventually being replaced by a restaurant which, at
one time, held the world record for the largest chippy in the world.
On one day in 1952, it sold ten thousand portions of fish and chips.*

Thanks to Harry Ramsden and tens of thousands of other chippies around the country, fish and chips was to become the 'national cuisine' of the UK. And it is a truth universally acknowledged that the best part of any takeaway is the 'scraps' of deep-fried batter you find in amongst your chips.

Chipster

Feeling tip top after hip hop tabata
and a quick trip down the Turkish barbers,

he dons his Paco Rabanne flip flops
and slip slops to the fish and chip shop,

six o'clock, every Wednesday evening.
You could set your pocket watch by him.

He stares at the board and wonders
what to have with his chips. He ponders

the tofu scallops and deep-fried sprouts,
the ale-battered halloumi. He doubts

the rogan josh sauce is fair trade.
He strokes his beard, applies fresh pomade,

before ordering laconically.
He eats his vegan prawns ironically.

21st December

The first crossword puzzle, created by Arthur Wynne, was published on this day in 1913 in the newspaper New York World. *While Wynne's puzzle was diamond-shaped and contained no black squares, it otherwise embodied many of the features we see in crosswords today. It took off so quickly that, within a decade, crossword puzzles were featured in nearly all the American newspapers and had spread around the world. They finally reached me in the nineties when I encountered the* Guardian's *1993 Christmas Bumper Cryptic Crossword. I was instantly captivated by it, to the extent that I now only have four clues left to solve.*

Mope About (4)

Before commencing, ensure you have a hot mug of tea,
one sharpened hb pencil and all twenty volumes
of the *Oxford English Dictionary* to hand.

Stare uselessly at the across clues for several minutes
before working your way forlornly through the down clues.
Doodle a picture of a cat upon a skateboard.

Identify trigger phrases. Words such as 'confused',
'mixed up', and 'abandoned' may all signal the presence
of an anagram, as well as your state of mind.

Boil the kettle for fresh tea and think again about 11 across.

Might the wording indicate an acronym? Decide against looking up the word 'GPOTLYD' in the dictionary.

Briefly consider attempting the Japanese number puzzle on the adjacent page. Have another crack at 23 down. Mope about. Observe the lengthening shadows.

Draw a picture of a house without lifting your pencil from the page. Celebrate with another cup of tea and a hopeful forage for Hobnobs.

Write a rude word in the squares of 7 across. Smile to yourself. Fill in the puzzle with similar profanities or nonsense words until the grid is complete.

Repeat daily.

22nd December

....

The first medical X-ray image was produced on this day in 1895, created by Wilhelm Roentgen, the German professor who had discovered electromagnetic radiation the previous month. The image was of his wife's left hand, her wedding ring clearly visible on one bony finger. 'I have seen my death,' Anna Bertha Ludwig was to remark. Roentgen never sought to profit personally from his discovery, never registering a patent and donating his Nobel Prize money to his university. Financially, their married life was a struggle but it did not matter to Anna, who saw what others couldn't see in her husband, just as he was to see what others couldn't see in her.

X is for . . .

As a writer of alphabet books,
I'd just quickly like to say
thank you, Professor Roentgen,
for inventing the X-ray.

I never liked the xylophone
that we had to use instead.
All it did was confuse the kids
cos it sounds like it's a zed.

The same applies to xenophobe
while no one's heard of xylem –
neither sits right in our books
when we're trying to compile 'em.

So, thank you, Professor Roentgen,
you have earned my full respect,
for allowing me this option
when I'm illustrating X.

x

23rd December

....

*It was on this day in 1986 that Chris Rea reached Woolley Edge
motorway service station on the M1 in his marathon attempt to reach
Middlesbrough in time for Christmas. Having set out from Cookham*

seven days previously in a tropic-green Reliant Robin, the gravel-voiced singing sensation had endured a torrid journey, including an altercation with a policeman in Horton-cum-Studley, a prang with a Ford Cortina near the turn-off to Alfreton, and three days of driving around the Spaghetti Junction. At Ashby-de-la-Zouch his car radio had packed in, and he was forced to continue the long journey northwards with only a cassette tape of Paul Young's No Parlez *for company. There were to be no further sightings of him after he was seen leaving Woolley Edge services with a Twix, a packet of Quavers, and two cans of cherry Coca-Cola.*

A Short Poem Concerning the Proximity of Chris Rea to Home as He Drives Back for Christmas

Chris Rea
is nea

24th December

....

For those who celebrate the Christian holiday of Christmas, all should now be ready – for today is Christmas Eve. Gifts have been panic-bought and inexpertly wrapped. A vegan nut roast sits in the fridge awaiting the microwave. The Radio Times *has been marked up using a complex system of highlighter pens to indicate competing family voting preferences. And, at the centre of it all, there is the Christmas tree, fully bedecked and bebaubled, sprinkling its needles over the carpet, the cushions, the cat, because you bought it three weeks ago and haven't watered it since, and yes, next Christmas, you will get yourself an ethical, sustainable living tree in a pot, it's just that things have been incredibly busy recently, what with Christmas and everything.*

Needles

<pre>
                    I
                  wrote
                 a poem
               in the shape
              of a Christmas
            tree but then forgot
          to water it and only a few

                    days
                    later
                    there

      were

                  words

                                          over

                          all

          the   carpet
</pre>

25th December

....

Today is Christmas Day, traditionally the most Christmassy of all the days. It commemorates the birth of Jesus Christ, although today it has come to mean many different things to different people. This can be seen by the poem below, which has been constructed from

auto-completed searches on Google involving the word 'Christmas'.
To my mind, this 'found poem' is interesting in that it gives some very
real insights into contemporary preoccupations concerning Christmas;
not only that, I didn't have to write a single original word in the whole
thing, just rearrange the words of others. For that reason, it's a form
of poetry I am looking to do more with in the future.

Searching for Christmas

is christmas in the bible
why does christmas make me cry
is christmas dinner tax deductible
do christmas elves ever die

christmas is a time for giving
christmas is a load of crap
christmas is a coming
and the geese are getting fat

can christmas pudding make you drunk
can christmas lights kill a cat
can christmas island crabs be eaten
is christmas skins coming back

christmas is a hippopotamus
christmas is a rockin time
christmas is a proper noun
christmas is a state of mind

can christmas trees smell of urine
is christmas celebrated in Peru

is chris **packham related to jools holland**
is christmas m**usic bad for you**

*christmas is all **around bill nighy***
*christmas is a **time to share***
*christmas is **just around the corner***
*christmas is **in the air***

26th December

Today is the second day of Christmastide, more commonly known as Boxing Day. No one quite knows for sure why it's called that. It may be in reference to the alms box that would be placed in churches to collect donations to the poor, or to the tradition of tradesmen and servants receiving a Christmas box from their employers. Or perhaps it was so called because many of us spend the day sitting in front of the television 'box', unable to move from all the food and excitement of the day before (just made that theory up). Although it seems most likely that it comes from the quaint Victorian tradition of exchanging boxer dogs on this day, as a signal of goodwill and friendship (also made that one up).

Debrief

OK, OK! Simmer down, simmer down!
Believe me, I don't want to be here any more than you do –
I'd rather be reclining with a piña colada

on a sun lounger in Florida
but if we don't get this done now, we never will.

Right, Blixen – yesterday's KPIs.
99.7% of presents delivered on time? Good work, team!
That's a 0.2% uplift on last year in the happiness stakes.
Accuracy is trending down a little, though.
Yeah, I know about that problem with 26 Masefield Drive –
the elves in Customer Services are working on it –
but if you move house two days before Christmas, what do you
    expect?
We also had one parcel left on the sleigh.
If anyone knows of a kid who's short of a Slime Blaster 5000,
please let Track and Trace know.

OK, what else? Ah, yes, Rudolph.
Seems we've had a few complaints about the brightness
of your nose. Light pollution, apparently.
Any chance you can turn that thing down by a couple of lumens?
If not, we're going to have to go back to lanterns
and that's gonna mean even more fire safety training for us all,
and after last year's three-day course
on the recent changes to chimney and flue regulations,
I don't think any of us want that.

Finally, Steve in Data Compliancy tells me
that, as from next year, we will need the children
to opt-in to any lists we put them on,
and they have the right to request from us

any data we hold on them
as to whether they are naughty or nice.

OK, that's it! Thanks again, team!
Mission accomplished. Enjoy your long break
and I'll see you back here presently.

27th December

....

Restaurant critic, food writer, and Britain's original celebrity chef,
Fanny Cradock died on this day in 1994. She is best remembered for
her TV appearances, where she would often be accompanied by her
bumbling, woebegone husband, Johnnie, and on which she introduced
the British public to such exotic dishes as the pizza and the prawn
cocktail. Fierce and formidable, her dreadful behaviour towards the
menus of Gwen Troake, a Devon 'housewife', led to her downfall;
Cradock's sneering, condescending responses outraged the public and
effectively ended her television career.

Recipe for Midwinter Happiness

One crisp and cold winter afternoon
with two tired legs
and the prospect of a long, improving walk
behind you.

One cosy sitting room
with one comfortable sofa,
one sleeping cat or dog (according to taste),

and the crackle of logs
in the fireplace.

Three or four hours off
with no phone calls or deadlines
or visitors to attend to.

One good book*

* or one good lover, if book not available.

28th December

*The American comic-book writer Stan Lee was born on this day
in 1922. At Marvel comics, he was responsible for creating a raft of
memorable superheroes, including Spider-Man, the X-Men, Iron Man,
Thor, the Hulk, and Ant-Man. As his characters were turned into
blockbuster movies in the Marvel Cinematic Universe, Lee would often
appear in cameo roles, including a FedEx postman, a bus driver, and
an annoyed neighbour. When asked what superpower he would like, he
answered, 'Luck! Because if you're lucky, then everything falls into place.'*

Sloth-Man

There are worse radioactive creatures to have been bitten by.
I mean, imagine if it had been a spider –
I'd have been climbing the walls in no time,
getting myself in a right tangle.

Or an ant – all that scurrying around!
It makes me exhausted just thinking about it.

I do a lot of thinking. That's one of my superpowers.
I can think about something for days,
weeks even. It doesn't matter where I am –
I can be lying in bed, on a bench, or simply reclining
on my chaise longue – I'll think it through.
And when I'm done, I'll think about something else.

It's no wonder I sleep so much. That's another
superpower, along with the slummocking,
and being able to surf up to eighty channels a minute.
Like all superheroes, I have a costume:
tartan wool dressing gown with medallion of egg;
bed socks; slippers, in case of emergencies.

But should my sloth senses start to tingle
with the thought of you in pain or peril,
I will spring up with the agility of a broken mattress
and be at your door, as quick as bus times allow,
to prop you up more surely
than any man scurrying around in a stretchable ant suit
lifting fifty times his bodyweight.

29th December

A blizzard swept across the south-west of England and Wales on this day in 1962. The country had already suffered heavy snowfall a few days earlier and the blizzard left drifts of up to twenty feet of snow in its wake. It heralded the beginning of the Big Freeze, the coldest winter in Britain since 1840, with snow blanketing the country for two months. Rivers and milk bottles froze over, while a cup game between Stranraer and Airdrie was called off thirty-three times. It wasn't until 6th March that morning arrived without a frost. It's not known exactly how many snowmen were to lose their lives in the Great Thaw, but some meteorologists calculate the figure to be in the tens of thousands.

Snow Poem

words

        fell

from   the

             sky

today

        i   stood

       and

    watched   them

     snowin'

and as they settled on the ground,
they turned into this poem.

30th December

Rudyard Kipling, the English poet, short-story writer, and novelist, was born on this day in 1865. At the age of forty-one, he became the first English-language writer to win the Nobel Prize for Literature, and he remains the youngest. He wrote exceedingly good stories, but his reputation was to suffer as the twentieth century wore on, due to the inextricable links between his writing and British imperialism.

If (Conservative Party version)

If you can keep your job when all around you
    Lies ravaged from what it is you've done;
If intellect and common sense confound you
    And if integrity you have but none;
If you can lie and not be tired by lying,
    And pretend you act for the public good,
But then leave the people to their dying
    And say you did, sadly, all you could:

If you can dream – of nothing more than power;
    If you can think – but only of yourself;
If you believe this country's finest hour
    Is when the chosen few can gain more wealth;
If you can flout the law with bluff and bluster
    And not care whether you are believed
Or deny with scorn every single blunder
    And not care how many you may deceive:

If you can stir up hatred, fear, and violence
    To create division to suit your ends;
And answer cries for help with silence,
    And then laugh about it with your friends:
If you can stretch this country to its limit
    Or until it is you've had your fun,
Yours is this land and everything that's in it,
    And – as you wished – you'll be PM, my son.

31st December

....

*For those of us who operate in the context of a Gregorian calendar,
today marks the end of another year. New Year's Eve is celebrated
traditionally with parties, fireworks, and alcohol – or, for those of a
quieter disposition, Jools' Annual Hootenanny and alcohol. But
more than that, it's a chance to reflect on the twelve months just gone,
to take stock of all your achievements and accomplishments, and to
feel amazed at just how far you've come.*

This was the year that was not the year

This was the year that was not the year
I repaired the bathroom tap
and emptied out the kitchen drawer
of a lifetime's worth of crap.

This was the year that was not the year
in which I launched a new career.

A West End hit eluded me
as did *Time* Person of the Year.

This was the year that was not the year
I became a household name.
Action figures were not sold of me.
I wasn't made a dame.

This was the year that was not the year
I spent less time on my phone.
Nights of passion did not happen
in boutique hotels in Rome.

This was the year that *was* the year
I didn't get that much done –
much the same as the year before,
much like the one to come.

Acknowledgements

Given the potential to get dates and facts muddled up in a book of this nature, I would like to express my thanks to all those who labour to ensure that the World Wide Web remains up-to-date and 100 per cent error-free. Any inaccuracies or misrepresentations in the daily entries are entirely of my own making. I'm obliged to Prof. Frank McDonough (@FXMC1957) whose 'This Day in History' tweets provided me with a constant stream of events and stories to pick from each day; while, elsewhere on Twitter, brilliant jokes by trouteyes (@trouteyes) and Guybrush Tweetgood (@philgibson01) served as inspiration behind my poems on 5th March and 12th April respectively. A debt of gratitude, too large to ever be settled, is also owed to all the poets, songwriters, comedians and other wordsmiths who have inspired me over the years, and whose influence shines through in many of these poems, although hopefully not in any kind of plagiaristic sense.

Thanks, as ever, to my wonderful agent Jo Unwin and her all-star supporting cast of Nisha Bailey, Donna Greaves and Milly Reilly. At Picador, I'd like to thank the editorial team of Philip Gwyn Jones, Don Paterson, Salma Begum and Nicholas Blake for all their guidance, insight and expertise; as well as the mighty Camilla Elworthy, Queen of Publicity, whose communications never fail to brighten my day. My thanks also go out to the Sales and Marketing teams for all they do in bringing my books to the attention of booksellers, librarians and readers – and again, to those selfsame booksellers, librarians and readers for supporting my books in a way that never fails to amaze me.

I would like to thank my family for their support, stoicism and forbearance in allowing me to do this kind of thing rather than have a proper job. I couldn't think of anyone else I'd rather have been locked down with. I love them very much.

And finally, thanks to Buttons, my much-loved, much-missed cat, without whom this book wouldn't have taken half as long to write.

Index of Poems